AN EMPIRE OF INDIFFERENCE

: SOCIAL TEXT BOOKS

Edited by Brent Edwards,

Randy Martin, Andrew Ross,

and Ella Shohat

RANDY MARTIN

An Empire of Indifference

AMERICAN WAR AND THE FINANCIAL LOGIC

OF RISK MANAGEMENT

Duke University Press : Durham and London : 2007

© 2007 Duke University Press
All rights reserved.
Printed in the United States of America
on acid-free paper ∞
Designed by Cherie Westmoreland
Typeset in Minion and Arial types by
Keystone Typesetting, Inc.
Library of Congress Cataloging-in-
Publication Data appear on the last
printed page of this book.

Contents ❖

Acknowledgments ❖

There have been many responses to the wars prosecuted by George W. Bush's administration in the aftermath of September 11, 2001. Some can be found in the streets, others in the battlefield, more in the cities and countryside visited by the war on terror, and still others on the airwaves, screens, canvases, stages, and not least of all, the page. This book, therefore, stands in very good company. I myself have been just as fortunate. I have enjoyed a generosity of mind and a plentitude of opportunity at myriad occasions of teaching and learning, meeting and writing. Stanley Aronowitz, Michael Brown, Patricia Clough, Bill DiFazio, Mark Driscoll, Larry Grossberg, Stefano Harney, James Hay, May Joseph, Arvind Rajagopal, and Ella Shohat have provided keen insights and key venues in which the ideas for this book have germinated. My dear colleagues at *Social Text*, an editorial collective with which I have been affiliated for over twenty years, provide a milieu where thought and writing can flourish. The Brecht Forum, an independent left school and cultural center, offers a ground where contemporary political concerns can be worked out directly with those engaged in efforts to effect radical change. Some of the material in chapters 1 and 2 appeared in the journals *Transitions* and *Cultural Studies*; my thanks to the publishers of both. My academic home in the Department of Art and Public Policy at the Tisch School of the Arts, New York University, has been an extraordinary place to develop curricular applications for intellectual commitments. The writing of this book corresponds with the completion of my term as associate dean of faculty, and I am thankful to the school's dean, Mary Schmidt Campbell, for her support over the years, as well as to Anita Dwyer, Emily Stephens, and Theresa Smalec, who have made it possible to research and write amidst my administrative duties. I have been sustained and enriched beyond words by Ginger Gillespie and our children, Oliver and Sophia, whose small voices have already made themselves heard against the wars. Reynolds Smith, at Duke University Press, saw a book before it was written and Fred Kameny provided the expert copy-editing that gives the book its finish.

Introduction ❖

Empire is back. But like a long-running cinematic franchise, the sequel is always already in production. An imperial unconscious percolates up from a desire for domination and an urge to see the whole complexity of the world. The long-standing attention to imperialism in the Marxist tradition was interrupted by the promise of something new. The new term was globalization—conventionally seen as the transnational spread of markets and commodities or, from a more critical perspective, what it means for the idea of the global to be implicated in social life.[1] Discussions about globalization raised concerns that the integrity and authenticity of local cultures and experience would be lost as the world became flattened. Typically, however, globalization talk underplayed the military adventurism involved with making the world one.[2]

When used in a celebratory sense, globalization was associated with the spread of democracy—free markets were harbingers of expanded choice— and hence the return of local wills by means of political participation.[3] Whether its effects were to be embraced or resisted, whether they were homogenizing or differentiating, globalization offered an inclusive view of the world. The war on terror cast aspersions on this presumed inclusivity, as it provided cover for imperial reassertion. The spread of a particular ideal of the global could be violently rejected; exclusion and isolation could become generalized values. Force would be required to sort things out. Order would demand imperial rule and not simply the reason of the market. Imperialism became a widespread topic of public discussion and various political perspectives, from liberal and conservative apologies for it to left critiques of it.

A century ago Rudolf Hilferding formulated the Marxist anti-imperial critique. The key term of his analysis was finance capital, the fusion of productive capacity with the circuits of credit and debt by which products are brought to market. From the start finance capital was seen as a hybrid construction of banking and industry, the two pressed together in pursuit of continued profits. The general formulation of capital is that money becomes an end in itself. Finance is capital for others. This intersection of various kinds of wealth-making activity beyond the capacity of individual owners or local sites constituted a centralization of capital that was expressed territorially in terms of an expansionist policy. Finance licenses the right of monopoly and is expressed as a national chauvinism that displaces democracy and the right of self-determination.

Hilferding observes that geopolitical domination is naturalized along lines of racial difference. "The economic privileges of monopoly are mirrored in the privileged position claimed for one's own nation, which is represented as a 'chosen nation.' Since the subjection of foreign nations takes place by force—that is, in a perfectly natural way—it appears to the ruling nation that this domination is due to some special natural qualities, in short to its racial characteristics."[4] While the principles of territorial expansion and geopolitical domination have certainly changed over the past century, the displacement of problems of economic monopoly into racial terms is an underlying continuity of imperial formations.

The present terror war joins the complex legacy of empire-making race war that Hilferding identifies. The threats to democracy and the cultural inflection of imperialism justified by terror are still very much with us. While not reducible to the interests of finance capital, war today takes on a financial logic in the way it is organized and prosecuted. War is a means of destruction, but also the occasion for reconstructing a region along specific lines for particular ends. War destroys, but it also bears forms of life that render perceptible capital's inner machinations. Any more detailed consideration of what social wealth is, of its forms and effects, of what the world looks and feels like from within its optic, is most typically dispatched with an efficient examination of economic interest. In practice, interest may be way too narrow a perspective from which to understand the consequences of imperial interventions for all those involved. The interest in wealth may be serviced while global authority is undermined, and peoples around the world may be subjected to new strategies of subordination while they organize their capacities for ways of living together in ever more expansive ways.

Nikolai Bukharin wrote another key Marxist text, *Imperialism and the World Economy*, in 1915, when the world was forced to be alive to the rivalries of countries that each sought to anoint themselves "chosen nation." He understood imperialism as both a policy of finance capital and an ideology in its own right, one whose consequence was to simultaneously nationalize and internationalize capital.[5] The complexity, prominence, and significance of combinations of capital today argue for a closer look at the kinds of geopolitical and cultural rivalry that are governed under the sign of finance. With imperialism thrust again into focus, there is now a sense that the world has entered a phase more elevated than what Lenin understood imperialism to be in 1916: capitalism's "highest stage," marked by the preponderance of monopoly over free-market competition.

The renewed attention to imperialism from disparate ideological quarters has tended to omit the most basic element in a now presumably transcended classical formulation.[6] Lost is the opportunity to examine afresh what the present incarnation of finance might mean for the contemporary imperial polity. While the imperial dream of infinite territorial expansion faded long ago, today's catalepsy imagines joining a war without boundaries in time or space, where enemies are to be anticipated and preempted—in short, a rapidly moving, self-limiting war without end. If finance still forces together production and mutual indebtedness, grasping its current manifestations will aid in understanding the significance of the attendant assemblages and divisions around the globe today.

My concern is to look at imperial ambitions in the context of the powers of finance, not simply as a form of capital but as a set of protocols for organizing daily life. The intricate acrobatics of high finance that occur somewhere in the stratosphere have all manner of parallel expression in dances on the ground. Designs for living as brought to us by imperial agencies trace their blueprints to the realm of finance. Self-management is the watchword of personal finance, and this framework illuminates aspects of the present occupations of Afghanistan and Iraq and the concept of preemptive war. Enemies are to be defeated before they can make their antagonism manifest. Contingencies of the future are to be lived out in the present, blurring the distinction between the not-yet and the now. By converting potential threats into actual conflicts, the war on terror transfers future uncertainty into present risk.

Preemption, bringing the future into the present, has since the late 1970s been the guiding principle for fiscal policy. Under the influence of monetarism, which emphasizes regulating the amount of money in circulation, federal economic intervention has been chiefly concerned with controlling inflation by adjusting interest rates. Inflation, like terror, need only be present in prospect for its menacing effects to be felt. The mere specter of inflation scares people away from risk-taking investment. Confidence that the worth of investment portfolios will grow is undermined by inflation. Inflation is treated as a distortion to the economic environment that renders loss unpredictable. Risk can be distinguished from uncertainty as an expected outcome whose likelihood or value can be quantified. For risks to be reliably calculable, the future must look like the present. Inflation makes the difference between present and future more than a matter of extrapolation based on clearly discernible parameters. In terms of the experience of time, preemption means that the future is profaned. The future no longer holds a promise that the constraints of the present can be transcended or transformed. Without a conviction that the future bears our dreams, the idea of progress becomes difficult to sustain.

Imperialism once held this utopian promise for both its victors and its vanquished. New frontiers would be conquered so that enlightening and civilizing possibilities would be opened. The United States was founded as an imperium on this utopian ideal of devouring what lay before it to generate unimaginable heights of power and strength. Once the westward expansionary destiny had become manifest, new imperial imaginaries cast their eyes around the world.[7] The older approach of modernization promised that all nations would become wealthy if they embraced the market-driven formulas of development. But rather than convergence along prescribed paths of general welfare, poor nations experienced dependency and uneven development. The confident universalism that the world should imitate its imperial masters was challenged by myriad movements for national liberation—none of which went unchallenged. Military intervention and aid are highly selective. Some populations receive external attentions whether they want them or not. Others are left alone to suffer the consequences of previous colonial attentions. The reassertion of imperial ambition has come with a pervasive indifference toward many places once snugly inside the imperial envelope. The results have been very mixed, with many Latin American nations rejecting neoliberal nostrums while many in Africa have been provoked or abandoned to internecine conflict by imperial powers.

Foreign and domestic policy now coalesce around a potent indifference. This indifference is not attributable simply to greed, stupidity, or neglect—although these have long been means and ends of global rule, and even though the administration of George W. Bush would seem to take these as its idols.[8] Rather, there is a comprehensive rejection of the difference that previous imperial enterprises had wrought. The vast interdependencies of humanity in all its diversity are not seen as a resource to enhance the scope and capacity of global society. Instead this richness of population historically forced together by conquest is treated as a menacing entanglement from which imperial might must flee. Intervention is a way not simply to extract resources or control territories but also to effect a separation from unwanted attachments and attentions—precisely what is meant by terror. Liberation is for and from others. Specific demands of others are converted into an abstract calculus of risk. Paradoxically, the disenchantment of the United States with its own colonial legacy also establishes conditions of opposition to empire. Negating the imperial regime takes the form of any number of constituencies and movements affirming their ability to co-operate without giving up their specific differences. The mobilizations against the war in Iraq (from before it started early in 2003 and continuing since) can be understood in this light. The world is presented with another perverse form of domination, an empire of indifference. Far from being accidental neglect, this indifference is a reaction to the diversity of experience and capacity that people have made for themselves, and an unwitting invitation on the part of the imperium to create more.

While certainly disordering to the world's peoples, the present imperium needs to be understood for how it seeks to make the world cohere in light of certain problems and desired solutions. Governing distant lands, supporting unsustainable regimes, controlling markets for energy and raw materials, have become expensive and burdensome. Afghanistan and Iraq, models for a new approach, are to be liberated from their earlier entanglements and reconstructed along the lines of leaner and more highly leveraged foreign controls. The self-managerial entailments and exclusions that finance sets in motion reveal a fuller extension of labor into many habits of life. People are to ponder their financial security into the wee hours and work their investment portfolios, consumer debt, and accruals for their retirement and their children's college tuition accordingly. The gap widens between the wealthiest nation's capacity to provide health, education, housing, subsistence, and public participation and the political will to do so.

Financial investment, war, and development are no longer rationalized by the administration as inevitable acts and natural consequences of progress but taken as discretionary activities advanced by states and markets.

Colonial histories have differentiated people along lines of conditions of labor, race, nation, and civilization so as to create unconscious geographies of opportunity. Every category into which humans have been partitioned as a matter of social organization and identification carries a dream of what the world could be—socialism's emancipation from toil, black power's reparations from slavery, national liberation's reversal of colonial domination, civilizational progress worthy of the name. Even while the imperium discredits utopian schemes, repressed desires condense fresh fields of possibility. Racism, sexism, homphobia, xenophobia, and exploitation are some of the names given to these hierarchies of value. But what once seemed a basis of reliably channeling human abilities to advance imperial wealth is now a limit to its expansion. In their turn colonial administration and monopolized markets present costs that the imperium becomes unwilling to bear. Difference is therefore not simply a means of classificatory distinction—to be in one race, gender, sexuality, or another—but the factor through which value is generated and assigned.

Value is an equivalent that moves recognizably in some medium of exchange and what is substantively consumed in use—a meaning discernible in Marx's account of the commodity and Saussure's exposition of the sign.[9] I hope to show that difference not only is a basis of division, partition, and exclusion but also constitutes specific kinds of recognition of rights, disbursements of resources, and elaborations of what social life entails. Some aspect of difference gets reincorporated into cultural commodities, niche markets (that fall into a demographics of style delineating those interested in hip-hop or golf), and expanded demand (for the legions of new consumer goods). Yet there is also a remainder, an unabsorbable share made tangible in some bodily mass or population that imagines life beyond the induced scarcities of the profit-taking market. It will become clear that the result of the present turn against value-generating difference is a not altogether novel approach to global power's management of social wealth, one that cleaves population from sites of capital accumulation. Surely this is capital's historic pattern, to excise money as an end in itself from the social basis of cooperative labor that makes growth possible in the first place.

Contemporary finance and its intricate quantifications of risk refine the process of differentiation of value by breaking up or bringing together what were once treated as stable affiliations of people and place, geography and history. What is referred to in this book as financialization is the process by which social affiliations are reconfigured to extract wealth as an ends by means of risk management. Conceptually, financialization is at the intersection of the socialization of capital and of labor. Socialization refers to the double process by which control of wealth is concentrated and centralized and people are dispossessed of independent means to create their own lives and instead are pressed more and more into mutually interdependent productive relations. Historically, as Giovanni Arrighi has shown, finance has gained prominence at various times over the past several hundred years during periods of general economic turbulence, restructuring of the social contract, and shifts in global power.[10] Finance is the subject and object of contemporary capital in its present incarnation, the domain where capital is joined to create fresh opportunities for wealth and where risk management and credit are part of labor's burden in daily life.

Politically, I am interested in a reading of Marx that emphasizes socialization over the more prominent leftist ideals of equality or liberation more commonly associated with his work.[11] The ideal of liberation has certainly been co-opted by a hawkish evangelism that wishes—in the name of one tradition—to free people from all manner of traditions, including the expectations of continued livelihood. Minimally, liberation's meanings need to be opened up and contested, but the terrain of freedom as an unquestioned political good needs to be evaluated as well. The value of a politics based upon the mitigation of inequality has faced a similar fate, with many on the right endorsing its eradication, even if this means ending social entitlements as a source of untoward dependence, or eliminating special rights as a type of minority privilege. Tax cuts, the privatization of social security, the promotion of private schooling are from this perspective invariably presented as solutions to poverty, even if these policies are recipes for propagating misery.

The intricacies of cooperation, mutual interdependence, and association on a world scale, the entanglements generative of difference and political demand, together create the rich vein of socialization that can be mined by a critical rereading of Marx's critique of capital.[12] Socialization refers to the thickening capacity for "material intercourse" by which persons and their worlds are made. Marx's feat is to enter capital's way of making sense of the world and to give expression to that sensibility from within—a kind of self-critical phenomenology of social wealth. Against the efforts to dismiss Marx as passé or discredit the basis for a close encounter with his work, a similarly robust phenomenological reckoning is required today to come to terms with the social forces being assembled in our midst.

: FROM SECURITIZATION TO INDIFFERENCE

The book starts with the view of the world at home and abroad captured by the war on terror, moves on to show how this view has been anticipated in the planning for war, looks at how this plan got applied in Afghanistan and Iraq, and provides a political theory of the empire of indifference. Chapter 1 explores what the most recent ascent of finance means for the commingled approaches to domestic and foreign policy. As it has arisen in the world of finance, securitization refers to the process by which individual notes of credit or debt, like home mortgages, credit card debts, automobile loans, and hospital bills, are bundled together and traded as securities. Amalgamating debt of various kinds from around the nation (or in some cases internationally) displaces local ownership. Securitization also interconnects strangers in a contemporary instance of imposed mutual interdependence or socialization.

Simply put, finance divides the world between those able to avail themselves of wealth opportunities through risk taking and those who are considered "at risk." This sorting of the population amounts to a kind of leveraged hegemony, by enhancing wealth-making opportunities for some portion of the working population so as to affect the general terms by which all would come to understand their chances of getting ahead financially. This risk-based repertoire of the arts of the possible has gained currency as an array of policies and approaches to governance in the United States over the past twenty-five years. The principal consequence of these various risk strategies has been a reorientation away from what was, beginning in the mid-twentieth century, the principal way by which individuals saw their future in terms of capitalism's prosperity. Popular consciousness shifted away from identification with the working class and toward an ideal of a middle class defined by its present capacities to consume and its ability to pursue the American dream. Today, instead of a consumer-defined middle class, the population is divided into the self-managed and the unmanageable. An articulation of the state with finance, this initiative of rule amounts to a shift away from citizens and consumers and toward investors, and as a new way of framing participation in public life and social policy as a public good. The investor becomes a model for the ideal kind of beings, who manage their affairs and take care of their own future.

The war on terror is modeled on earlier wars against crime and drugs and various populations (youth, the poor, the underperforming) considered "at risk" of social failure. The shared approach to managing threats to homeland security isolates and excludes one segment of the population against another, internally dividing national space so as to efface ideas and locations of the foreign and domestic. With no clear delineations between a shared inside and a discernible outside, the very idea of uniform national interest is brought to a crisis. The state is left to represent the nation through wars. These are wars of exclusion rather than capture. As a consequence, populations are liberated to manage the mess that has been visited upon them. Following the Vietnam debacle, the emergent strategy of dominance is based not upon the symmetrical global balance of power that was maintained through the cold war, but upon a hegemon's view of the world according to which power is distributed asymmetrically, and relatively weak opponents are seen as more likely to act antagonistically. While Bush's regime has claimed authorship for the war on terror as policy, the strategic approach to asymmetrical power and war has been brewing over several administrations.

Chapter 2 examines parallels of logic and operation between circuits of finance and of the military that seek to leverage narrowly focused interventions and investments to more general global effects. Starting in the 1930s with the work that would lead to the development of computers, and more commonly in the 1950s, the same mathematical models used to predict the outcome of decisions said to drive stock market behavior were also applied to simulate battlefield situations and aid in weapons development. The resulting approach to information processing in an environment where a number of factors or variables can be moving simultaneously in several directions came to be known under a variety of related rubrics such as cybernetics, operations research, and systems analysis. From the 1970s through the 1990s systems approaches to information processing provided the conceptual basis for the revolution in military affairs, an effort to achieve military domination through technological superiority. Military and financial planning are joined by the logic of arbitrage, the management of highly volatile small differences in value that are leveraged to large effects. Bush's national security policy of 2002 is significant. Between September 11, 2001, and the invasion of Iraq in 2003, the administration formalized a national security policy that combined preemptive war with the need for allies to embrace anti-inflationary monetary policies. A preemptive approach to managing military and economic affairs would create twin pillars of national security, since domestically it can be said that the principal defense against inflation also follows a preemptive logic. When the Federal Reserve Board observes or even anticipates unemployment falling or economic growth escalating it will likely increase the prime lending rate to dampen the creation and flow of money through the economy. For its part, the military practices what it calls "forward deterrence," a policy by which it deploys troops before a threat to the United States becomes manifest.

Central to these attentions, even before terrorists became the stuff of trading cards and dart boards, were the problems of what military observers call dispersed warfare. The narrow targets such as Osama bin Laden or Saddam Hussein that occasion intervention cannot be territorially confined and keep slipping away after the strategic objectives of regime change are declared met. As a result, new battlefield tactics rely on concentrated, relatively small deployments of soldiers (in particular, the array of élite military units called Special Forces) to have a more widely distributed effect. Special Forces are meant to eliminate targets before a formal battle is joined. They are trained to undertake greater personal risk in exchange for the prospect of substantial politico-military reward. In this regard they are the military's arbitrageurs. The volatility of war is isolated and contained by concentrated and precise interventions. The small-scale operation of the quick and clean surgical strike on highly focused targets is leveraged to the larger strategic ambitions of the entire war theater. The technologically sophisticated, precise applications of force perform a kind of arbitrage, an exploitation of small variations in the environment to achieve large-scale gain, that makes for a parallel between theaters of war and financial markets.

The use of arbitrage, or quick shifts in deployment of capital to leverage larger money-making effects, is also the logic of the financial derivative. The derivative is a risk-managing contract that links one value to another based on an expected outcome. A derivative contract can be drawn, for example, to hedge against the risk of an unexpected fluctuation in currency rates when a contracted product is manufactured and ready to be shipped for international trade. The agreement to exchange a certain amount of currency at a particular future time can then itself be put on the market in the present and sold. Let us say that a furniture manufacturer in Oregon gets an order for five hundred tables from a Japanese distributor. When the order is placed, it is costed at $500,000, and priced at an equivalent amount of yen according to the exchange rates then in effect. The manufacturer calculates costs and revenues based upon what the exchange rate between dollars and yen is at the time of sale. But the tables will take six months to complete, and the exchange rate can change in that time. If the yen declines against the dollar, the manufacturer stands to lose money. To protect the firm against the possibility, the manufacturer takes out a derivative contract to exchange dollars for yen on a certain date at a specific price. Once drafted, this contract has a certain price, and it can itself enter into exchange as a tradable commodity. The initial contract for tables sets in motion another exchange whose value is derived from the first but then comes to have an economic existence of its own. The result of all these transactions is a burgeoning growth in derivatives and their exchange.

Derivatives both anticipate and encourage volatility. Within a few years of the new millennium, derivatives markets traded contracts with a face value of more than $200 trillion, yielding billions in revenues for savvy arbitrageurs—investment bankers who exploit small price differentials in equities from different places to reap large profits.[13] By bundling local debts into globally marketable securities, securitization enlarges the scope of mutual indebtedness not only in strict financial terms but socially as well. The derivative disassembles and differentiates those collected financial bodies by taking one potential variable from the pricing of a commodity, isolating it, and marketing it as a distinct bill of exchange. Together securitization and derivatives, principles of assembly and disassembly, account for the push and pull of finance's inner social life.

Similarly, the preemptive approach to foreign policy, characterized by self-described opportunistic risk takers, needs to be coupled with the military problem posed by the need to combat terror. The terror war operates by leveraging particular attacks and interventions to a universal condition. Specific proxies for the cold war (as al-Qaeda and the Taliban were in Afghanistan) or for the subversion of Islamic governments (as Saddam Hussein was in Iraq's war against Iran during the 1980s) were converted into general figures of global terror. Particular interventions against former allies were to stand for a general condition of the world terror trade. The justification for the wars against Afghanistan and Iraq and the timing of them masked the histories that led to the conditions of belligerence, very much along the logic of a derivative. Specific investments stand in for and affect generalized results. So too, the multiplier effects are difficult to contain or control. Wars fought to preempt future attacks by unknown and unrelated enemies craft a link between hitherto unrelated conflicts and render present fighting a stand-in for any possible future battles. By attacking potential enemies anywhere at any time, war shifts from one place to another. But as a way of justifying how the state should properly relate to the people, as the basis for a generalized social contract oriented toward living by and with the risks that come with terror, war goes on without end.

Ultimately, terror wars make more of what they fight, as is evident in the increased number of attacks worldwide since September 11, 2001, and the sustained insurgencies in both Afghanistan and Iraq, characterized by the United States as the work of terrorists. The urge to cut and run from an investment gone bad while proclaiming victory, known in military and business circles as an exit strategy, becomes obligatory to formulate yet impossible to execute. Consequently, a debt is amassed that circulates but can never really be closed or canceled. In this Afghanistan and Iraq emerge from very particular histories, or economic or energy instrumentalities. In addition, their reconstruction plans are emblems of financial and military design by which risk is being made into a way of life.

Chapter 3 takes seriously the Bush administration's presumption that bombing can unleash the democratic spirit. Again, the rightist appropriation of the trope of liberation should give pause to the left regarding the way it uses this term. Purging Afghanistan and Iraq of bad leadership is clearly not to be followed by a new Marshall Plan, as even promised reconstruction funds in both countries were largely withheld months after victory was hastily declared. Two years after Bush declared the war in Iraq won, even the fraction of money approved by Congress that had actually been released as aid was being redirected from building water, sewage, and power plants to training Iraqis as soldiers and police.[14] The discovery that some of those involved in reconstruction were skimming and stockpiling cash was certainly scandalous, but the malfeasance also mirrored that of the failed regime that the United States was seeking to replace.[15]

The reconstruction of lands devastated by invasion will be eclipsed by security needs generated by failures of occupation. The intervention in these countries is not reducible to maintaining control of oil supplies, the history of which betrays a willingness to jeopardize access by installing governments whose corrupt and repressive practices foment instability and unrest. While it is a compelling slogan, "No blood for oil" can assume a Malthusian computation of scarcity that makes war appear inevitable rather than avoidable.[16] Accordingly, there are too many people jostling for too little oil, and some will have to go. Nor is war simply explained by the admittedly nefarious instrumentality of the connection between Halliburton and Washington (through which billions of dollars' worth of contracts were awarded noncompetitively to the firm once headed by Vice President Dick Cheney). The practices and presumptions of contemporary war are replicating themselves in all manner of life's domains.

Military planners' risk assessments provide a key text for evaluating the war's financial reason. When the United States was going to war, Paul Wolfowitz, then deputy defense secretary, promised Congress that the occupation would pay for itself, because of increased revenue from Iraqi oilfields. While Iraq possessed no weapons of mass destruction, it was subject to the most sophisticated means of destruction available on the planet. The idea that those subject to violent and massively destructive regime change are responsible for financing their own reconstruction under a blueprint deposited with them by their invaders needs to be addressed as its own kind of developmental discourse. For Afghans and Iraqis, soldiers of the occupation, allies, and majorities of citizens in the United States and around the world, the war has gone on far too long. But by design and in relation to other colonizing actions, the occupations were meant to be short-lived. The hit-and-run occupation belies a strategy of disoccupation that aims to actively dispossess population from sources of social wealth. Those left without jobs, houses, and utilities are treated as expendable, damage that is a collateral asset of the invasion. This relative surplus population is not simply a check on pressures for rising wages but also presents the contrary principle of population for its own sake. The liberated must find ways to reattach themselves, to affiliate along lines of an idea of homeland security distinct from the brittle models flung at them.

Chapter 4 draws upon the concrete analysis of war and finance to explore how an empire of indifference works. In contrast to earlier imperial models that banked territorial expansion like savings in an account, the American imperium now oscillates between invasion and isolation. Occupation is not an end in itself, intended to hold a population and fix it to a place so as to siphon off wealth. Rather, intervention disperses people from jobs, cities, homes, and other productive resources associated with a colonized area. Compared to earlier imperial forms, the empire of indifference stands as a massive flight from commitment, urging an embrace of risk and self-management to others as it would to its own domestic subjects, then ignoring, incarcerating, or dispossessing those who cannot make the grade. The difficult political questions are how these exempted populations locate their own means of affiliation and what social entanglements cut across the securitized risk divide.

As in the influential work of Michael Hardt and Antonio Negri, especially their books *Empire* and *Multitude*, I underscore the expansive political base that emerges from people's interconnections and capacities to formulate how life might be lived. Hardt and Negri, along with Michel Foucault, Achille Mbembe, and Giorgio Agamben, have sought to understand the social capabilities of affiliation, population, and movements of people in terms of rule or sovereignty. As it is frequently presented, sovereignty is discussed as something outside the question of political economy —the question of how value is rationalized and how social capacities are responsible for creating wealth. The last chapter of this book explores what happens to the critique of capital in light of an emphasis on problems of sovereignty in a global context. My hope would be to make good on some of the initial philosophical promises of political economy as a general framework for thinking the social. Rules engage a population, and production rests upon labor. The accumulation and circulation of capital join people's ability to create and to participate in what they have made. But capital also sunders that link, as it leaves people out in search of some newly free and disposable capacities to work.

The basic tension in capital is that its accumulation requires the creation of particular social conditions and associations that it ultimately cannot abide, a social surplus beyond alienable wealth. Historically, people are dispossessed of their particular means of subsistence; for example, they might be pressured to sell a family plot or common land and instead work for a wage. When people are forced to give up what they had and obliged to come together on a new basis, capital certainly profits. But people also bring into being new ways of living together: they form unions and other associations, they make communities from strangers. This organizational muscle costs employers money, but it also reinforces the belief that people can manage their own affairs. The managers are not left alone to decide what is best for business. The question of how to best manage life has become the axis of policy, as well as a touchstone of political strife.

Consequently, capital flees not just persons and places but its own categories and forms of development—such as cities, nations, races, and civilizations. More abstractly, the promise of a better future and the interest of capital in its own utopian aspirations have largely been abandoned in favor of a rather disenchanting ethos of self-management. Despite the advertised enthusiasm that all should be managers of their affairs, the ethos of responsibility is not shared, and people are left to manage the mess that the imperious investors deposited before taking flight. The perverse effect of financialization in daily life is to exchange security for volatility, to recast the recently revered ideals of middle-class stability in terms of risk. Government becomes the arbitrageur of disinvestment from the old ways and the retailer of embracing the new. No longer assuming a unified national interest that applies to an entire citizenry, the interventionist, privatizing, evangelical state leads with its taste for opportunistic war.

The promise of a self-managed world is a very contradictory one. If the future has been jettisoned in favor of ongoing intervention in a perpetual present, the ends of that capacity to do anything one chooses, anywhere, for any purpose, are also up for grabs. If info-wars rest upon intelligence that cannot succeed, increased volatility and targeted opportunity will result. Capital is hyper-mobile; it speeds around the world, hastening transactions to increase its mass. So too, labor is freed to move from job to job, place to place, retooling itself along the way. Labor mobility is not simply part of the dispossession of ways that people have had to make a living. The movement or circulation of labor is socially creative. It is also constitutive of population: people are brought together with a particular experience and sense of being together—they fill, inhabit, populate, so as to differentiate a particular space from others and from what might have been before. Labor circulates in response to the peregrinations of capital but also the machinations of the state. But it is not a passive victim devoid of agency, or an object of desire that can do no more than refuse and resist. Labor's creative capacities to forge a particular population, paint its own dreamscapes, and weave together an address to state and capital constitute political projects that are at once political, civic, and productive. Recognizing the value of these capacities is the task of political theory.

While neoliberalism denied the significance of the state, the privatizing state (a neoconservative trope of government action for moral effect) dwarfs the old leviathan. Liberalism and conservatism, whether old or new, share a dialectic of global intervention and nationalist isolation that illuminates various historical expressions of imperialism as well as the regime of globalization.[17] Yet today's imperial attitude is striking in its attention deficits. Efforts at rule proceed without knowledge of whom they would subordinate or even knowledge of who resists domination. The absence of intelligence field operatives in Iraq, the uncertainties after several years of occupation as to who the insurgents actually are, the use of torture to extract information—all point to a pervasive flight from a will to knowledge that was once thought essential to global rule. The irony of this program is that the rejection of knowledge comes through a sturdy confidence in the power of calculable information under the sign of a techno-scientific intelligence war.[18]

The refusal by the imperium itself of certain histories of difference departs from previous conceptions of international hegemony but is also common to the rejection of so-called special rights like fair wages, affirmative action, and queer unions. This rejection of the need to know others in the midst of ruling them opens routes to new expressions of sociality and solidarity, assertions that affirm the rightfulness of difference. The anti-imperial movements in this regard not only are strident refusals of discretionary war but can be read as a population's own politics of securitization and the derivative. Polled opinion has become an obsession of contemporary rule, designed as much to track volatility as to consolidate acquiescence in particular approaches to governance. Given the incessant making and unmaking of opinion, polls would seem to present their own version of intelligence failure. How to notice and validate the resonant if oblique agglomerations and interdependencies in our midst and how to make much out of what may seem to be too little becomes a conceptual opportunity, a value-enhancing return of theoretical attention to the political scene.

From Security to Securitization ⚞ 1

In the language of homeland security, economic normalcy has become seamless with political emergency. Security is an investment—a term that has changed its meaning from its initial, ecclesiastical one, dating from the seventeenth century, of putting on robes to assume spiritual powers: among powerful nations it was once enough to drape oneself in the flag to be imbued with the attribute of security. "Investment" by the nineteenth century was used in military engineering to denote the isolation of a hostile force or fortress by blockade. Just as old is the sense of the term, in colonial commerce: the use of money to purchase goods. Subsequently, eighteenth- and nineteenth-century economists would distinguish investment, the acquisition of property, from speculation, a distinction that eventually would largely disappear. The idea of security is still older than that of investment. Use of the word to mean safety or freedom from danger goes back to the fifteenth century. Already at this time security could also refer to a bond, a pledge to fulfill a debt; these bonds would develop, by the seventeenth century, into exchangeable documents, bills of credit among firms sold in specialized markets.[1] The roots of credit in faith, evident in the general appeal of financial services today, constitute what Marieke de Goode calls "a genealogy of finance," whereby our confidence in money is established through all manner of religious and artistic representation.[2]

Homeland security is best understood from the perspective of the original double meaning of safety and debt, but the concept moves in a world where the political and the economic are most commonly separated in public conversation. Pressing on the political meaning of security brings its economic double to the surface once again.

The wisdom of finance wrought as a way of life now guides foreign policy, the simultaneous othering and remaking of them into us. The ascent of finance, its insinuation into daily affairs, and its primacy of self-anointing investors compromise the abilities of the state to unify its population around a national principle even as this process rests upon a hypervigilant regime of regulation and intervention. To wit, controlling inflation necessitates continuous action that is necessarily preemptive. This is both the logic and the public rhetoric of interest-rate adjustments by the Federal Reserve Board.

Before the supremacy of strategic intervention, the Fed had long mastered the art of the preemptive strike. Investors would want to think of themselves in these terms as well. While acting in one's own interest assumes a stable present to mitigate an uncertain future, preemption acts to turn a presumed certainty about the future into a present suddenly made uncertain and therefore open to opportunity. Cutting interest rates treats the specter of future inflation as a tangible presence, just as does the panoply of financial products that issue from the credit economy, especially the class of securities called derivatives. When preemption drives foreign policy, the same logic is at work. Potential threats are actualized as demonstrations of the need for further intervention. Preemption is the temporality of what will be explored here as the political and moral economy of securitization, the future made present. Whereas the history of securitization is an incorporation of the foreign in the domestic, the reaction to risk brought home, the terror war as foreign policy directs this ambiguous domesticity outward.

: THE MORALITY OF RISK

Risk management bridges security and finance. Financial risk is the prospect of a greater than expected return on investments. Security is the converse: "preventing adverse consequences from the intentional and unwarranted actions of others."[3] Security as a sense of entitled protection readily slides into the calculating logic of financial securities. As has happened many times in the past, moral and political economy—the production of value as right and as wealth—have become entangled. Like the usurers once subject to sanctions, the figure of risk, once a bad subject to be avoided, must now be presented as right and true. Safety is a public good whose ultimate preserve is legitimate warfare. This moral achievement of the well-governed state is transferred to an ethical subject who does good and well by accepting risk. To make sense of the present conjuncture of imperial dis-ease, with preemption auguring small interventions meant to have large effects, the articulation of finance and military authority, of economy and polity, needs explanation.

In the world of finance, the consolidation or bundling of local, individual debts (such as mortgage loans) into certificates of ownership or indebtedness (stocks or bonds) that can be publicly traded or sold elsewhere is called securitization. Securitization was the "revolution" in financial services meant to mitigate the risks that came from these violating insecurities.[4] Mortgages, car loans, and credit card debt are securitized when some financial interest purchases them from the issuer and then reorganizes this debt according to its risk characteristics. High-risk mortgages or credit card debt—those whose debtors are beyond a certain debt-to-income ratio—can be separated and packaged as a distinct commodity or derivative. Risk is the measure for the rate of exchange among debt commodities. In the simplest terms, securitization assembles credit, derivatives disperse risk.

Securitization, far from being a reduction of polity to economy, announces an intricate affiliation between the two. It interweaves particular circuits through which wealth is amassed, the deployments of force to forge the shape of social life, and the whole repertory of engagements at people's disposal to transform abstract beliefs into credible practice. There is no question that financial sectors flourish during moments of imperial trepidation and turnover.[5] In this the present bears the signs of other eras. Much effort to wrestle the present into some serviceable political coherence oscillates between the poles of the all-is-new and nothing-has-changed dichotomy, complicating the task of knowing what difference a critical intervention might make. Novelty is but an aspect of the present. Not all is new, and it would seem that little of the past ever fully departs. One temptation is to postulate the advent of new times in which everything moves in syncopation to the old ways, freed of their burdens and bad habits, but the challenge to critically oriented political thinking is to notice what is different in the present so as to revalue what now seems possible.

Caveats aside, just what does make the present ascent of finance any different from the dull march of the market's ways over the past five hundred years? What has shifted since the days when security and its double took shape as the morally requisite means of building the common wealth? And with marketization, commodification, consumerism, neoliberalism, neoconservatism, privatization, and deregulation, aren't there enough words already to describe what capitalism does to our lives without weighing in with one more—financialization? The treatment of how finance affects politics, of how fiscal policy infuses foreign policy, is both a specification of those other terms and an invitation to notice what has been added to the pot. While analytic clarity can be very quickly compromised by the complexity of what it actually encounters, let me present a very preliminary schematic distinction between the generic reason of the market and its present elaboration in finance, and what kind of ideal self is implied by the recent shift.

Fundamental to classical liberalism is a faith that the urge to truck and barter resides in human nature and is something that the artifice of the state can only impede. The neoliberal turn, said to reign for the past twenty-five years, paradoxically enlists that very state to spread market values throughout the realm. According to Wendy Brown, this colonization of liberal democracy, in which the state acts to promote liberty by a neoliberal market reason, in turn situates "citizens as individual entrepreneurial actors."[6] Her account of the neoliberal turn is worth quoting at length:

> While this entails submitting every action and policy to considerations of profitability, equally important is the production of all human and institutional action as rational entrepreneurial action, conducted according to a calculus of utility, benefit, or satisfaction against a micro-economic grid of scarcity, supply and demand, and moral value-neutrality. Neo-liberalism does not simply assume that all aspects of social, cultural and political life can be reduced to such a calculus, rather it develops institutional practices and rewards for enacting this vision. That is, through discourse and policy promulgating its criteria, neo-liberalism produces rational actors and imposes market rationale for decision-making in all spheres. Importantly then, neo-liberalism involves a normative rather than ontological claim about the pervasiveness of economic rationality and advocates the institution building, policies, and discourse development appropriate to such a claim. Neo-liberalism is a constructivist project: it does not presume the ontological givenness of a thoroughgoing economic rationality for all domains of society but rather takes as its task the development, dissemination, and institutionalization of such a rationality.[7]

Hence the triumph of the market cannot be assumed. It must be achieved. Moral responsibility is equated with the ability to be a utility-maximizing actor forever weighing cost and benefit. Government must be vigilant in intervening among those too mentally or morally weak to act on their own behalf. Privatization has a didactic function of showing how the market intervenes better. Perhaps it is fair to ask what happens when the "neo" itself is no longer new, or when its magic seems to have faded in the laboratories of the South, especially Latin America, where once Argentina, Bolivia, Brazil, and Ecuador were crowded together as its poster children. Now each of those countries—either in fiscal policies or in foreign affairs—has defaced the poster. As astute a left business observer as Doug Henwood has asked, "Neoliberalism, RIP?"[8]

It should be remembered, however, that neoliberalism never stood alone. Moralizing was not left to the market, but had a strong cultural and religious bent, evident in neoconservatism. The expansive use of military spending makes both Reagan and George W. Bush look like Keynesians convinced that the state had to step in and stimulate demand for goods where the market could not. The moral imperatives to reshape domestic life, like the war on drugs and the educational policy No Child Left Behind, always came with a state-wielded stick that was costly to hold. While the shorthand for neoliberalism is small government and free markets, the neoconservative menu serves a privatizing state and interventionist markets. The state must act to control indolence-inducing public sectors and the market must be spread (forcibly if needed) to effect human liberty. Economists of most stripes continue to believe that economistic behavior is rooted in human nature—a classical specter that continues to haunt all constructions—but the nature of the state meant to conform to this nature varies widely.

More than admitting that life is a cocktail of contrary tendencies, I want to add an ingredient to the mix. With the advent of a marketplace of values, finance over the same period (roughly thirty years) has come to qualify reason with risk. Risk is not simply a calculation that benefits will exceed costs, but a wager on accumulating beyond expected returns. When every cost and uncertainty can become an opportunity, the secure precincts of happiness are left behind for the dizzying heights of risk. Risk is not simply a construct that one abides but something somatized as a way of being. The gauge of risk tolerance is not "What will it cost me?" but "Can I sleep at night?"[9] Risk also performs a moral function, by sorting out those with the disposition to embrace it from those relegated to being bad risks. The risk taker is a righteous agent of history; those at risk are left in the ashcan.

Market values as described imagine a universe of value-neutral and fair rules of the game by which citizens are willed to take possession of themselves as free individuals and entrepreneurs. By contrast, financial values torque the sovereign subject into a sales agent. Financial reason focuses not on the free citizen but on the bonded investor. Rights are not given a priori, but gains are made because one is fully vested (recall the ecclesiastical meaning of investment), a portal of absent authority from which one derives one's own. The successful investor is also touched by good fortune, as if the recipient of a blessing in this seemingly secular domain. If the citizen's interests can be represented by transparent rules watched over by the state, investors are the kind of people who play the market, which means taking whatever bit they have, dispossessing themselves of it, and seeing in what form it might come back.

Leverage takes precedence over ownership, and the arbitrageur, one who preys on marginal fluctuations in price, balances with alacrity where once the entrepreneur stood fast. Whereas the entrepreneur decided for himself, the arbitrageur is embedded in the decisions of others, surfing the waves of decision and deriving unseen value from the undertow. The entrepreneur respects the boundary between property and speculation. The arbitrageur can no longer. No more moving property on and off the market, speculation has moved in full time. In the process of securitization, financial reason assembles these little bits of value, these tiny interventions, and links them to a universe of exchange.

Market value touts the individual: the owner, the utility maximizer, the secure, the free, the self-possessed. By contrast, financial reason continually references a social force that it can appeal to but not abide: the dispossessed, the leveraged, the derived, the securitized. Nothing could be more artificial than finance, or capital for others, but it does suggest a social ontology where once nature had its day. For those with the right moral fiber, a new being—or at least one born again—is on the horizon. The arbitrageur looks to trounce plants like an amoral elephant, but really he's just zealously spreading seed. No wonder that the most objectivist calculus of finance can share the mantle of power with latter-day evangelism (as the Texans Bush and Lay once did before the fall of Enron). Financial reason is a logic of agglomeration, of association, of far-flung interconnection. Its religious affinities are not Calvinist ascetic accumulation but something closer to animist cosmologies of the new evangelisms. In this light the terror war presents itself as a liberation theology grounded in risk.

The history of market society has entangled moral and political economy in a variety of ways. But time and again, moral codes compensate for social traditions that have been rent. Joyce Appleby has written of the moral economy that would be swept aside in the late seventeenth century by a money economy: "The salient features of the biblical economy were sufficiently congruent to the ordering of labor in the sixteenth century to invite belief: the world could be made fruitful through labor; labor came to man as both a punishment and a gift. As a gift it tied human society to God's charity. As a punishment it forever harnessed men and women in God's will."[10] Economy would maintain equilibrium in the person of God, who would balance good and evil on the body of labor. The depersonalization wrought by the market severed this moral order. This break was conceptualized by John Locke, who would ground value in a natural law of money resting upon the universal consent of mankind—the money that a man possessed represented his due proportion of the world's gold and silver. The link between population and wealth would find acceptance in the natural order of which the fixed quantities of specie were the visible evidence.

A century later Adam Smith would objectify wealth through economic exchange as a process located in the productivity of labor rather than as a static quantity. Morality would be secularized in the social space of impartial observers through interpersonal engagements. The parallel and conflicted constructions have been observed by Michael Shapiro, who argues that Smith's "perspectives are as notable for what they treat uncritically, formalize, and render static as they are for their critical recognition of dynamics and their displacing of static objects with human actions."[11] Ultimately Smith abetted the move from mercantilism, characterized by naturally constructed national boundaries, to industrialism, characterized by the setting of populations to labor by means of objective rules for exchange. This faith in objectivity and impartiality supported a monetary regime based upon convertibility and measurability and created an affinity between market equilibrium and moral harmony.

The currency shocks of the late nineteenth century that eventuated in the formal termination of the gold standard (at the London Conference of 1933) continued the fissure between economic and ethical valuation characteristic of capitalistic development.[12] Jean-Joseph Goux has articulated the crisis of realism in art that gave rise to abstraction with the end of the gold coin's universality. He understands the subsequent inconvertibility of the monetary sign as a "historical crisis of the general equivalent form."[13] This confluence between economic exchange and representation raises questions of moral fraudulence, as the authenticity of token and reference are placed in doubt. Such challenges to capitalism itself would require new forms of capitalist legitimation, be they socialist states, welfare states, fascist states, radically autonomous artistic movements, internationalist revolutionary movements, or liberationist impulses (especially along racial lines) within national states. The recognition that abstract tokens like paper money could wreck depressed or inflationary economies was met with moralistically grounded social economies. Crisis in this regard was not terminal but constitutive, in this case a reknotting of profit-driven wealth and its legitimation in increasingly abstract terms.

The breach of what had been accepted as a natural order of things must then be repaired by moral affirmation. The move from the concreteness of soil, to the objectivity of metal and convertible exchange, to the money token, to the ethereality of financialization captures a spirit consistent with control by the cosmos. The relation between neoliberalism and neoconservatism, both responses to the crises of Keynesian legitimation of mass-based growth economies that produce the moral stability of the citizen consumer, can be placed in a longer context. The risk-driven accumulation of finance that neoliberalism offered as its political economy would meet its moralizing faith in the neoconservative commitments to evangelizing intervention. The investor would become the holiest figure in the trinity of personhood completed by citizen and consumer. By millennium's end the abstract money token had itself become concrete, and the world of bonds and promissory notes between firms that Marx had described as "fictitious capital" was becoming part of a master tale of economic life. The revolution in international finance yielded a "new geography of money" that looked amoral for all its mathematical sophistication but relied heavily on various forms of warfare to restore the moralism lost to the vanishing ideals of the unified nation.[14]

While clearly contingent on an ever-expanding market, financialization introduces its own terms of critical evaluation that can allow us to notice social possibilities. Left critique of neoliberalism provides a narrative of what the state has taken away from the social contract. In this respect at least, neoliberalism only advertises loss to which neoconservatism is the moralistic compensation, and the older entitlements of the welfare state are viewed with nostalgia. So how is privileging finance any different? Finance is, after all, nestled in the market, even as it facilitates the accrual of wealth where money is not immediately to hand. Finance speaks not to sovereignty but to mutual indebtedness, and debt always foregrounds the force of obligations to others. At a time when all that seems visible is naked self-interest, rugged individuals, and winners taking all, there is something cunning to finance's reason. It encumbers us to the social principles in our midst, the necessary cooperation on the backs of which so much damage is done. We can flee debt, manage it, pay it off, but we can also learn to notice that what else it suggests is already at hand, the myriad encumbrances tendered. Precisely when security is breached and life is risk, together-ness has a recombinant aspect. In tracing what the rise of finance has wrought for habits foreign and domestic, there is an opportunity to discern what the present imperium has to offer the rest of us—rather than simply mourn better days.

: THE FINANCIAL ANGLE

Narratives of finance are always shadowed by a belief in the naturalness of the business cycle—a regular and predictable oscillation between economic growth and stagnation, leading to stable periods of prosperity and recession. Accordingly, the relative prevalence of money in speculative circulation versus money invested in production varies over time so as to describe a cycle of dominance of financial over industrial capital. More money changes hands in a month on international financial markets than is attached to a year's worth of global production of goods and services.[15] More significantly, dominance means that the reason of finance permeates and orients the activities of markets and social life. In the present incarnation of financial dominance (since the mid-1970s), the cycling is not simply temporal but also takes on a spatial aspect between the foreign and domestic, much like the reaction formation when the domestic infests the foreign. As the story is most commonly told, the United States held the cards and the cash for the international financial system after the Second World War.[16] The rules of the game were established in July 1944 through the Bretton Woods Agreements, named for the location in New Hampshire of the Mount Washington Hotel, where plans were made for the International Monetary Fund, the World Bank, and terms for conducting global exchange subject to American authority.

The crux of the international currency system was that the U.S. dollar, backed by gold reserves, was the guarantor of all monetary exchange. In 1960 gold was set at a fixed price of $35 an ounce, with set ratios for the amount of dollars in circulation and the amount of gold held in reserve. As the currency to which all others could be converted, the dollar achieved what in financial terms is called sovereignty. The solidity of the dollar was linked not only to the strength of the American economy but to the sense that behind the paper in circulation stood secure coffers of gold which naturalized the dollar as a universal store of value. When American money made the world, a national emblem took on a life of its own outside the nation. Not only did international exchange denominate its movements in dollars, but speculation in dollar equivalents (such as Eurodollars) placed unsupportable strains on the sovereign entity, leading to the suspension of convertibility from dollars to gold in 1971. Industrial nations recovered from the devastation of war while ex-colonies underwent the process known as development, which promised that they would follow the same path to riches (but without the benefit of colonies of their own) if only they followed the prescriptions and swallowed the pill of Bretton Woods and subsequent cold war policies.[17]

Between the fissuring of the Bretton Woods agreements, as world trade outstripped the mandated quotas for gold supply, and the flight from Saigon in 1975, this postwar Pax Americana underwent a seismic shock. Rather than make too much of the fallen sovereignty of the dollar or military defeat, standard reckonings of the new "visionary capitalism" place the blame in the developing world. By these accounts the trouble for the banking nations began when the Organization of Petroleum Exporting Countries (OPEC) raised oil prices in the 1970s, leading to mounting debt among the less fortunate nations, whose borrowing soared from $300 million in 1970 to $13 billion in 1977.[18] With oil-producing countries awash in dollars and no solitary power or hegemon to control their flow, interest and currency rates could float on the waves of new borrowing. Further, OPEC's ability to do for one strategic commodity what the United States could impose on the market as a whole was blamed for inflation, the blast-off of price without reference to value.

Domestically, labor shares with the third world the attribute of having its efforts to improve its lot considered inflationary by fiscal policy makers. Labor militancy and strike activity in the early 1970s or legislatively guaranteed entitlements (like Social Security, which was indexed to inflation in 1972) could be recast by financializers as serving special interests and therefore being unhealthy for the economy as a whole. Regulation Q, enacted during the Depression, limited the interest rates that banks could offer on savings accounts. In response, mutual funds (marketed to corporate clients seeking a hedge against inflation) offered higher returns and began to draw consumer accounts. Consequently, federal fiscal policy was pushed to alter its regulatory framework.

The movement of money from the security of insured deposits to the open fields of speculative risk became a first step in a process in which, as Joseph Nocera has explained, "the middle class joined the money class."[19] The American dream was being recast with the investor as its central figure. Paradoxically, when the third world acted on the promise of development by assuming the debt that would fund its industrialization and consumer expansion, the consequence was to destabilize the established patterns of money lending back home. As the veteran business writer Charles Geisst observed, "Ironically, adjustable rate home mortgages put the homeowner in much the same position as Mexico and other developing countries had been in a decade earlier."[20] The enticements of credit and the entrapments of debt removed the clear path from rags to riches, from dependent child to mature adult that development once advertised for all.

The efforts to make the skies friendly again to the united of capital would fall to a series of government initiatives with the disingenuous name of deregulation. While he would get no credit for the celebrated reformulation of government, Jimmy Carter got the ball rolling with the passage of the Depository Institutions Deregulation and Monetary Control Act of 1980, which phased out interest ceilings, facilitated interstate bank activities, and permitted thrifts to expand into credit card and commercial services. Carter's appointment of the monetarist Paul Volcker to head the Federal Reserve Board in 1979 was equally significant.[21] Volcker's tenure signaled a shift from encouraging growth to curbing inflation as the prime target of fiscal policy. In monetarist hands, the Fed's principal regulatory activity was the perpetual adjustment of interest rates (in particular, the prime rate at which banks lend money to one another). Constant intervention to control the monetary supply should properly be seen as characteristic of a state hyperactively involved in the economy—contrary to neoliberal self-portraits. Instead, interest-rate adjustments were presented as government mimicry of the market, which constantly modulates prices to achieve equilibrium.

Narrowly speaking, monetarism is associated with tight control over the money supply on the premise that rapid expansion of money in circulation is inflationary—and that inflation destabilizes prices and compromises economic and social stability. The mandate to limit monetary growth proved untenable during Bretton Woods and even more so afterward. As increasingly large sums of money were placed in circulation by financial transactions initiated throughout the global economy, monetarism came to have a greater afterlife, less because of an obsession with the amount of money in circulation per se than because inflation was feared as a damper on the entire fiscal environment. The conviction of the new economy was that money itself could grow without being inflationary, as long as growth did not carry the burdens of development.

Not simply growth in the monetary supply but debt became a contagion that washed back from third world to first. But although debt was a sign of moral weakness among the less developed, it became a credential of adroit risk management among the financially mature. In 1982 the United States was the world's largest creditor (at roughly $250 billion). It ended the decade a net debtor. The reversal from creditor to debtor was sudden, a shock that devalued security, no longer an aim of government policy and now an attribute of the weak and feeble. By 2001 the United States was in hock to foreign creditors to the tune of $2.3 trillion.[22] Consumption, based on the expanded capacity to buy on credit, would come to drive global economic activity in the form of exports to the United States, and concomitant dollar-denominated surpluses would be reinvested in the United States (for example in the stock market). The ability to sustain debt, and the willingness to continue lending, were portrayed as signs of strength. But the debt of the third world, inert and immobile, was treated as bad.

When the loans made in the 1970s could subsequently be repackaged as securities, these newly amalgamated assets made good the vulnerabilities of development, turning fixed debt into a promissory note of credit that could be turned over and reinvented as infinitely exchangeable bonds, futures, contracts, and other financial niceties. The flush of dollars from oil producers and European banks had fueled a credit-driven third world boom for about six years in the 1970s. As Robert Guttmann explains: "But then, in 1979, the Islamic Revolution in Iran triggered another worldwide hike in oil prices. Amid surging global inflation, speculation against the dollar became rampant. Six months later U.S. monetary policy switched dramatically toward restraint. Shortly thereafter the world economy entered its worst downturn since the Great Depression of the 1930s. This sequence of events hit the [third world] with a double whammy. Their borrowing needs and interest payments exploded, while their debt-servicing capacity eroded precipitously at the same time."[23]

The U.S. Treasury, the International Monetary Fund, and the Bank for International Settlements arranged a three-step bailout that included short-term bridge loans, domestic austerity, and myriad loan restructuring agreements with private banks that profited handsomely from fees on new loans, longer-term debt agreements, and later the ability to resell the debt on the open market in what were called debt-for-bond swaps. As Guttmann explains, "The first swap, negotiated with Mexico in February 1990, lowered that country's annual debt-servicing charges by $1.5 billion—a reduction of about 12 percent."[24] While the results were decidedly mixed for the debtor nations—formerly stable Venezuela, for example, faced major unrest when the austerity measures were rolled out—lending banks now had a rich loam of opportunities from which to craft securitization, including loan sales, debt-equity swaps, and debt-for-bond swaps.

Unlike the late 1960s and early 1970s, when imports also exceeded exports, the fixed quantity of American gold reserves stood as a kind of ballast that was intended to adjust for differences but ultimately sank the dollar. In the fifty years preceding the turn of the millennium, gold went from nearly 70 percent of international reserves to but 2 percent, much of the remainder in dollar-denominated foreign exchange.[25] Now monetary movement was being freed to spread the wealth. Equilibrium—key to Bretton Woods and early monetarist currency controls—was no longer a condition of exchange. The dollar's spread, the expansion of debt and speculation, fostered disequilibrium and its attendant risks as a new horizon of opportunity. Fixing exchange to a physical standard perpetuated the image of the economy as a closed system. It could grow in proportion to the balance of inputs and outputs.

The fear of inflation retained the organic metaphor. An economy could become overheated and melt down or explode.[26] The social sciences more generally were predicated on this image of a closed system. The system adapted to internal strains by growth and differentiation. It maintained boundaries, kept out threatening uncertainties, and externalized unintended consequences from its internal decisions. As financial reason overtook the system-based moral and political economy, as the investor who knows no country elbowed out the consumer-citizen of the nation-state, the organic closed system, result of the social sciences' unacknowledged metaphorizing of the social, was morphing into a different kind of beast.

The models for open, far-from-equilibrium systems went back to the 1950s and gained currency among organizational studies in the 1970s and 1980s.[27] With clearly bounded demarcations between inside and outside now lacking, uncertainty became risk. Rational-choice theories, which described a world of individuals processing information (discrete inputs) to effect preferred outcomes, envisioned society along market and computer-decision lines. The conceit was that the logic of calculation, the ordered addition of data in a controllable series, could be translated into a more general conception of human temporality and the treatment of information could be used to forecast the future, here simply a desirable outcome in and of the present. Systems may have been opening, but the confidence that human activity was best modeled by the design principles of certain machines remained. The easy flow of ideas between financial and military thinking that now underwrites the war on terror has long been organized through the metaphors and models of systems.

: DERIVATIVE DEVELOPMENT

The finance-driven path to development posed a double bind, in the words of one account: "The trading partners of the United States now face the choice of continuing to invest their dollar surpluses in U.S. dollar-denominated assets despite very compelling reasons to doubt the security of such investments, or else converting their dollar surpluses into their own currencies, which would cause their currencies to appreciate and their exports and economic growth rates to decline."[28] Hence countries like China that manufacture much for the United States also purchase government-issued U.S. bonds to secure the solvency of dollar-driven exchange. This is a very precarious situation for maintaining the status quo. Debt dependency forced an opportunity on developing nations that meant eschewing security for greater and greater risk.

When the mischief of foreign policy comes back to haunt the homeland, it is called "blowback."[29] The wave of debt was blowback of a very different sort: a menace to security at and of the home that would turn productive. The mountains of dollars dispersed in the name of development were coming back as little pebbles. Management of others by means of indebtedness was converted to industrial production of debt in a manner that recalled colonial exchanges of raw materials and finished goods, but with a new geographic twist. Securitization served as raw debt extraction—derivatives named the production of debt machinery in the form of financial instruments. The new international division of debt culled labor from populations around the world and fed it into a spider's web of financial exchanges that spread from New York, London, and Frankfurt, to Tokyo, Singapore, and Johannesburg.

Derivatives remove reference from the commodity. They allow debt to serve as a productive medium from which countless commodities can be spawned. Derivatives are promissory notes issued between firms. They represent a prime vehicle with which industrial corporations undertake the function of banks by engaging in financial services. The derivative is a sign of the shift in the beneficiaries of development from populations or nations to other economic actors. Those who can steward risk will advance. Those who cannot will remain underdeveloped. The capacity for financial decision making trumps democratic involvement to decide political representation. Dressed in the objective garb of mathematics, risk technology cloaks its own cultural references. Edward LiPuma and Benjamin Lee have described how derivative decision making trumps democratic development by promoting a culturally specific concept of risk. "This concept of risk promotes asymmetry because it inscribes western ideology, specifically an acultural notion that modernity is a set of enhancing transformations that every nation-state can, should, and no doubt will be forced to go through."[30]

The derivative is in effect the apotheosis of the new financial regime, a "financial abstraction whose value is derived mathematically" from anything, asset or not, on which a contract can be drawn for some variation in price.[31] As noted earlier, a firm selling a product overseas that will not be deliverable for several years will create a contract to fix currency exchange rates for the time when the product is finished. The expected difference between current and future exchange rates can then be sold as a separate commodity. A similar contract could hedge against a change in interest rates, or the price of raw materials, or delivery costs. The single exchange of goods for money multiplies into an interconnected series of denominated notes worth particular amounts that can be traded in specialized markets. Over the past twenty years, the market for derivatives has undergone staggering growth, such that now the face value of contracts in interest-rate, currency, and credit-default swaps far exceeds the global value of goods and services. In 1998 the principal markets for derivatives amounted to $96 trillion, and eight years later they surpassed $200 trillion. All this is part of what the *Economist* called "a two-decade-long transformation of the financial markets and a new approach to risk."[32]

High risks fetch higher returns, which transform poverty from a public burden or blight into a highly profitable investment opportunity. The poor have long paid more to borrow money or gain access to financial services, a disparity defended on the ground that they are more likely to default on their loans. What was once the local knowledge of the loan shark is now the province of multinationals. Michael Hudson provides as an example of what he calls "the poverty industry" the reinvention of the industrial giant International Telephone and Telegraph (ITT) as a consumer financial services company that grants small loans at 21–30 percent interest: "Deborah James thought ITT was helping her dig out of debt. She was wrong. It was digging her deeper. Her problems began with a $300 bill at a waterbed store that ended up in the hands of ITT's Jacksonville, Florida, office. From there, ITT persuaded her to refinance her loan five times over two years–and ratcheted her debt up to more than $4,000."[33] Poverty has also been made into an asset by means of modest ($200) loans from banks or nongovernmental organizations (NGOs) that have become known as microcredit. Micro-credit, initiated in Bangladesh by the Grameen bank in 1976, has now become a global movement with its own world summit that solicits individual investors to help create 100 million small businesses for a slice of the world's poor.[34]

Financialization has expanded the attention that financial corporations pay to the poor and the middle class. It introduces internal divides between those able to embrace its ways and those it considers unprofitable risks. For the financially literate and self-manageable middle classes, the plethora of securities and enlarged access to markets have meant the emergence of trade in smaller lots, discount brokers, and eventually home-based e-traders. The first instances of these exchanges (beginning with the International Monetary Market in 1971) were for foreign currency, but eventually all manner of domestic consumer debt—from mortgages and college loans to credit card and medical bills—would be subject to the same protocols and the mandate to hedge future volatility against present rates of exchange. The resulting futures contracts fixed some anticipated rate of exchange for the wealth of the other and brought it into the domestic present. A derivative contract could hedge against a rise or fall in the exchange rate. The broker of the contract can gain simply by charging fees to package and sell it. The one who owns the contract and bets correctly that the exchange rate between, say, dollars and Euros will rise the predicted amount can profit because the contract itself (like insurance) costs less than the money to be made in the transaction when it occurs. Conversely, exchange rates can decline and the owner of the contract will still make a profit if the transaction is properly hedged. The derivative thus tends to destabilize price and simultaneously increase speed and volume in circulation. Properly ascertained risk, not growth per se, is what yields rewards. The trade in risk avoidance devolves into a profit on risk itself. Other currencies are reduced to minor differences, no longer a strain to the closed system.

Securitization not only stripped debt of its initial content but also delocalized debt, severing the sense that its repayment installed creditors and debtors in a particular place. Local differences are reconstituted as variable risk, which because it is connected to a larger asset pool can have substantial ripple effects. The thickening derivative economy increases the density of interdependence. Small is no longer beautiful—an object of contemplation—in its own right, isolated and left to its own devices as a uniquely local experience. David's pebble can bring down its share of Goliaths. The previous geographic logic was evident in the model of the savings and loan, which localized the consumer's relation to capital so as to provide financial activity with a domestic face. Granted, this domesticity was part of a federal financial architecture—the interior security to which Bretton Woods was the foreign policy. In any event, with derivatives on the rise by the 1980s, the neighborhood thrift, shrine of the homeowning dream, was in deep trouble. Despite the advent of adjustable mortgage rates, many S&Ls struggled to turn a profit. In the ten-year period ending in 1984, fifteen hundred S&Ls went out of business.[35]

From a banking perspective, the rise of securitization was the result of poor nations' "debt crisis which led to a perceived deterioration in the credit standing of the major banks."[36] The wall of security between consumer and commercial banking and between domestic credit and foreign debt had been punctured. The debt crisis did not bring the expansion of the financial services sector to a halt: it was treated as another opportunity. The old guard began to whistle new tunes, and new recruits joined the ranks. Beginning in 1982 the Kansas City Board of Trade introduced stock index futures contracts, which made it possible to buy a unit or contract of the whole Standard and Poor's 500 portfolio of stocks at a fixed value and point in time, a way to hedge the volatility of the markets. Derivatives picked up steam partly as a result of legislative initiatives, and new forms of credit ownership began to flourish.[37] Soon other stock markets and exchanges were getting into the derivatives business, looking at the future as the present. Risk hedging, long a prophylaxis, became a new way of life for the burgeoning financial services sector, to be embraced at considerable profit.

The American dream unfolded in space and time. Homeownership anchored the spatial dimension, providing a physically bounded unit of domesticity. The pension had equivalent status with respect to temporality. It was meant to assure a heaven on earth, a life free of labor that would begin after the home was bought and paid for (presumably on a thirty-year mortgage). While half the population never attained this package, this dream (like that of development) would come to those who would work hard, accumulate, and wait. Until the 1980s the most common pension scheme, the defined-benefit pension, granted the pensioner a fixed percentage of salary upon retirement. A career of hard work would be rewarded with the certainty of knowing that one's calling in life had been found. Defined benefits delivered on the futurity of the Protestant ethic, a godlike assurance from the employer that labor had done good and the retiree would do well.

But if one had to wait for retirement to know that life had been well lived, people would become passive about their future, dependent on the judgment of others, lacking moral self-definition. Better to take control of one's fate to master the future now, to prove one's mettle a day at a time. Gratification and judgment would no longer be deferred. Judgment day came with each dawn. This morning in America, associated with Reagan's reign, was a moral imperative underwritten by a redesign of the financial plan for living. Concomitant with other changes in the financial architecture, the passage of the Employee Retirement Income Security Act (ERISA) in 1974 shifted pension capacity and responsibility to the individual under the rubric of the Individual Retirement Account (IRA).

Eight years later the first 401(k) accounts were developed, and within twenty years these accounts totaled $1.8 trillion with 42 million participants. IRAS were a crucial conduit, not simply for funding pensions but for broadening participation in stock and other financial markets. Before ownership was popularized by defined-contribution pensions (which have individual accounts, and no guaranteed return), holding stock, while not formally restricted, was largely a preserve of the élite, limited in 1982 to slightly more than one in ten households.[38] While promoters of the first retirement accounts championed a diverse investment portfolio to hedge risk, they also fostered the idea of the worker-as-owner, and employees averaged a fifth of their holdings in their employer's own stock. The financial services business for consumer accounts was quite highly concentrated, with twenty firms (including Fidelity, Vanguard, Prudential, and Merrill Lynch) managing over three-quarters of all retirement assets. This ownership sought to seal an interest between labor and capital generally by reinforcing the employer-employee relationship.[39]

Defined-contribution plans provided the crucial bridge between pension financing and stock market investment and helped change attitudes toward ownership that had been jaundiced by the lackluster returns of the 1970s.[40] Again, fate was not given by a corporate father but lay in one's own hands. The early spirit of capitalism had borrowed an ascetic religious disposition. The new spirit was that of the televangelist, with daily performances required to assure that the calling is heard. This moral activism had elected Reagan. Now it could be applied to those who would elect risk. Religious conservatives and financial self-managers were not necessarily the same people, but they belonged to the same moment when a contributing self was being defined. No longer would you wait until the end of a career to measure your worth: you would need to measure it day by day. In practice, defined contribution schemes are private (employer-sponsored), but they create a spirit of voluntarism for the worker.

Roughly half of all households in the United States have some kind of private retirement scheme. By 1993 more than half of those employees with pensions had the defined-contribution type (up from 19 percent in 1984), in large measure because of the perception that the risks were equivalent to those of the defined-benefit type while the rewards were likely to be greater.[41] The sway of defined-contribution plans over defined-benefit plans had to be seen in the context of ongoing prophecies that the Social Security system was going bankrupt, but also as an assault on even private conceptions of corporate benefit. Defining a contribution for labor's savings meant that workers were being enlisted directly into the circuits of finance—nominally at least as owners of the means of its production. Peter

Drucker had famously and hostilely forecast that the growth of pension funds was an insidious, creeping socialism. Accordingly, the spread of financial participation would undermine managerial controls and place labor's needs over profit. At the same time Robin Blackburn exposed the profitability for financial services of the trend toward greater longevity. He proposed a notion of sustainable development over the course of workers' lives that would restore universal access to public pension benefits.[42]

The shift from defined benefits to defined contributions was not restricted to pensions but intended to essentially end social welfare. The Keynesian welfare-state notion of the public good stood for a committed universalism to an entire population. State-recognized residence conferred citizenship, and with it the determinate basket of benefits defined by the social compact. The shift to a consumer society, evident in the 1970s, could be considered a transitional form of public identification that detached welfare from the state and applied it to the market. The id-like me-ness fit the inflationary decade, a plea for a soft-market intimacy that recognized the consumer as still the somehow passive beneficiary of a vague, expansionary horizon of satiating goods. But although inflation was the mother of a consumerist ethos, it was also a sign of excess, a government-induced fiscal indiscipline (according to monetarist doctrine). For monetarists, what had been sired by government had to be slain by the state to protect the honor of what a dollar might buy, to shore up the mass of goods that the money was chasing.

In place of the citizen or consumer, the figure of the investor loomed as the new focus of government policy. Consequently, personal investors would need to assume responsibility for themselves and make their own contributions, albeit with the state paving the way. More than this, however, the investor type assumed a self that had already been dispossessed of a secure past, present, and future. Citizenship under the welfare state secured not only fixed benefits but a determinate amount of space and time that the ideal type would occupy. Subsequently, to occupy the kind of time and space once readily conferred on personhood, one would need to make an investment, and then continually contribute to see what one was amounting to, how big a place in the world one was taking up.

We are, of course, still addressed as citizens and consumers, but it is investors that are at the edge of policy and at the interface of the well-tempered self and the machinery of state and economy. By shifting the inflection from citizen to investor, defined contribution elides the universalism once claimed for all Americans. The faith that if you live in the freest nation on earth you must be free is no longer an unbroken circle. While the old universalisms imposed a range of exclusions, the new ambitions for progress would be partial and permeable. The half of all citizens who participate in defining their future now stand for the whole, or at least the universe of all who count. This half turns out to be quite a fateful proportion: in addition to representing the share of all households who hold stocks, it is also the share who have personal computers, and who vote.

The investor category, while less inclusive than that of citizen or consumer, is a kind of political derivative, since particular gains result from national policies like tax cuts or interest-rate adjustments. The "investor class" expands still further when homeownership is treated as one of the criteria for membership, insofar as management of home equity, credit, and debt is of strategic importance in financial self-management more broadly. Homeownership, now characterizing over two-thirds of American households, has effectively passed over into a defined-contribution logic.[43] The government's version of defined contribution is to shift social entitlements to a policy of tax cuts and incentives as a means of effecting a distribution of wealth that creates its own version of who is inside and outside the nation. If the ever-cheapened computer is the icon of consumption, its installation in the home opens the domestic haven to the heartlessness of market speculation. At the same time, participation in the life of the country will be redefined as the achievement of self-management.

: RISK WARS

What began as the financial service industry's embrace of risk-management tools in the face of overexposure to foreign debts has been refigured as a subjectivity of consumer finance that infuses domesticity with risk. The space of security is now that of securitization. Risk is not unilateral but operates as a kind of moral binary, sorting out the good from the bad on the basis of capacities to contribute. The prototype financial instruments and regulatory mechanisms were introduced in the 1970s for the life of risk that would rise in the 1980s. Those who cannot manage themselves, those unable to live by risk, are considered "at risk."[44] The epidemic that began with the 1980s, AIDS, is defined by moralizers as caused by "high-risk" behavior, a definition likely to last until, with the help of pharmaceutical largesse, the disease can be properly managed and (helped by epidemiological shifts in who is getting sick) some of the homophobic stigma fades. Those who are subject to risk, as opposed to those who can make of it a subjectivity, are treated to various modes of domestic violence or wars. Unlike the War on Poverty (1964–68) during the Great Society years, which aimed to assimilate the poor to middle American affluence on the model of new immigrants, the risk wars have turned pathology into social partition.

Much of the Patriot Act, enacted in 2001 shortly after the September 11 attacks, was anticipated by changes to conceptions of privacy and criminality brought about by draconian drugs laws and federalized law enforcement. In particular the Racketeer Influenced and Corrupt Organizations (RICO) Act of 1970, initially meant to combat Mafia activity and to encompass both extortionists and their victims (the passive instruments whose lives or businesses were threatened if they did not pay protection fees), was subsequently applied to businesses, political organizations, and terrorist groups that were connected more indirectly to a racketeering activity, for example by laundering money.[45] RICO can now be used to treat virtually any organization as a suspect medium or front group for unwanted activity. The Mafia, neither an individual nor a business, was an organizational form without legal status. By imputing intent to a nefarious network, the state was able to assign enemy status to a domestic organizational entity. The war on crime, which delocalized and federalized prosecution, could be applied to other activities identified as domestic threats.

Military means and metaphors connected foreign and domestic policy, and featured incarceration over rehabilitation as the preferred means of dealing with bad risk.[46] Monitoring, intervention, and punishment for failure became the watchwords of domestic warfare, whose casualties were effectively disappeared from the civic fabric. The war on drugs and crime militarized law enforcement and fed expansion of the prison complex. The culture wars marginalized public interest in the arts and depicted minority discourse as dominant—all as justifications for intensified federal vigilance. An assault on education, purportedly to combat poorly managed failing schools, reached its militaristic apotheosis with the enabling legislation of 2002, No Child Left Behind. This act analogizes low-scoring students to wounded soldiers—a kind of *Black Hawk Down* meets *Saving Private Ryan*. Federally mandated testing is used to withhold funds, punish failing schools, and control curricular content—all elements of the zero tolerance that makes for a generalized state of war. The eradication of welfare as we knew it was similarly based upon the purported need to drum erstwhile cheats out of the system.

What often combined all this bellicosity into one category was youth, figured as a culturally depraved group undeserving of a future.[47] The "scapegoat generation," sketched so effectively by Mike Males, was the silent majority counterpoised with the yuppie poster child.[48] For every young urban professional making a killing on The Street, nineteen members of the same cohort were seeing real declines in wages, rising college costs, and dismantled social services. Those who couldn't make the cut would encounter stiff discipline. So much for the winsome days of youth. In each at-risk category, something excessive lurks. It does not matter if drug use goes down or test scores go up: the pressure of failure to embrace risk is itself inflationary. It threatens to bring about a scarcity of goods and to introduce other criteria for valuing risk, a problem well understood by those who have studied crime waves and moral panics.[49]

This division between good risk and bad, which prepared the way for the speculative 1990s, operated as a matter of government policy, business initiative, and professional culture. The now-famous run on the stock market amassed more wealth, $17 trillion, than had been amassed in the two hundred years prior.[50] It has become common sense across the spectrum of economic opinion to view this accumulation as momentary irrational exuberance, explained with animalistic metaphors of herds and feeding frenzies.[51] But it is worth inquiring into the more durable effects upon habits of life and social organization of these ways of finance. The speculative bubble may have made some people rich, but it also extended participation in the stock market, once the province of the affluent (12 percent of households in 1982), to the better—or at least the upper—half of households measured by income.[52] Much money was lost when the bubble burst after its peak in August 2000, and investment priorities have shifted among stocks, bonds, and real estate, but remarkably, an exodus from speculative financial markets back to conventional savings accounts has not ensued.[53] The low interest rates that fuel real estate investment make the conventional savings accounts unattractive, with rates of return lower than the rate of inflation. The defined-contribution genie has not returned to its bottle. In 2004 George W. Bush campaigned on the promise of an "ownership society" and began his new term by pushing for the privatization of Social Security.

The underlying continuities of government financial policy between the administrations of Bill Clinton and George W. Bush have been forcefully documented by Robert Pollin. Both presidents abetted financial speculation and the redistribution of wealth to the wealthiest through tax policy; Clinton's partial restoration of prior tax cuts had an aggregate effect similar to that of Bush's cuts, further concentrating wealth and stimulating consumption in the upper income brackets.[54] Low inflation was the chief goal of fiscal policy. Whether during Clinton's boom or the Bush recessions (both father's and son's), minimizing inflation was a constant for the Federal Reserve under Alan Greenspan, perhaps the best survivor of the new economy markers (he was appointed by Reagan in 1987 and retired under George W. Bush in 2006). With Bush, growth could again be an economic good so long as it was underwritten by a "stable macroeconomic environment, characterized by low and stable inflation" which promotes "economic freedom" by allowing people to "plan for the future."[55] The heroes here, according to Bush, are the "risk takers and entrepreneurs" who create opportunity for others.[56]

The habits of risk and the measures of participation have remained the markers of middle American success and the concomitant blight of the American dream.[57] The expansion and sophistication of consumer credit have meant that the restless dream has been replaced by the work of acquisition. The increased rate of homeownership mentioned above is significant. Rent money is just as difficult to scrape together as a monthly mortgage, but mortgages are the gateway to a whole range of further decisions and transactions. The activation of the home as an object of speculation is less a first leaf in a get-rich-quick scheme of further property acquisition than a prosaic means of using equity to pay off credit card debt.[58] By 2004 plastic surpassed paper as the preferred medium of transaction, and the average cardholder in the United States had 7.6 accounts. While 40 percent of these accounts are paid off monthly, the rest are not, in part because 43 percent of households spend more than they earn. In the aggregate, for every dollar earned, $1.22 is spent. But if the average household holds over $8,000 in credit card debt, most cards are far from being tapped out. Per capita, $6,185 remains unused on the little plastic rectangles.[59]

In contrast to home values, which are presumed to increase over time, household income is not univariate. For four-fifths of the population income over the past thirty years has been largely stagnant, and the experience of this stagnation has been increasing volatility. The loss of jobs and medical insurance means that year-to-year income changes are greater now than in years past, a statistic tracked by the Panel Study of Income Dynamics at the University of Michigan.[60] As in the stock market, increased volatility assures that those who can make an opportunity from risk can quickly fall prey to uncertainty's blows. Nonetheless, the formulation of the "high-risk society" establishes equivalence between "workers, businesses, and countries," all of whom "must start thinking like investors in the financial markets." In a sunny scenario painted by the business writer Michael Mandel: "each person's main asset will be his or her willingness to take *intelligent* risks. Those people best able to cope with uncertainty—whether by temperament, by talent, or by initial wealth—will fare better in the long run than those who cling to security."[61] In effect, the embrace of risk is a subjectivity that knows no country.

Whereas prior constructs of stratification advertised directional mobility, the risk divide is far more miasmic, and can seemingly be crossed at any moment. According to the economic historian Michael Perelman, the intrinsic volatility of corporate profit fuels ever-more-risky speculation that ends in the reparcelings of property known as mergers and acquisitions.[62] What happens when the investor takes home this way of life? The anticipation of loss must be built into any calculation of risk, rendering contentment a particularly scarce commodity. In the face of imminent loss, the corporate body must be forever supplemented, reassessed for redundancy, and put back on the block. A question often asked by a financial adviser to those selecting among various investment schemes and options is, "What is your tolerance for risk?"[63] Unfortunately, one is never in a position to be intolerant, and what assumes the garb of choice is in actuality a labyrinth of decision. The decision is over which level of risk to accept at any given moment, on the assumption that nonacceptance is not an option.

In this regard, self-management is the ultimate faith that further securitization will eventually lead one home. As with the self-vigilance accompanying the war on terror, nothing assures that the investment-making, contribution-defining risk taker will stay put. Bad consequences of even good decisions can slide anyone into the at-risk category, just as kindness inadvertently misapplied can put anyone in league with terrorists. Maintaining moral integrity will require strip searches down to the very core of our beings. Proper morality can be achieved by conversion to risk-as-a-way-of-life; core values have adjustable rates.

Homeland security claims to snugly fix people to their places in the face of terrorist threats. On closer inspection, homeland security has been a means through which one arrangement for attaching population to geography has come unglued. Where is this sense of home that resides neither in the house nor in the nation? What does it mean for both to have moved from sites of security to scenes of securitization? The dispossession of fixed savings, home as a place for connecting elsewhere, life as a manageable volatility, suggests a more dramatic rethinking of what it means to be part of the nation than allowed by the notion of a secure, internal, and shared space.[64] The modern idea of the nation-state is grounded upon the premise that territorial boundaries, even if artificially imposed, engender an abiding connection among people that they recognize in the form of a shared interest. This common interest in the nation entwines a people together, conferring upon them a fate sealed by the actions of the state. But while the nation-state remains, it is far from clear that populations can be mobilized to common purpose and a sense of shared future under the rubric of national interest. This is a key consequence of the shift from security to securitization, a realignment in the political and economic work of interest. While the idea of national interest persists, it is important to trace through the problems that it now faces.

Interest of the monetary kind and interest as a political concept would seem to be independent. As Albert Hirschman famously traces the term, however, the two references are entangled from the start. The notion of interest begins to circulate widely in late-sixteenth-century western Europe as "the totality of human aspirations," given predictability and direction through reflection and calculation.[65] As the notion migrated to England, it would be made singular and consolidated in the seventeenth century as national interest, a concept tied directly to the acquisition of wealth. Interest allows political and economic attachments to form by subordinating anarchic passions, like avarice, envy, or greed. These passions subvert the coalescence of individual action into a sustainable social order. This at least is Hirschman's account of the triumph of capitalism as an assertion of reason incorporated into state authority. The state's knowledge of what the people need and of what threatens them allows it to act under the banner of national interest.

Ultimately, however, the notion of national interest rises above any public service. Grounded in Machiavelli's ambitions to consolidate Italy, the state embodies the highest principle of morality sustained by power. Preservation of the state justifies even immoral means of exercising force. The twentieth-century notion of national interest as a form of political realism grounded in naturally based objective law is credited to Hans Morgenthau. Realist rules transcend individual motive or ideological preference, such that scientifically adduced rationality is the only judge of historical success. According to Morgenthau, "political realism considers a rational foreign policy to be good foreign policy; for only a rational foreign policy minimizes risks and maximizes benefits and, hence, complies both with the moral precept of prudence and the political requirement of success."[66] Minimizing risk is necessary both to maintain security and to conserve power, the capacity for control and domination over people. Morgenthau defines state rationality as that which preserves rather than squanders power in the course of its deployment. Strategy is to be measured according to its successful outcome. Where power is insufficient, strategy is infeasible. Realist national interest is a machinery for the massive accumulation of power and is obliged to be risk averse.

The problem is that interest by this light can only be known after the fact. Writing to those who will conduct military affairs at the U.S. Army War College, Michael Roskin warns that "to get an accurate fix on the national interest it would be necessary to travel into the future in a time machine to see how things worked out under a given policy. The real national interest is sometimes knowable only many years after the fact."[67] By this reckoning, national interests require a clear delineation of present and future, where the present consists of a self-justifying pragmatics of power (I will because I can) and the future requires a "time machine" to vindicate the decision. The forward glance which allows decisions to become historical is called strategic. Strategy, in turn, affirms "vital" interests which pertain to the life of the state as such, and are differentiated from secondary interests which can be considered discretionary. Vital interests give primacy to preserving the state against threat instead of furthering power as an end in itself. Even as securitization has crashed the time machine by bringing the future into the present, the terror war has certainly effaced the distinction between strategic and secondary interests. The preemptive leap in time treats the secondary as vital, as a means and end of state that obviates a strategic dimension to interest.

This loss of the longer view, what in international relations is called "grand strategy," is treated by realists as policy failure. Their aim is to maintain the authority of a hegemonic state during a historical inter-regnum and to propose a new era of rule. The drift of grand strategy is that great nations require worthy rivals. Whatever the reasons for the disap-pearance of so-called great power rivalry, its return is treated as inevitable. The naturalization of rivalry affirms the necessity of the nation itself. In one typical account of America's lost glory by the realist Charles A. Kup-chan, "The tendency for nations to compete with one another is intrinsic to the human condition. It stems from basic human drives—the search for security, wealth, and dignity. Humans form nation-states and other types of communities to pursue these goals, and these communities then mani-fest the same essential drives in relations with each other."[68]

Such transcendental pronouncements have been challenged within the field of international relations, itself divided between realism, which views states as acting out of rational self-interest under conditions of interna-tional anarchy, and constructivism, which presupposes a norm-generating international order that tends toward stability. Recently, for example, Benno Teschke has surveyed the field and concluded that "the elevation of anarchy and the balance of power to transhistorical principles that deter-mine geopolitical behavior in a mechanistic way rests on a series of un-founded assumptions and generates behavioural propositions that are eas-ily falsified."[69] But as with many axioms of realpolitik, the ideas are more durable than their norms of falsifiability would allow, especially among the scientists charged with sustaining the grandeur of those self-anointed na-tions that have treated the world as their strategic field. Realism treats empire as an axiom of national interest. Those who provide the strategic firmament for military planning are in a position to propose realism that may be put into practice. Their proposals disclose much.

Proposals for grand strategies continue apace. So rich is the lode that they have been grouped into typologies. One prepared for the U.S. War College by D. Robert Worley has four types which have been applied throughout history in various combinations. First there is primacy, a con-dition of uncontested dominance based on "preponderant power" that establishes the United States as a singular "benign hegemon." In this condi-tion all other nations balance against the United States, which attempts to avoid an imperial overreach that can lead to isolation. The second type is neoisolationist, with a clear separation between military buildup to defend the country from prospective attack (a goal seen as legitimate) and the promotion of American values abroad (a task seen as best left to the private sector). Ultimately, increasing global militarization can be tough to square with the purported avoidance of foreign entanglement upon which isolation rests. Third is "selective engagement," aimed at preventing war between great powers and the proliferation of weapons of mass destruction (WMDS). Selective engagement assumes the ability to fight two medium-scale regional wars simultaneously. It also rests upon the capacity to act unilaterally and minimize peacekeeping as a long-term commitment, approaches that depart from the history of such interventions. Finally there is "cooperative security," which interweaves the nonproliferation of WMDS with advancing the peace internationally. This strategic type is identified as "indiscriminate in its willingness to intervene" and would require raising military force levels without any clear ceiling.

Assuming that grand strategy as the big idea in international relations is at a crossroads or hiatus, the question arises of where to intervene next, understanding that the choice will be a signal to the world about the strategic formation to come. Current friends and foes do not provide a powerful enough basis to orient global alignments, in the way that Britain or the Soviet Union once did. But there is strategic promise among those nations once called third world. Around the world there are an estimated thirty "failing" states—too many for nation building that is externally funded or based on intervention or occupation. Instead there is a need for unilateral strikes of limited scope to destroy threatening capacity. According to this diagnosis, terror is the product of states that are failing to remain part of the western secular system. Two military options are open: preemption when an attack is believed imminent, and prevention, under which an enemy is itself attacked before it becomes too strong. By this revisionist logic preemption is nothing new and most interventions are actually preventive, part of a continuing "counter-guerilla war."[70] By extension, preemption is the divine right of the hegemon.

For a military concerned about its institutional viability, selective engagement is the Goldilocks choice of grand strategy. Both uninational primacy and internationalist cooperative security will risk exhausting military forces, or overextending military capacity beyond what is allocated for the present and planned for the future. Research and development, once interrupted, can be difficult to put back on track. Military planners are especially concerned that open-ended deployments and military proliferation can politicize the military and jeopardize future budget allocations—

their version of the Vietnam syndrome. Without a great rival to keep at bay, defense and deterrence become a bit quaint, as the United States cannot sit and wait for the next attack. When little failed states act out, their behavior must be righted. "Compellence," the word of preference for Robert J. Art, "is the use of military power to bring about a change in an adversary's behavior; it is designed to force an adversary to stop the objectionable actions it has already undertaken."[71] When as a result of small-scale intervention an adversary changes its behavior in accord with the dominant state or hegemon's norms, selective engagement provides a valuable demonstration effect. Where opportunities to use the military to spread democracy are concerned, "demand far exceeds supply," Art says of the targeted interventions of compellence: while "small in number, these tasks are large in scope and importance."[72]

These overseas interventions are not ends in themselves, but are to be leveraged so as to create a totalizing effect in the absence of a political entity potent enough to mirror the scale of dominance. Military bases are to be sprinkled throughout the world to achieve this leveraged hegemony. Hegemony is the ability to set the terms of what passes as politically possible or realistic at a given moment. Leveraging suggests that the means for achieving hegemony have themselves run into limits, so that the appearance of global dominance is maintained by relatively small investments with large multiplier effects. This grand strategy prioritizes action according to a fixed hierarchy of interest. First is vital interest—preventing attack on the American homeland. Next are preventing Eurasian wars and securing cheap oil, followed by achieving an "open international economic order," advancing democracy and human rights, and protecting the environment.[73] Certainly there is an intent to conserve political power, but elevating leveraged intervention against a prospective threat into the principal orientation for American force represents a marked shift away from Morgenthau's risk aversion.

Compellence is an affirmative approach to risk management which operates similarly to the financial grand strategy of securitization. Without the epic, system-affirming world war or the era-affirming arms race and proxy battles of the cold war, the small intervention that makes a rogue of a weak state hedges against systemic failure. As if hegemony had moved from the realm of brutal necessity to obligatory freedom, the discretionary crusade, selected from among dozens of candidates at risk, assumes the mantle of grand strategy. The little war executes the failed state and isolates one risk in the hopes of sending liberatory ripples throughout the world. This derivative war pulls out one differential at the margins to leverage against a more general loss of control. Preemption steps in where great ordering antagonisms are missing. The preemptive terror war follows on the heels of the lost monetary sovereignty that was represented by Bretton Woods. With the United States no longer able to maintain equilibrium between national and foreign currencies, alien risk rushes in—bundling the small and domestic into potent new opportunities. Financialization made a virtue of this necessity. Now the terror war offers compensatory morality for a violated domestic state. It is not that every risk turns out to be good, or that each person placed at risk is harmed by intervention. The lines are no longer so easily drawn. Safety has given way to dizzying opportunity. A move from security to securitization.

꞉ SECURITIZING THE STATE

With the advent of the risk regime, the state is not merely an instrument: it is also transformed in kind when inside and outside know no boundaries. The most explicit interweaving of foreign and domestic was achieved by Bush's national security policy statement of September 2002. This is also the official articulation of the war on terror as the new grand strategy, one in which the small, preemptive intervention is elevated to great heights. While seemingly occasioned by September 11, many changes incorporated by Bush had been set in motion since the cold war's end. Preemptive military doctrine was made consonant with its equivalent in fiscal policy. Bush made a speech on 17 September to announce the new policy. The argument in his speech is characteristically compact yet sweeping. It is worth looking at an extended passage of the document to see how the rhetorical elements are assembled:

> The gravest danger our Nation faces lies at the crossroads of radicalism and technology. Our enemies have openly declared that they are seeking weapons of mass destruction, and evidence indicates that they are doing so with determination. The United States will not allow these efforts to succeed. We will build defenses against ballistic missiles and other means of delivery. We will cooperate with other nations to deny, contain, and curtail our enemies' efforts to acquire dangerous technologies. And, as a matter of common sense and self-defense, America will act against such emerging threats before they are fully formed. We cannot defend America and our friends by hoping for

the best. So we must be prepared to defeat our enemies' plans, using the best intelligence and proceeding with deliberation. History will judge harshly those who saw this coming danger but failed to act. In the new world we have entered, the only path to peace and security is the path of action.[74]

The document makes a number of claims that bear interrogation. The monetarist state makes defense its first priority, its own version of a defined contribution that displaces the sense of domestic security based on social welfare. Yet defense is complicated by the diffusion of enemies and their refusal to recognize the reasonableness of prior norms of deterrence. The end of the cold war will require a new arsenal of justifications that do the ideological work once provided by an ill-defined communism. As Harry Harootunian has observed, "In re-writing the script communism was replaced by terrorism, paradoxically making a method into an ideology, and effectively retaining the received binary between 'good' and 'evil.'"[75] Terror (like finance) is technique elevated to the status of belief. It would seem that the method is the ideology and that while Manichaean terms have been retained, the binary has got a bit slippery. Without defense capabilities of their own, "shadowy networks" lack organizational materiality but still have capacities of appropriating power. This enemy is at once spatially dispersed and temporally ambiguous, removing an end to its existence from sight and rendering the terror war of "uncertain duration." Yet uncertainty of form will be mastered by risk.

While terrorists are unaccountable, nations through which they pass will be held "to account." Homeland security means denying not just place but the state of being called "home" to terror. The ontological difference between those with a homeland and those without allows the "gravest danger"—the intersection of "radicalism and technology"—to apply only to others and not to the novelty of this national security policy. Further, while other nations can be attacked to purge them of terror, the United States is purportedly already under assault, meaning that the nation can be at war with itself and hold itself to account for the terror in its midst. All this leads to a response to history's harsh judgment, a future world made present by "the path of action."

Ultimately, the means for realizing defense will shift from deterrence to preemption. It is as if the very existence of enemies threatens the prospect of security, rather than necessitating a capacity for intervention. This is more than analogous to the obsession in fiscal policy with eliminating inflation. The mere presence of inflation undermines the will to participate in securities markets. The call to live by risk is threatened by a difference or distortion to the environment that subverts means to make rational calculations about the future. The preemptive strike is different from the elaborate regulatory environment enforced by mutually assured destruction during the cold war, its treaties, inspections, and mutual surveillance.

Preemption is closer to the privileged instrument of monetary policy, the manipulation of the prime rate by the Fed. In Greenspan's arsenal, adjusting the prime rate can usurp inflation before it has the chance to appear.[76] The mere presence of inflation is the bad other raising doubts about the future which will dissuade investors from participating in markets. It would seem that American foreign policy has arrogated to itself the same intolerance of difference, a national security based upon keeping rule-defying uncertainty at bay so that risk can thrive and the United States can reap profitable rewards. For the rest of the world, the carrot behind this stick of national security, as outlined in the Bush administration's National Security Document, is a fiscal policy for other nations lifted from Bush's own domestic agenda:

- pro-growth legal and regulatory policies to encourage business investment, innovation, and entrepreneurial activity;
- tax policies, particularly lower marginal tax rates, that improve incentives for work and investment;
- maintenance of the rule of law and an intolerance of corruption, so that people are confident they will be able to enjoy the fruits of their economic endeavors;
- strong financial systems that allow capital to be put to its most efficient use;
- sound fiscal policies to support business activity;
- investments in health and education that improve the well-being and skills of the labor force and population as a whole; and
- free trade that provides new avenues for growth and fosters the diffusion of technologies and ideas to increase productivity and opportunity.[77]

The point is not that possessing or even deploying weapons of mass destruction is at odds with inflation-fighting fiscal policy.[78] The United States is the supreme instance of that fateful combination. At the same time, Russia's freighted market transition can be twinned with its deflated nuclear capacity to remove it from consideration as a threat. And Iraq, by even representing some contrary logic of deployment, contests the sooth-ing claim that the world is safe for risk. Acting against Iraq is an interven-tion against any possible distortion to realist presumptions, one that forces an acknowledgment of shared accountability to a singular rule. Imperial interventions seek to ensure that the future can be extrapolated from the present, so that risks taken by military adventure can yield predictable outcomes. Converting risk into a productive opportunity would be as true for peacekeeping interventions sanctioned by the United Nations as for financial markets.

No doubt many other factors apply to the prosecution of war against Iraq. The particular point at which security blends into securitization buttresses an otherwise tenuous connection between the war and the war on terror (before the invasion, a few contacts between Iraq and al-Qaeda hed been a basis for insinuating that Saddam Hussein was behind the September 11 attacks).[79] Iraq could readily be seen as a distraction from the limited conquests in the war on terror, a planned effort demonstrating that the war could be won. When Iraq is placed in relation to other global efforts to destroy terrorism, the war on terror can be viewed as one against an axis of evil. The axis composed of states and shadowy networks would run along a dimension ranging from high- to low-technology destruction (bombs borne by missiles or human bodies) and large- to small-scale configurations of the mass (whole countries or tiny cells).

The alleged presence of weapons of mass destruction in Iraq, one of several misstatements used to justify the invasion and occupation, was not merely a cynical act of bad faith (tell the people what you want them to hear). The fugitive Osama and Saddam and the elusive and inscrutable WMD were derivatives in a global campaign to make terrorist threats pre-dictable. Investment in these particular risk profiles fit the eternal displace-ment of security assets, whose circulation into a netherworld of elsewhere occasions the perpetuation of the terror war. Terrorists disappear on con-tact or are made to run—the tactic of bringing terrorists to justice by prosecuting a war against them does not put an end to the problem but only places terrorism in circulation. Small wonder that the UN inspectors, those best prepared to locate the weapons materials and evidence of con-tinued capacity to make WMDs, had themselves been banished from the scene. By means of these disappearing acts, the specific politics of interven-tion, the moral imperatives to be instrumentally opportunistic, morph into globally diffuse effects of locally derived risk in a securitized world.

While the cold war had its hot double in the range of revolutionary nationalist insurrections around the world, the terror war is hot on both ends of the state-network axis. The cold war assumed that all liberationist movements aspired to internationally recognized state power, while the terror war imagines an equivalence between political entities with disparate aspirations—states that harbor terrorists, nonstate actors, and rogue states. No longer is government legitimation of violence decisive—now the accusation of terror is what matters. If being named "against us" or "against the United States" is enough to confer the appellation of terrorist, the notion of an axis will sustain an indifference between legitimate state authority (as conventionally conceived) and unsanctioned violence.

As the Taliban and Saddam Hussein learned like many before them, falling (or being pushed) from the grace of state power is grounds for turning an opportunistic friend into a foe. In the language of the National Security Document, "shadowy networks of individuals" bring chaos and suffering to our shores, a phrase that as readily describes Osama and his lieutenants as it might the fifty-five intimates of Saddam, key figures of the fugitive Iraqi state, depicted on the deck of cards issued by the Coalition Provisional Authority. The shadowy networks of financial radicalism and technology that brought down the likes of Enron, WorldCom, or ImClone may have resulted in indictments, but those accused escaped a similar fate.

At the same time, the imbrication of foreign and domestic policy by means of securitization culminates with the terror war. Since the first Gulf War, Iraq has been a laboratory of American foreign policy, as well as the most explicit thread among the past three presidential administrations. Clinton had shifted tactics from the Bushes, but not bellicosity. His Iraq Liberation Act of 1998 paved the way for his successor's actions by making forcible regime change an official policy. The war between the wars was marked by continued bombings, while Clinton's Strategic Command advocated "preemptive response" with nuclear weapons if appropriate.[80] More importantly, strategic intervention seems to have reversed the edict of Carl von Clausewitz that war, which supposedly has a distinctive language but not a unique logic, is politics by other means. Diplomacy, humanitarian assistance, and support for human rights—what might seem to have once been the nonmilitary wing of foreign policy—are soaked in warring ways.

Just like the unmanageable at home, the world is full of rogues who can't take care of themselves. But unlike the amalgamating designations of third world or developing nations, the lexicon of failed, failing, and rogue states introduces a logic of risk assessment for highly differential treatment. Robert Litwak, for example, urges politicos not to lump the rogues and renegades together, but to develop a "repertoire of targeted strategies under the 'differentiated containment' rubric."[81] Targeting risk is certainly part of the language of derivatives: collateral is an asset not to be damaged. The terror war focuses on the isolatable risk without attacking the underlying values that give rise to terror in the first place. Success in the war has led to an increase in the number of terrorist acts, just as securitization has fostered growth in the derivative economy. As is evident in the other policy initiatives against those considered at risk, war is simultaneously metaphorized and literalized. The unmanageable are treated to military tactics and understood as requiring redemption by means of war.

Military intervention is not the only weapon in the anti-terror arsenal. Diplomacy and economic reason can also play a part. Applied to the arena of international diplomacy, weapons of intervention also have to become selected, targeted—in a word, "smart." In the minds of their deployers, these techniques do what smart bombs do. According to Joseph Stephanides, director of the Security Council Affairs Division of the Department of Political Affairs in the UN Secretariat, "multilateral sanctions could, if properly targeted, impact culpable decision makers, with minimized collateral damage to civilian populations and affected neighboring states."[82] Smart sanctions are not considered necessarily more effective than sanctions of the comprehensive or dumb variety, but they have fewer side effects. Implementing these sanctions requires a high degree of coordination between state and finance, government regulation and industry policing, which are interwoven into a single surveillance network. Indeed, sanctions help to laminate public and private.

Consider the U.S. Treasury's Financial Crimes Enforcement Network (FinCEN), created in 1990. FinCEN prepares a list of what it calls Specifically Designated Nationals, or SDNs. In one example, a bank in New York with 115,000 transactions from around the world screens for SDNs by computer program. From all the transactions, 27,000 are flagged and held for further scrutiny. Of these, thirteen are blocked and turned over to the Treasury Department.[83] Lest the Treasury treat this information as proprietary, sec. 314(a) of the USA Patriot Act requires it to share information on terrorist acts or money laundering, effectively equating the two from a systems management point of view. According to the FinCEN web site, during 2003 ten federal agencies submitted 64 terrorism and 124 money laundering cases that covered 1,256 suspects and resulted in 407 subpoenas, eleven search warrants, and three indictments.[84] Financial circulation is, by means of this surveillance, a medium where the wars on drugs and terror commingle in a space at once foreign and domestic.

The move to smart sanctions that are now part of the homeland security apparatus was in many ways a response to the failures of prior sanctions against Iraq. While the justifications for the sanctions were Saddam's crimes against humanity, the evident humanitarian costs of the general trade sanctions against Iraq were generating what was seen by the United States and the UN as a backlash of support that was fraying compliance. International carriers were resuming flights to Baghdad, illicit trade was on the rise, and Jordan had stopped monitoring trade altogether. While part of the UN Iraqi Sanctions Committee, the United States and the UK had arrogated to themselves the enforcement of the sanctions and placed holds on $2.3 billion of other nations' goods. This early expression of the coalition of the willing exposed the inequity of authority in the international community.[85]

In an episode that anticipated the charges of price gouging leveled against the oil contractor Halliburton in December 2003,[86] the Iraqi government had demanded that purchasers of its oil pay a surcharge on each barrel, the money to go into a special fund uncontrolled by the UN (now evidently the basis for funding resistance to the American occupation). In response, the architects of smart sanctions, writing in early 2001, suggested that corrupt practices of this sort be rectified by a "private oil brokering firm": "Such a brokering operation would add greater transparency and control to the marketing of Iraqi oil, and make it more difficult for purchasers to pay illicit surcharges to Baghdad."[87] Privatization was proposed as a solution to the problems that we now associate with privatization—a vicious turn in the virtuous circle by which the state, supposedly cleansing itself of inappropriate economic interest, devolves its responsibility for good government to the corrupting market.

Issues of transparency and corruption aside, Halliburton's designation as the contractor of record for the Iraqi occupation and reconstruction evokes hallowed mercantilist traditions from what was supposed to be a neoliberal state. The smartness in sanctioning a private firm to do the state's bidding points to another domain where security meets securitization. The idea of chartering companies to manage daily colonial affairs was a staple of British Empire presumably overturned when the English East India Company's tea was thrown into Boston harbor in 1773. Mercantilism today goes by the name of government-sponsored enterprises (GSES) and is largely a multi-trillion-dollar mutant of the trade in mortgage-backed securities. The largest players are the Federal Home Loan Bank System and the Federal National Mortgage Association (affectionately known as Fannie Mae), both rooted in efforts during the Depression to prop up banks' bad loans on mortgages. Joined by the Federal Home Loan Mortgage Association (Freddie Mac) in 1970, these are now highly profitable securitization outfits. Ironically, just a fraction of their portfolios are in assets backed by real estate. Investors (either other banks or, in the case of Freddie Mac, individual investors) are offered consistent returns over 20 percent.[88]

While their practice is securitization (including agricultural and student debt), GSES are markers of a privatizing state. Standard corporations register within, say, New York or California and are subject to its laws and taxes. But because they are deemed to perform a public function (compensating for market failure), GSES enjoy the status of "federal instrumentality" that exempts them from state and local tax on the one hand and regulation by the Securities and Exchange Commission on the other. They cannot be forced into bankruptcy and can only be terminated by federal action. Even though they are privately held, profit-making entities, GSES have protections and exemptions suggesting to potential investors that the government is backing these special corporations, and that risks of failure are thereby minimized.

The investment assumption is that periodic financial debacle will be met with government bailout, taken from those placed at risk by enterprise operations. In practice, GSES can carry far lower cash or equity reserves than are legally mandated for other corporations. Their business in highly leveraged derivatives carries the imprimatur of the state. The government is therefore sponsoring elevated risk and providing a spectral subsidy that never appears in the federal budget.[89] The federal chartering of the Maes and Macs not only immunizes them from local control but links them to the register of foreign policy that republican structures lack. Whatever gets reconstructed in Afghanistan and Iraq, we should look toward what sponsored securitization in the homeland has yielded for clues as to its logic of administration and the foreign interest that it unleashes. That these once stable entities have been clouded by scandal is less a result of managerial malfeasance than enthusiasm for risk of the sort that now walks in the tracks where development once trod.[90]

⁝ LEVERAGED HOMELAND

Unmaking the nation has been a fairly bloody affair. Colonial subjugation was hardly a friendly matter, but arguably it advanced the welfare of the populace under the banner of a developmental state.[91] Where once conservative national interest vied with radical national liberation to win over the masses, now the prize of state power has been stripped of its universalist pretensions. In practice, the 1980s were times of military adventures when nary a socialism or liberationist nationalism was encountered that the administration could abide. Nicaragua, Grenada, and Panama were assaulted in turn by proxy, occupation, and decapitation—and that was just Latin America. Reagan's security doctrine as articulated by his defense secretary, Caspar Weinberger (and later by his military advisor Colin Powell), urged vital interests, overwhelming force, clear military and political objectives, good prospects of public support, and flexible applications of force as a last resort.[92] Today the last resort has become the first.

The cold war could claim some credit for limiting these interventions. Colonial spheres of influence or socialist support for liberationist movements could place a damper on expansionist designs. Certainly after 1989 there was less to show for a globally capable interest in national formation. The colonial telos of national independence rested on some support for development even as an imperial interest. The implosion of the nation-state where once development had been promised—especially in Africa—turned the social body in on itself. Liberation from development had still more ambiguous consequences for subjugated peoples than colonial emancipation had done. States failed to contain wars, which erupted over the body of the nation. Between 1989 and 1998 there were 101 civil wars, as compared to seven interstate wars.[93] With the development train derailed, the second and third worlds suffered a major collision. National interest was on the wane, and private interest—the appeal of accumulated wealth—was injected where the confidence that neocolonial states could provide development had flagged most.

Instead of populations developing within the womb of nations, individuals would ascend to universally recognizable human rights. The interventions of former imperial and colonial powers would continue, but now they would roll out a humanitarian welcome mat, what Noam Chomsky has called "the new military humanism."[94] Rolled out as well, however, would be an assessment of the capacity to embrace private enterprise, which would become the arbiter of a nation's future viability. Political risk would be redefined in financial terms as "the probability of politically determined losses for an investment in the future."[95] Financial derivatives could be designed to hedge against these outcomes. Internal chaos could fetch a premium return for those willing to undertake the risk. National instability would become a market opportunity. A repertoire of risk management strategies would include avoidance, negotiating concession agreements, transferring risk through shared ownership, keeping local affiliates dependent on vertical integration, keeping R&D capabilities at home, and maintaining production at multiple sites.[96]

The advent of political risk insurance abetted the financial management of post-colonial states. In 1971, seeing the havoc that foreign policy could wreak on foreign direct investment, the U.S. government formed the Overseas Private Investment Corporation (OPIC), a fee-for-service government entity and state correlate of the government-sponsored enterprises that would eventually generate $3 billion in profit. OPIC has partnered with the likes of Enron to facilitate "market entry" in developing nations.[97] Similar symbiosis can be found in the realm of government-precertified and licensed private security firms like Gurkha Security Guards and Sandine International, staffed by former members of Special Forces. The private soldiers are less likely to defect or desert, and their employers, unlike the UN, have a financial stake in success. Yet even for supporters of outsourced mercenary services, not all is rosy. Like private prisons that maintain an interest in extending the carceral experience in perpetuity, peacekeepers-for-hire depend upon the continuation of strife.[98] Hence privatization introduces what is called "moral hazard," the encouragement of unsustainable risk or negative behavior on the promise of a bailout or rescue. Moral hazard exists whenever the mere perception of government remediation threatens the righteous punitive action of the market, as occurred with the meltdown of Asian stock markets in 1998.

For the true believers, the fury of the market tempers undue risk, here defined circuitously as subsequent failure to succeed. Because it is the sum of all information, knowledge, and decision, the market is always right, and those who fail have no one to blame but themselves. Productive risk, on the other hand, is invited, and at this point the moralizing market is left behind for the ethos of the arbitrageur. This is the world inhabited by those who bet with equal enthusiasm on gains or losses in future securities prices, and can profit from either when hedges go their way.[99] The contradictions of risk management are blamed on the state as it serves to further open markets to opportunities that mortals dare not seize. These humanisms are the private dreams that will land with the troops in Iraq.

So much of what passes as neoliberal rhetoric seems an expression of government self-loathing. As Donald Rumsfeld, two-time secretary of defense (1975–77 and 2001–), has put it, "government does two things well— nothing and overreact."[100] What if we were to take seriously the pronouncements of every president from Reagan to Clinton and the Bushes that government is the problem? Its existing model must be terminated and reengineered. Their attack on the potential knowledge of state posits that government is the enemy of the people. Its gifts only bring the pain of dependence. Freed from the yoke of entitlement, citizens can realize their capacity for attaining wealth. The old habits cannot be left simply to atrophy, for the decay will spread. Those who would refuse to see that government is in their way must themselves be attacked. But the conservative impulse that has swept into government is not unitary.[101] The neoliberal confidence in ending government can chafe against the neoconservative messianic mission for the state to forcibly liberate people from their moral and cultural turpitude.

Given this tension between political and moral economy in the voicing of the state, we should expect domestic warfare of every stripe. Tax cuts and tax-deferred accumulations reinforce the distinction between those at the top of the economic ladder and the rest.[102] The risk divide produces a public constituency for concentration of riches through investment that hollows out citizenship and recalibrates consumption as the ability to shoulder debt. Risk tolerates the amalgamating of the moral and the politico-economic, the neoconservative and the neoliberal. Investors may benefit from fiscal policies, but their only social responsibility is the tautological invocation to invest, to maintain business as usual in the face of heightened threats.

The self-loathing can now be clarified. The government cannot possibly take up the nation as a whole when some part of it must constantly be under attack. The national population cannot be made one when some part of it is to be sacrificed on the altar of risk. We should also expect, under these conditions, that government could not possibly embody a national interest. In the absence of an affirmative role based on a more inclusive commonwealth, the state could only establish itself vis-à-vis the nation by means of war. Hence Bush's assertion in the previously cited National Security Document that war making is the "first and fundamental commitment" of federal government. No doubt nationalism is made of nothing less. But there is a reason why the "imagined community" by which strangers get the sense that they live and work together in the nation is always stated in the past tense. This condition renders nationalism reactionary in the strict sense of harkening back to an earlier, less problematic moment, whatever popular ambitions it may bear.[103]

While patriotism is being enforced in the United States, it is difficult to see in the forward-looking calculations of risk that homeland security alerts us to anything as gauzily retrospective as Reagan's reelection campaign slogan in 1984, "It's Morning in America."[104] In fiscal policy, in the domestic wars, in the populations "at risk," securitization is already well under way, but still with a nationalist incantation. Bush has parted Reagan's mists and done to America what area studies had once done to the world: now population is assembled into areas or concentrations of risk, not geographical regions. These areas have frayed the domesticity of the United States, so that the foreign in our midst, figured by the terrorist, can now be generalized to the population left behind. The terrorist represents the nexus of risk embrace gone bad and the other who places the self at risk. Organized by risk, the war on terror allows the foreign and the domestic to be treated with equal opportunity.

One implication of partitioning the nation into two imagined communities along the lines of risk is that American studies would become an area studies, something that quite fine minds had recently assumed to be illogical if not unthinkable. Paul A. Bové, for example, has observed that there is "no U.S. desk in the State Department," and that American studies is for hegemony, not policy.[105] State power would be required to see the nation as "both a competitor and alien about which it needs specialized and authoritative knowledge on the basis of which it can direct its own policy toward that object."[106] Hegemony is achieved both by making a particular social arrangement appear as if it marked the limits of possibility, as received reality, and by providing the material supports for participation in a given way of life (such as federal subsidies or tax abatement for homeownership). When the divide between risk managers and those at risk cleaves the population into investors and others, participation for some gets leveraged as a more general condition. Leveraged hegemony rests upon double policy regimes, one oriented toward reward and the other toward punishment of the excluded populations. Domestic policy assumes its own selective engagement. American studies would need to know this other kind of being as well, the kind of resident alien that is the object of homeland security.

Granted, the desk in question is not in the State Department: it now has a home all its own. If ever there was a bureau whose value was derived from the work of others, it would be the one from which Tom Ridge first spoke to us—bidding us to go about our business in the face of risk. Billed by the Bush administration as a major initiative, a reinvention of the scope of government as we know it, the Department of Homeland Security (DHS) is a derivative institution of state. It was assembled from some twenty-two offices in existing secretariats like treasury (the U.S. Customs Service), justice (part of the Immigration and Naturalization Service), health and human services (the Strategic National Stockpile and the National Disaster Medical System), and agriculture (part of the Animal and Plant Health Inspection Service). With the exception of a tiny slice of the FBI, the heavy hitters of intelligence, the CIA and the National Security Agency, are noticeably absent, despite a claim that the formation of DHS was "the most significant transformation of the U.S. government since 1947, when Harry S. Truman merged the various branches of the U.S. Armed Forces into the Department of Defense to better coordinate the nation's defense against military threats."[107] Of course pegging this great transformation to the organizational shift that gave birth to the permanent military-industrial complex not only reaffirms the primacy of defense as government's key mission but also elides domestic initiatives past and present. Omitted from consideration are the expansion of the welfare state during the 1960s and, over the past three decades, the broader insinuation of finance into what the state is and does.

In fiscal terms, the transformation is strikingly modest. In 2003 $6.7 billion was appropriated for DHS, of which $2.4 billion would go to airlines to cover security costs and over $2 billion to states and municipalities to cover their existing security costs. A proportionately slim $150 million goes to the department itself for counterterrorism investigations and activities.[108] For all the fanfare, the "most significant transformation" of the past half-century is striking in that so much political mileage could be got from a government initiative whose internal resources are slightly larger than the budget of the National Endowment for the Arts. Homeland security bundles together the work of others, advancing securitization in the name of enhanced security. More money passes through the agency on its way elsewhere than is spent directly on its own operations.[109] Under threat of forecasted doom, our business is to continue. No wonder that when the weather gets rough, as with Hurricane Katrina in September 2005, homeland security is nowhere to be found. No result of mere cronyism, the walls of the institution were built to be breached.

Beyond an assessment of reinvented government, homeland security needs to be understood not as insulating fortress America but as providing yet another portal of risk. One group of experts have concerned themselves with how to cost out a preventive strategy based on an "EZ-pass approach," which would allow those who use protection most (and have the most to gain from it) to pay more, but at discounted rates.[110] The experts acknowledge that there is no end to what could be spent in a preventive market for security, and they are concerned to parse out what a proper government role might be. Their findings are instructive, as they offer the following scenarios: (1) Terrorists steal biochemical materials from a private facility and deploy them elsewhere. The public bears the costs of a private failure, constituting a "negative externality." (2) Material damage is done to a privately owned public facility (like a sports stadium or trade tower), exposing a vulnerability in the homeland that undermines the nation's sovereignty. (3) A firm can't assess risks from all potential threats individually, so it needs to use government standards (such as a building code). (4) Private-sector liability is limited by bankruptcy laws. (5) The private sector neglects security because the government can't convince it that it won't be bailed out (the airline industry's version of moral hazard). (6) Insurance companies are unwilling to transfer risks, a consequence of "incomplete markets."[111]

While aimed at preempting terror by advancing markets for risk, these scenarios point to the possibilities of loss that markets find terrifying. Securitization, even this prosaic type that aims to protect against loss, places security in circulation as a tradable commodity or exchangeable risk factor. Ever lurking on the horizon is market failure, which acts as a general condition of advancing securitization, a preemptive bailout that merges and bundles hitherto discrete risks. We have become accustomed to focusing our concerns on the loss of privacy that is a consequence of the regime's ever greater surveillance.[112] Certainly we would want to be alert to how much privacy we had in the first place, and what a focus on gaining it back might preclude. Whatever it once was, privacy now is hardly a sanctuary from the forces of discipline and control. Perhaps the most mundane effect of the war on terror is to make clear how much we have to fear from the advance of the private itself.

With the war on terror it is not simply specific populations but the nation itself that is placed into the category of being at risk. Homeland security is a political art that aspires to a science. For counter-terror to be scientific, it must give reason to terrorists. No longer seeing terror as an irrational act without benefit of state legitimation, a comprehensive approach to combating terror as augured by Homeland Security brings prospective acts into our midst to model them into submission. The prevention and preemption of terror render it a permanent condition of the present by imagining future threats in terms of how they can be lived now. The suicide bomber would seem to present a pointed challenge to grand strategies of deterrence based on a calculus of risk aversion. Without fear of self-destruction, primacy loses its pop. If self-preservation is a natural impulse that extends from the individual body to the nation, terrorists may walk on terra firma, but they have already departed the world of rational actors for another. While public sentiment can be mobilized around the notion that the terrorist is a nonhuman sort of being, or is part of a civilization with values alien to our own, scientists are not so willing to let these subjects out of their grasp.

The suicide bomber would figure as the labor-intensive version of risk embrace, financialization's opposite number. The deployment of one or a handful of individuals can be leveraged to the heavens, just as the derivative isolates bits of risk that can shock entire markets. Leave it to that stalwart of neoliberal journalism, the *Economist*, to make terrorist rationality clear for us: "Counter-intuitive though it may seem, terrorists also regard suicide attacks as low-risk, given the scale of devastation they can inflict. As Ayman al Zawahiri, Osama bin Laden's right-hand man, has put it, 'the method of martyrdom operations [is] the most successful way of inflicting damage against the opponent and least costly to the mujahideen in terms of casualties.' No accomplices are needed for rescues or getaways. Nor is there much danger of bombers betraying their comrades."[113]

On this account, the method of successful terror understands the relation between risk and return, a minimal investment for a maximum outcome. It is this play of input and output on the assumption of maximized utility that is modeled by decision theorists as a game, where actions and consequences are broken down into variables whose possible combinations can be forecast.

In the aftermath of September 11 the nation's leading organization of scientists, doctors, and engineers, the National Research Council, wrote to President Bush to offer their expertise. The contributors included the future procounsel of Iraq, L. Paul Bremer III, and a mix of academics and consultants like the sociologist Neil Smelser and the former admiral and CIA chief R. James Woolsey. Their report, *Making the Nation Safer: The Role of Science and Technology in Countering Terror*, reviews the range of "systems" (nuclear, agricultural, infrastructural, informational) that could be objects of attack. The report proposes integrating each target type into a "system of systems" with metadata as a "rational data structure."[114]

The two resulting modeling approaches incorporate the shift from closed to open systems, the turn in thinking that was initiated half a century ago with military and stock market models and that the terror war now legitimates for mainstream social science research. Applying what has been learned from financial services and geophysical exploration (as in oil), the modeling approaches purport to counter terror by forecasting its occurrence. The first approach is called "complex adaptive systems": "This process results in evolutionary, emergent, and adaptive properties that are not exhibited by the individual agents themselves. For example, an animal may be an agent in a formation of a herd of animals, and herds of animals may become a species, and the species may be part of a particular ecosystem. There is a clear analogy here to the characteristics of our society's critical infrastructure and its associated adaptation, emergence, and evolution."[115] While the model and others like it cannot predict outcomes, they are seen as simulating the processes used to come up with a result. It might seem curious to base a mathematical approach to human reasoning on an analogy with animal behavior, but the herd analogy is something of a master trope in financial services. The model also seeks to explain why speculative bubbles get formed, as people ignore information offered by the market and get caught up in fits of "irrational exuberance."[116]

The second approach to modeling is based on system dynamics, which "take a top-down approach to system analysis by compressing the many variables of a large, complicated system of systems into a relatively small number of overall attributes."[117] This approach to risk assessment focuses on the nonlinear responses and chaotic dynamics associated with terrorist threats. Unlike conventional modeling, in which the boundaries for analyzing variables are defined before a specific problem arises, here boundaries are "defined by the system level problem or issue."[118] Making the boundaries contingent represents a shift away from a priori interests and reasons of state within a problem set to a flow of decision that continually sorts and reshuffles what is inside and outside its purview.[119]

The fuzzy rhetoric by which the firm boundary between foreign and domestic, inside and outside, is effaced meets its opposite and equivalent number in mathematical precision. It should now be evident that the drawing together of hitherto disparate elements—rendering them into a universe of exchange where volatility drives measurement and management—goes by the name of securitization. By no means have these mathematical games slain the purported singularity of interest that keeps the nation together. They merely suggest how terror is an occasion for further insinuating risk parsing and protocols into that increasingly differentiated field of the homeland.

Twenty years ago, the careers of risk as a referent for society and for economy seemed to operate on separate tracks. Sociologists such as Ulrich Beck and Anthony Giddens were concerned with technological and nuclear threats, and economists were rationalizing the new market opportunities.[120] Financialization augured the embrace of a calculus of opportunity while the risk society sought damage control or ablution of moral contaminants. By means of securitization, the war on terror aims to bring economy and society into a grand, nonlinear matrix where the movements of risk trace something like the internal tracings of the political. To see risk as now pervasive and productive across a number of domains where common techniques of management have also been adopted is not an assertion that all has become one. But securitization enables us to see what joins otherwise disparate elements, and to appreciate, as with the derivative, how seemingly small interventions are linked to widespread effects. The anticipation of risk is always meant to be self-fulfilling, a preemptive action that makes its imagined future come to pass. The ultimate terror may be that we are condemned to live this perpetual present. Unless of course we can derive some other value.

The cold war's demise was supposed to have brought the very idea of revolution to a close. With communism gone, the historical alternative to progressive reform had effectively left town, and all that remained was for the market to perfect itself on its own terms and in its own time. Competition was no longer between socioeconomic systems but was now the internal means by which the only system left standing advanced itself. All that remained were cultural or civilizational differences, but if these existed within domains of common values there would be little strategic interest in expansion and nothing to fight over. The freedom of choice that made markets sing would make politics hum as well. With the enemies to liberty gone, there was enough democratic goodwill to go around for all the world to enjoy.[1]

Somehow the victory parade got lost en route. In quick order (and doubtless before the celebrated collapse came to pass), the world once again looked like a very dangerous place. The cold war triumph was credited to an arms race that had sapped its opponent's strength from within. Consequently, a war that was never joined was rendered the ultimate instrument of politics. The thermonuclear weapons buildup was like massive piggybank savings for a future that would never come. The dull weight of accumulation in this savings plan ultimately crushed the opponent. Consequently, the terms of accumulation and even the logic of saving were thrown into confusion. Instead of expected triumph, confusion crept into military quarters. As one military historian, writing when the cold war's end was new, put it: "A ghost is stalking the corridors of general staffs and defense departments all over the 'developed' world—the fear of military impotence, even irrelevance."[2]

For the military whose stockpiled capacity was the basis of victory, the embrace of revolution was not banished. Revolutionary fervor burst forth where the old revolution lay smoldering. The term that gained currency to describe and direct this emergent state of being was the "revolution in military affairs" (RMA). Poised as a self-justifying juggernaut of military planning and expenditure, RMA became a policy rationale and a historical lens through which to apprehend the accelerating pace of technological and organizational change in how wars are fought. It was promoted as a techno-logical and managerial solution to long-standing problems of warfare—the most significant of which was the prospect of losing. With the Soviet Union out of the way, victory over an enemy became an abstraction without a proper name. The military could nevertheless achieve an epochal break-through—to defeat the very idea of warfare as an encounter of equally matched rivals. Instead, war would realize the idea of unipolarity. Since the winner was known in advance, the proof of domination would be in the application of war, the ability to dictate its terms, rather than a measure of outcomes. The military would finally be free to pursue war opportunis-tically and without reserve as an end in itself.

To achieve this, the military was being asked to compensate for the loss of a great power rival by demonstrating how unipolarity could be achieved, even if there was no one willing or able to contest American dominance. Military superiority would now signal the capacity to defeat the prospect of any challenge to the way the world was being ordered. The futuristic promise that military technology will put an end to war has a longer history. Bruce Franklin traces the entanglement of superweapons and cul-tural fantasy back to the submarine during the Revolutionary War, the development of Robert Fulton's ironclad steam vessels, and the schemes of the flying ace Billy Mitchell during the First World War to use airpower to destroy cities—technological fixes claiming to end war by absolute domi-nance.[3] In the absence of a political principle against which our own superiority as a system might be tested, the perfectibility of military prow-ess became sui generis. Typically, imperial triumphalism requires some other country or enemy to play the role of vanquished. Without this other, and for triumph not to turn into stagnation, an inner dynamism would need to be found to impel imperial might forward.

The new military protocols amount to a grand concept of Hollywood proportions, and are something like the evil twin of the new economy— that other great fable of the 1990s. Separated at birth but rejoined in adolescence (through cold war informatics), both concepts imagined fric-tionless, perpetual expansion on a surface of their own design. Curiously, while a mega-idea during the 1990s, the RMA amounts to a discovery that moments of dramatic change and opportunity have always been available to those wise enough to grasp them. It is a revisionist history of the nature of war in the service of the present. Similarly (at least while info-tech stock prices soared), the laws of nature as understood by conventional economists had been revised. A new gravity-defying physics promised that what went up no longer needed to come down. Growth could go on forever, the business cycle was over and had taken inflation with it. Low unemployment would no longer put pressure on wages, as productivity could compensate for tight labor markets indefinitely.[4]

The burst stock market bubble that heralded the next millennium may have disproved the factual basis for a paradigm shift. Yet collapsing stock prices did little to shake the faith in the primacy of finance to the economy or monetarist approaches to fiscal policy. Interest-rate fluctuations and further elaborations of the machinery of credit and debt remained the order of the day long after boosterish confidence in the speculative economy had been betrayed. Even though the information technology euphoria had burst, its ethers were released into the minds of military planners, generating a veritable war dividend. Thinking in systems, the preeminent cold war doctrine, saw information science nurtured by intellectuals under military contracts made increasingly profitable when the internet turned civilian. The defense department then repurchased what the markets had borne in the form of military hardware and managerial approaches suffused with info-processing.[5] As Paul Edwards has shown, through the emergence of informatics from the 1930s through the cold war, this intricate military and civilian tango sought an "operational equivalence of humans and machines" that could enclose "the globe into a single world."[6] With the cold war's end these boundaries were sundered and the RMA sought to maintain the systems utility when equilibrium was far away, even as enclosure broke down, as always, and allowed its insides to seep out. In Afghanistan and Iraq both order and stability seem to have escaped the systematizers' clutches.

Whereas the first Gulf War ushered in the military's futuristic dream, the war redux a dozen years later brought that dream to earth—but not before placing faith in its fantastical realization. Tracking the transformation of war doctrine affords an insight into how the self-understanding of deployment became aligned and infected with a calculus of risk. Warfare has been packaged and produced along the lines of the financial instruments known as derivatives, and a concept of leverage discussed in chapter 1 as securitization. If military deployment is the means of imperial accomplishment, if it makes manifest the supremacy of American power, then the inner workings of the new warring ways need to be engaged to unlock the secrets of the imperium.

Like many revolutions before it, this military one is the consummation of many prior aspirations. Less than a complete break with the cold war, the revolution in military affairs imagines that the condition of imminent threat has been generalized. But with the prospect of defeat removed, with every deployment an opportunity for gain, the diffusion of future threats into the present argues for deploying early and often. As politics is now the extension of war by varied means, the idea of war as eternally available and expendable must be accounted for. As with its financial cognates war must learn to make much of little, to derive value from seemingly minor movements (whatever their direction), to amass its victories through far-flung connections. War by this reckoning is not simply a way to extract wealth by conquest: like risk itself it undertakes to create the very conditions that make new wealth possible—one investment at a time. One can take a long historical view and see that war is productive.[7] A more immediate look at the drawing boards of military design can tell us what war now produces.

: BRIGHT MOMENTS

Derivative wars are prosecuted with the understanding that their limitations are their opportunities, that any situation of conflict can be joined for a gain. A seemingly minor fluctuation in world affairs, for better or ill, can be mined for a bonanza of desirable outcome. Derivative wars are small and quick, with extensive ripple effects because they can move through a network created by a medium of military and technical innovation. They benefit from the massive grade inflation in weaponry that has allowed what was formerly considered merely smart to become brilliant. This move to brilliance was indeed the narrative of the two wars against Saddam Hussein, a regional power elevated to a global threat.

Just after September 11 Robert Martinage, senior defense analyst at the Center for Strategic and Budgetary Assessments, quipped, "In the Gulf War, we had smart weapons. Now, increasingly, we are fielding brilliant weapons."[8] Smart bombs merely hit their mark. The target was a question to which the hit was an unequivocal answer. Force was decisive. Like an obedient child, smartness only spoke when spoken to. Brilliance, on the other hand, just can't shut up. Its intelligence is compulsive. It is complete, even if, like a bolt of lightning, fleeting and highly localized. It captures the enemy's orientation to space and time, entering into its antagonist's decision process and neutralizing it. Brilliance is a multimedia, ballistically induced sensory overload of noise and light that means to cancel cognition altogether. The world of the supine opponent is crushed, even if its surrendered body survives. All the while the vision of brilliance is unperturbed and focused.

Such opposition-canceling superiority is what was imagined by Harlan Ullman and James Wade Jr. when they prepared a report for the Institute for National Strategic Studies in 1996 under the title *Shock and Awe: Achieving Rapid Dominance.* In their words: "The goal of Rapid Dominance will be to destroy or so confound the will to resist that an adversary will have no alternative except to accept our strategic aims and military objectives. To achieve this outcome, Rapid Dominance must control the operational environment and through that dominance, control what the adversary perceives, understands, and knows, as well as control or regulate what is not perceived, understood, or known."[9] Although dominance is rapid, occurring before an adversary can react, it is also selective, as shock and awe only needs to be produced "at the appropriate strategic and military leverage points" to get the job done.[10] Hence shock and awe is not only economically efficient but humanitarian as well, as casualties are minimized on all sides. Brilliant!

Brilliance in this context characterizes a system that fixes what politics would otherwise have made a mess of through endless negotiation, perpetual compromise, and indecisive rule. Shock and awe is the cure for those impatient with power but destined to wield it. But if politics has become subordinate to war, then we would expect the revolution to have yielded its own magnitude of mess. Indeed that is the case. This is not simply a discrepancy between doctrine and deployment, theory and practice. Just as with the complex mathematics of the derivative, theory is forcibly applied. And as has been discovered repeatedly in the most advanced applications of financial derivatives—from Long Term Capital Management, the hedge fund that collapsed in 1998, to Enron, the energy futures trader that met the same fate a few years later—realization has been destabilizing.[11]

For those who would be the masters of war, the epic enemies—beyond any specific antagonists—have been friction and fog. Friction is the internal resistance to things going as planned. Soldiers will die or fail to advance. The weather will change. The enemy will be in the wrong place. Weapons will malfunction. Effective systems of control are meant to anticipate these problems and correct them. The uncertainties that emerge in combat generate noise in lines of communication. Messengers get it wrong. They are overly optimistic or pessimistic. Intelligence reports don't predict movements clearly. Information is dirty (inaccurate) or compromised. The commander's vision is clouded. Reason is enshrouded in fog.

Command is decision making in the face of uncertainty, the military correlate of management. The business analogy has its limitations. Competition in the marketplace is based upon hiring and firing labor. Soldiers —at least those enlisted by a state—may be salaried, but they are not at liberty to quit in battle. While soldiers like other laborers may seek control over their working conditions and productivity—they may resist orders, or "strike"—their bodies belong to the state for the duration of their tour of duty. Conversely the market, however putatively free, is in practice thoroughly regulated, so that the destructive effects of interfirm competition are somewhat ameliorated and underwritten by a more general cooperation of mutual interdependence. Combatants are characterized as having independent wills, not necessarily agreeing on the conditions of engagement or the moment of surrender or victory.

The ongoing fable of military command is that it could be wielded to perfection. The military historian Martin van Creveld has offered a more sober view. He has selected what have been considered among the greatest victories by the most accomplished military leaders and identified what could have been disastrous errors of judgment and failures of circumstance. For example, Napoleon, considered brilliant for his ability to assimilate massive amounts of information and quickly issue voluminous and decisive written dispatches, was at the height of his powers in his victory against the Prussian armies at Jena, Saxony, in 1806. Yet as van Creveld observes: "Napoleon at Jena had known nothing about the main action that took place on that day; had forgotten all about two of his corps; did not issue orders to a third, and possibly to a fourth; was taken by surprise by the action of a fifth; and, to cap it all, had one of his principal subordinates display the kind of disobedience that would have brought a lesser mortal before a firing squad. Despite all these faults in command, Napoleon won what was probably the greatest single triumph in his entire career."[12]

Napoleon's power was ascribed to his omniscience, his ability to directly observe a battle, see through its complexity, and render it whole through his capacity for synthesis. In military annals he is the affirmation that vision is truth. The ability to see everything from a single point clears the fog and renders the battlefield transparent. Clear-sighted, rational decision making with all the affect-less confidence of a mathematical equation would become the human model for artificial intelligence. But because, as Chris Hables Gray has observed, "reason has never been able to make of war a science," the technological solution to friction and fog would paradoxically be modeled on an icon of romantic genius rather than machinic efficiency.[13]

The scale of mass warfare that made direct observation by a single individual possible passed with Napoleon, who could scarcely command more than 100,000 troops at a time. The Prussian army developed a command structure based on the assembly of interchangeable troop formations from disparate points, a principle that anticipated Henry Ford's assembly line by more than half a century. As on the assembly line, technological advances such as deadlier breech-loading rifles made the battlefield noisier. Troops had to spread out to avoid getting mowed down. Junior officers lost a measure of control over their infantry, as "entire armies turned into clouds of uncontrollable skirmishers."[14] The Prussians too had their great general in Helmut von Moltke Jr. and their consummate campaign against Austrian forces at Königgrätz in 1866. Once again, van Creveld offers a corrective:

> The battle was an unforeseen one, fought as a last-minute improvisation against an enemy whose whereabouts had not previously been discovered for forty-eight hours even though he was only a few miles away. The chief of staff had no part in planning it, and it may indeed have been fought somewhat against his will. The commanding general of 1st Army refused to comprehend his own role as an anvil even when it was explained to him in so many words by Moltke; he launched pointless, premature attacks which he was then unable to control. The outflanking movement that Moltke had planned to take place on the Austrian left never materialized, and the arrival of 2nd Army was delayed by a string of misunderstandings until it was almost too late. Futhermore, as Moltke wrote in his post mortem on 25 July, "we should make no bones about the fact that our worst error consisted in the inability of senior headquarters to make its influence felt on its subordinates.[15]

Van Creveld's point in these examples is that command only succeeds when it recognizes its limitations. Given that recognition came after the fact, it is perhaps more accurate to say that it is the assessment of progress itself that is most problematic. With each apparent advance in command new problems emerge. When, for example, people are replaced with machines, war can intensify and increase in scope. At the same time there is a concomitant loss of flexibility, greater prospect of dysfunction, obsolescence, and dependence on increasingly sophisticated logistical support.

Since greater command tends toward a centralization of decision making that can concentrate uncertainty at the top, van Creveld advises distributing uncertainty among the ranks of the hierarchy by decentralizing decision making in self-contained units that can respond differentially to the circumstances they encounter.[16] These local variations would report in and out, much in the way that a derivative is traded independently even as it has a ripple effect on the various equities and positions to which it is attached. Against all the pressures to centralize, the challenge would be to find some way of distributing managerial intelligence downward, to assure that some discretion remained at the front lines.

The imperative to conquer uncertainty gives organizational solutions a lasting appeal. If uncertainty could be turned into a calculus of risk, making measurable the difference between expectations and actuality, battlefield management could take a great leap forward. This at least is the aspiration of command, control, and communications (C^3), an attempt to formalize military science. The emergence of this science during and after the Second World War is tracked very effectively by Manuel de Landa. He cites Norbert Wiener, pioneer of the computer, who developed cybernetics while helping to design the anti-aircraft machine gun's "servomechanism" to predict where the targeted airplane would be.[17] Mechanical models of thought and perception, operations research, and systems analysis had roots in the First World War but were elaborated by cold war intellectuals like Albert Wohlstetter and Ed Paxson at government-sponsored "think tanks" like the RAND Corporation. The think tank was based on the notion that the tank could be removed from the uncertainties of the actual battlefield and subjected to the controllable outcomes of mathematical modeling.

In 1950 RAND fellows developed the prisoner's dilemma, an example of the non-zero-sum game in game theory, in which the players can minimize their risk by cooperating. In the game, two criminals are interrogated separately with the promise that if one betrays the other the betrayer will be freed while the betrayed gets full punishment. If both remain silent (in solidarity), their punishment is minimal, and it is slightly more if they both confess. But if self-interest prevails over cooperation in the absence of shared information, the naïve player who cooperated while the other player did not will receive the greatest punishment of all. The game, modeled on unilateral coercion, means to tie reason to self-interest. But aside from the dream of making reason and enemies captives, reason and interest are tied in knots, as the game rests upon a decisive break between individual and collective interest that its own operation belies. This disavowal of cooperation is convenient when one wants to run an arms race by means of cooperative agreements, and at the same time violate those agreements in the name of self- (or national) interest.

Later simulations of war with the Soviet Union induced a "paranoid bias" of "thinking Red," with the result that planners in Washington analogized the Soviet mind to that of the United States.[18] Defense Secretary Robert McNamara founded the Office of Systems Analysis (OSA), which employed professional economists to apply to decisions in Vietnam the state-of-the-art mathematical models recently formulated to forecast stock market behavior. The result was a notorious "information pathology" that equated quantification with understanding. The systems analysts in OSA had no way of corroborating the inaccurate information passed on to them by accounting-oriented junior officers under the bureaucratic hierarchy of the Military Assistance Command.[19] That financial models apply uneasily under circumstances of command has not slowed the traffic between military and economic development. De Landa observes that the permutations of global trade and credit have been both a cause and a consequence of the further commercialization of violence dating back to the thirteenth century.[20]

As the systems approach was operationalized through information technology, computers were added to the arsenal, as were live information gathering of surveillance based-intelligence and formalized protocols of battle management. This expanded list of factors resulted in a rather cryptic acronym, c⁴IBM (command, control, communications, computers, intelligence battlefield management), meant to capture the military's managerial revolution. Subsequently, battle management came to be defined as informatics, namely surveillance and reconnaissance, and the acronym was changed to c⁴ISR (command, control, communications, computers, intelligence, surveillance, reconnaissance).

The proliferation of terms mimics the innovation in financial instruments and lends rhetorical credence to the military's incessant reinvention. The enemy may remain diffuse, but our own brilliant identity can be forever clarified. The number crunching of RAND and OSA and the communications among scientists funded by the Defense Advanced Research Projects Agency (DARPA, the federal entity that gave rise to the Internet) relied upon highly centralized mainframe computers.[21] By contrast, c⁴ISR applied the consumer model of personal computers that could be embedded in weapons systems and unit-level decision making. As with financial self-management, the repertoire of control and decision making, and the assumption of risk, were meant to be localized while still accountable to a central command. The ideal was to eliminate the fog of war by achieving information transparency, which like its financial counterpart was based on a set of accounting protocols imposed from without.

The futurologists Alvin and Heidi Toffler were closely read by technophilic military strategists in the 1990s. According to the Tofflers' forecasts, new military technologies would unleash a third wave of warfare, which for them corresponded to the rise of infomatics, an advanced basis for society that defied conventional dimensions of time and space.[22] In this technological utopia, precision-guided weapons would eliminate the inverse relation between distance and accuracy that had brought contending armies into contact. Like the Tofflers, all-seeing command would be married with infallible practice. Intelligence would go ballistic. Power would become knowledge, as the capacity to strike with impunity would be translated into the equivalence of seeing and touching or hitting a target.

The point of systems integration from a military management perspective is to render machines as smart as people and people as reliable as machines, on the assumption that the machinic and humanist ideals can be applied in practice to places where people work with technology. As such, the utopias are as much about labor that doesn't resist being told what to do as they are about frictionless machines. Self-managed soldiers on the ground would be able to use global positioning and surveillance technologies to see exactly where the enemy was. This proletarianization of Napoleonic omnivision was what Defense Secretary Donald Rumsfeld intended in taking up Ullman's and Wade's *Shock and Awe* as the archprinciple of intervention in Iraq, as will be discussed in chapter 3. This slogan of the second war against Iraq has visited many a cruel irony on its authors in terms of what was shocked and who was awed.

Managerial revolutions as we have come to know them are packaging devices with a significant dose of self-fulfilling prophecy sprinkled throughout. In this respect, the revolution in military affairs is no different. Military commentators on this doctrine have warned of the "risk of optimism in the conduct of war."[23] Steven Metz and James Klevit list a variety of aims for the RMA: to "rejuvenate the political utility of military power," to "delay the emergence of peer competition" as a "blueprint for technology acquisition and force organization" and as a rubric for "forward looking thinking." At the same time, they acknowledge that the amalgam of ideas "has no mature theory."[24] Before Kosovo and Iraq, the authors state, "In terms of strategic objectives, the more the United States stresses active engagement and the promulgation of open economies and political systems, the more the United States must be able to project power and sustain protracted operations."[25] According to the doctrine of what was then termed the "non-lethal," prophylactic use military of force, a little force early is better than a lot of force later. The surgical strike is by this reckoning a double metaphor—both precise and corrective (even if, to date, the patient never gets a chance to recover, and success is confined to the operation). Already preemption is a kind of unilateralist's palliative, a reductive effort to keep small things small.

The irony of the RMA as policy, at least in terms of its intellectual genealogy, is that what was touted as a brave new world after the cold war was in effect a realization of cold warriors' dreams. The person credited by Donald Rumsfeld as his intellectual inspiration, and the one commonly cited as the author of the RMA, is Andrew Marshall.[26] Marshall began working at RAND in 1949 as an analyst and eventually became its director of strategic studies, involved in developing the systems approaches outlined above.[27] He worked at RAND until 1972, left to work for Henry Kissinger at the National Security Council for two years, and then set up the Office of Net Assessment.[28] Net assessment is "the comparative analysis of military, technological, political, economic, and other factors governing the military capability of nations. Its purpose is to identify problems and opportunities that deserve attention of senior defense officials."[29] True to systems logic, net assessment takes all possible difference and subjects it to coeval calculation without reference to qualitative value. Part of Marshall's iconic status (he is known by the nickname "Yoda") derives from his ability to remain in his post as the Defense Department's oracle through seven presidencies, the Vietnam debacle, the demise of the cold war, the revolution in military affairs, and its successor, "transformation." Perhaps more impressive than his longevity is the list of those considered his protégés, who include Rumsfeld, Richard Cheney, and Paul Wolfowitz.[30] Ostensibly, net assessment is responsible for seeing how all the pieces of military operations fit into the whole. Intriguingly, the Office of Net Assessment is the only one on the Department of Defense web site not to have any independent link or web page.[31] Alone among the vast array of think tanks, study centers, and information offices that publicly release wave upon wave of reports and position papers, the Office of Net Assessment is all classified, all the time, and posts nothing electronically.

Initially the office's adversary was the Soviet Union, whose chief of staff, Field Marshall Nikolai Ogarkov, identified a military technical revolution in Washington's deployment of precision guided missiles during the Vietnam War. Ogarkov was fired for telling the Kremlin that the Soviet Union lagged way behind the United States in its weapons capacity. That was in the mid-1970s. Marshall credits the Soviet Union with a greater understanding of the changes taking place and inspiring reflection back home:

Although a number of people were aware in the late 1970s that the Soviet military theorists were beginning to write about a new military revolution that was already underway, it was only in the late 1980s that a major assessment focused on the core question: Are the Soviets right? Are we really in another period of major change in warfare? If we are, important strategic management issues face the top-level managers of the Department of Defense. Among these issues are how to foster innovation, and how to change the weapons acquisition process to make field experimentation easier. A strategy would be needed, one part of which would be focused internally on how to make innovation and change easier so that the United States would more likely find the right ways of exploiting what technology would make possible. Another part of such a strategy would be focused externally on obtaining competitive advantages with respect to potential opponents and on the management of relations with allies.[32]

In 1989 Georgii Arbatov, then director of the USA and Canada Institute in the Soviet Union, met with American officials and issued a proclamation about his country's dissolution: "[We are] removing your threat and the whole rationale for your military's being."[33] Marshall would have none of it. He appropriated the Soviet term of dread for its rival and applied it as a continued rationale for the military buildup of the 1990s. Although the term "transformation" was first used to define RMA by his predecessor, Clinton's secretary of defense William Cohen, Rumsfeld made transformation the umbrella concept for the present RMA.[34] According to Marshall, "Transformation is more of an imperative: *We've got to transform the force. I personally don't like the term. It tends to push people in the direction of changing the whole force. You need to be thinking about changing some small part of the force more radically, as a way of exploring what new technologies can really do for you.*"[35] Isolating a small part of a larger whole that undergoes volatile change describes once again the logic of the derivative. Marshall's formulation stays closer to the applications of RMA than more dystopian pronouncements of total control. The derivative logic lines up with the focus on deployments of Special Forces and selective weaponry where the élite particular carries the weight of the mass.

The gist of transformation is to use new technology as a cover for downsizing and outsourcing. While the Office of Net Assessment is stingy about the information it shares publicly, and its director parsimonious as to whose ear he's willing to whisper into, the Office of Force Transformation lays its plans on the table. The purpose of this office, and that of the assistant secretary of defense for networks and information integration (Linton Wells II in 2004), is to operationalize the network theory that had been the conceptual thread of military planning from the first days of RAND to the RMA. RAND studies are still contracted for by the office and inform what it does, but now computer modeling has been decentralized from the decision makers pushing the button for nuclear attack to the soldiers in the field. The network is meant to integrate people and things, machines and marines, labor and capital by converting the activities of all into the measurable output of information flows. Transformation, according to a statement by George W. Bush at the start of the Iraqi occupation, figures a military future "defined less by size and more by mobility and swiftness, one that is easier to deploy and sustain, one that relies more heavily on stealth, precision weaponry and information technologies."[36]

On the longer view, the expansion of the U.S. military has been massive. The army ranks numbered 186,000 just before the call-up for the Second World War (after which it swelled more than sixtyfold), while today the military force strength stands at just over 1.4 million, with 969 military installations in the fifty states, and over 725 bases and nearly half a million troops spread around the world.[37] But the RMA, which boasts to remove labor from the scene of battle, provided cover for substantial reductions in active duty military personnel not unlike the outsourcing and downsizing of labor that drove the new economy. Between 1987 and 1999 the army reduced its ranks by over 300,000, the navy by over 200,000, and the air force by nearly a quarter-million.[38] The 1990s saw demobilization of six divisions (from eighteen to twelve) and the loss of a known enemy. Subsequently, planning would need to be oriented toward using a more concentrated force for any number of kinds of intervention.[39]

The leaner, meaner force structure is a military version of "just-in-time production." This is one approximation of postmodern war, the standardized mass military replaced with a customized force configuration, managed informatically.[40] The military's emphasis on efficiency was but one of many efforts in large-scale organizations to tightly coordinate production and consumption so as to avoid the tendency to produce more than can be paid for. The shift to these new priorities has been described as that from Fordism to post-Fordism. Fordism tied mass production to mass consumption and was modeled after Henry Ford's idea, novel in 1914, that workers would be paid the then princely sum of $5 so that they could purchase the Model Ts they were making. With post-Fordism, relative stability is exchanged for flexibility, product differentiation through customized niche markets, outsourced labor, and minimal inventories.[41] Needless to say, civilian post-Fordism requires the equivalent of c^4isr to subordinate market uncertainty to wasteless profit.[42]

The military's term for this post-Fordist flexibility is "agility." Without an arms race to calibrate the capacities of an opponent, it is taken as a strategic axiom that "knowledge of adversarial capabilities and intentions is increasingly difficult to obtain. Rather, U.S. forces must prepare for increased uncertainty and ambiguity in the future."[43] Even if a great deal is known about an enemy, agility treats future uncertainty as a plannable aspect of the present. The deficit between what each branch of the military would like to have and what it receives has aggravated internecine competition. The solution to destructive interservice rivalry is captured by yet another of the military's neologisms, "interoperability," a principle for systems communications within and across the branches that bears on common procurement strategies. What there is of fancy machines and high technologies should be shared or "leveraged."

To soothe the competitive edge introduced by these relative scarcities id imposed uncertainties, a sort of New Age vocabulary is introduced. ;hared awareness" and "shared understanding" make for collaborative ecisions throughout the network. Finally, "shared sensemaking, the process of going from shared awareness to shared understanding to collaborative decisionmaking, can be considerd a socio-cognitive activity in that the individual's cognitive activities are directly impacted by the social nature of the exchange and vice versa."[44] Consideration should be given both to "organic information" from the grassroots of the unit and "shared information" derived from the network. In the end, the target is the same—to train soldiers to simultaneously apply local verbal commands and data fed remotely to increase their "kill ratios."[45]

: COERCIVE NETWORKS

Networking allows for the merger of present and future, planning and evaluation, accounting and assessment. All the human and mechanical inputs can be entered into a computer as variables in a three-dimensional model. The point is less to predict outcomes, as the earlier battle simulations sought to do, than to manage information flows in real time, to convert the model into the actuality of combat situations, and by so doing to maintain force superiority. Since deterrence and mutually assured destruction can no longer maintain the fixed exchange rates of global bellicosity, more agile deployments will be needed to affirm their own value. Networking takes the same resources and maximizes their utility, so that the process itself constitutes a "value-chain" that improves the effectiveness of a mission through its application.[46] Being right in where and how force is applied becomes the key to the demonstration effects of this value-adding activity.

Adding value is not limited to technological applications but pertains to the privatization of those applications as well. The director of the Office of Force Transformation, Art Cebrowski, was already thinking beyond Iraq when he testified before the Senate in March 2004 on how the dominance of space capabilities is being maintained. He spoke of "an expanded business base for space" in which small satellites launched privately (in this case by Rockwell International) are more cost-effective and allow corporations to "assume risk" for military ventures.[47] Space and in particular intercontinental ballistic missiles were the key to strategic deterrence and dominance during the cold war, subsequently elaborated as a kind of global prophylaxis through Reagan's Strategic Defense Initiative.

An equivalent superiority will be achieved through a plethora of intelligence satellites which connect surveillance to the ground so as to render space dominance a tactical tool for the average soldier. Cebrowski observes that between the two Gulf Wars, troop deployment declined (from 542,000 to 350,000) while bandwidth expanded (from 99 to 3,200 megabits a second), and concludes: "The nation's space capabilities directly impacted speed of maneuver, the tempo of the fight, and the boldness and lethality of our forces."[48] Yet the shift to tactical deployments of space-based systems has also meant that the United States and other great powers have abdicated their monopoly over aeronautics. Hyperbolically claiming a space race from below, Cebrowski insists that any small nation can now contract with an entrepreneurial university to deploy in space. Despite plans for offensive space weapons, Cebrowski cautions that the United States is taking a back seat to other nations in this smaller segment of the industry and must now reenter the field where competition is keenest: "As we are at the threshold of transforming ourselves into a network-centric military, using the coherent effects of distributed military forces and systems to achieve commander's intent, the newer smaller elements of space capability emerge as a toolset providing virtually unlimited potential."[49] Cebrowski may be concocting a fable, a latter- day counterpart to the "missile gap," but like the earlier myth this one is meant to be prophetic for planning. Smallness is not simply beautiful: it simultaneously defines the norms of superiority but also allows non-equals to be given the status of military peers in a business model sanctified by internal rather than external competition. A superiority based in the cold war is outmoded not because Russia no longer poses a nuclear threat (the American arsenal is never part of this calculus) but because big rockets have such high risks of failure that they pose obstacles to deployment.

In terms of national security, the usurpation of a concrete other anywhere so that America can spread everywhere, the most abstract medium of risk management can be traced to the lineage of the Strategic Defense Initiative, or SDI (announced by Reagan in 1983 and popularly known as the "Star Wars" program). The smoke and mirrors of Star Wars R&D carried an image of extraterritorial exclusion of the world from a putative American police function. SDI was a boondoggle lasting a decade and a half that eventually gave way to the Ballistic Missile Defense Organization (BMDO). BMDO proposes an "architecture" in which enemy missiles would be "hit to kill" from air or land or sea.[50] This hedge strategy is based upon years of failure to produce even a single encounter between an errant missile and its pursuer.

The promise of technological advance seen in the epochal, general terms of the RMA refigures interstate rivalry as a competitive edge over earlier systems. The harder they come, the harder they fall. The network in this regard is a medium for distributing risk so as to make it easier to keep systems in circulation. Whereas the ICBM system rested upon risk avoidance, webs of smaller rockets or "microsats" use risk management as a factor of their production so that they can be constantly in use. Whereas ballistic missile defense aims to prolong the fantasy that evil can be kept away, by imagining an enemy everywhere it represents a strategy of deterrence that is passive, and from the perspective of transformation outmoded. Stockpiling hugely potent warheads is passive and futile: little, derivative missiles can stay in active use. Continuous expenditure yields an environment where the dividends of risk can be exploited and deployment is maintained.

Tactical command of space follows a consumer model of deployment. No longer is the big bang of high tech reserved for the commander in chief: now that entry costs have been lowered by this new business model, anyone can play, each with a managerial role. "Rather than treating our operational and tactical level commanders as lesser includeds, this business model designs a capability to meet their specific warfighting needs."[51] These needs are established only in the "risk-tolerant" present, the real time of war, rather than by "predictive futures or scripted acquisition periods."[52]

Allowing battle managers to assume these risks is associated with a demotic collectivist impulse that is in keeping with the spirit of transformation. "While micro or nano satellites may not offer technologies that are groundbreaking, they can significantly alter the capabilities of a wider user base. The collective produces an understanding that is not replicated or deliverable by any single analyst or structured hierarchy. Leveraging space access by the entire defense establishment changes the methods and techniques that can be adopted by future users."[53] Here it becomes apparent that the system and not the machine maintains superiority. The global positioning system that the infantry uses is as prosaic as that found in their family car back home. No longer is the point of technology to be groundbreaking but rather to be generally applicable. The microsat is a flying toaster that allows access to even the humblest loaves. Because the decision taken and actions initiated anywhere in the network can make all the difference, the small investment is what matters most to transformation.

Since transformation is a kind of meta-managerial approach, it claims a generalizable applicability without reference to what needs to be changed and for what ends. In the absence of a strategic orientation for the military, transformation accommodates the amorphous mission drift that ranges from local peacekeeping to global war. In the face of this ambiguity, military analysts have been peripatetic in their search for the right name for the moment, by one count coming up with thirty labels for how war has changed since the middle of the twentieth century.[54] The principles of network control have been applied to peacekeeping and to combating the outbreak of severe acute respiratory syndrome (SARS) in Southeast Asia in 2002. The same mathematical models have been used to manage the military's $200 billion retirement and health care investment portfolios to maximize returns.[55] If cyclical or perpetual revolutions in military affairs are consummated in moments of heightened consciousness about the nature of change, then transformation amounts to a reflexive sensibility about the significance of its own effects. It is also a narrative of how small threats can be leveraged to a generalized sense of risk.

The aggression in risk management is that it is opportunistic—with every conceivable action yielding the prospect of return beyond investment. Transformation would be the theory and practice of this opportunism, with intervention defined by situational capacity—a speculative turning of what might be done into what happens. In the words of one military analyst, Juan A. Alsace, the transition to a post–cold war world entails moving from a "threat-based" to a "capabilities-based" force: "A threat based force was reactive and defensive in nature: the United States awaited the thrust. In contrast, a 'capabilities based' force carries with it an implication of offensive capability if not intent: the US focus is not on any particular threat as it prepares for any and all contingencies by adopting an aggressive forward-leaning posture."[56]

It should be clear that the faceless threat fits well with the war on terror. This capacity to lean forward on the world is evident in two key strategic documents prepared by the military. One, called Joint Vision 2020, is a plan to achieve cooperation among warring military branches subject to what they see as a Darwinian winnowing of their capacity for autonomous growth. Technological innovation, or awarding requests for new weapons systems, is a managerial carrot to achieve interoperability. Codependence is supposed to assure that the forces can work together. The carrot and stick of funding and defunding applies in the international arena as well. South Korea, for example, was pressured by the Pentagon to buy F-15K fighter jets made by Boeing over the preferred Rafaele built by the French firm Dassault, even though the order of non-American goods would have cost $350 million less. The Koreans were told by Deputy Secretary of Defense Paul Wolfowitz that the United States would refuse to install tracking systems or sell air-to-air missiles used by the plane. In bowing to the pressure to buy American, the Koreans cited interoperability as a rationale even though other allies like Britain fly just fine side by side with their own fighters.[57] Interoperability is a kind of corporate unilateralism that proscribes choices even as decisions are portrayed as local and collaborative.

: A FUTURE WITH A PLAN

The perfectly focused military vision is to wage what Max Boot calls "the savage wars of peace necessary to enlarge the 'empire of liberty,'" a designation that Thomas Jefferson had used for the breakaway republic itself.[58] Savagery characterizes the antagonists or what the protagonist will do to them. More specifically, Boot is pointing to a legacy of "small wars" (a polite term for neocolonial intervention, from native conquest to short-term occupation around the world). The key document is a Marine Corps manual from 1940 on small wars, for which there is a British equivalent dating back to 1899.[59] The Marines are themselves the smallest of the major services (and the one least affected by the demobilizations of the 1990s), and they anticipated the asymmetrical force structure that would come to prevail in military affairs. Until now small wars were treated as tactical skirmishes, wars of position to situate the grander maneuvers of great power. Now the small war is not simply for the expeditionary force but is strategic to the organization and application of military might. From the perspective of "jointness," as outlined in Vision 2020, the aim is to inflict harm without getting hurt, what is termed "full dimensional protection." Missions are to be fulfilled with an "acceptable level of risk in both the physical and information domains."[60] Stay safe and keep the network secure. To this end, commanders collect and disseminate decision-generating information; they now also "assess and manage risk."

The other key planning document, the presidentially mandated Quadrennial Defense Review, also offers what it deems a new framework for risk management. In actuality this framework is quite terse and scarcely explained. It amounts to a listing of risk types. Force management risks are the risks of having insufficient troops. Future challenges risks arise from the move to a capabilities-based approach to military deployment. Institutional risks are the risks of getting mired in bureaucratic controls. Operational risk is the possibility of not getting the money that has been requested. The review, published 30 September 2001, takes a sixty-year average of defense expenditure (so as to incorporate the major buildup for the Second World War, Korea, and Vietnam) and concludes that at 8 percent, this long-term average makes the 2001 allocation of 2.9 percent of GDP seem mighty stingy.[61]

But in the Quadrennial Defense Review as well risk is to be embraced and not merely avoided. Small interventions from the global network of American military installations are described as an imperative to "deter forward" in critical areas to achieve what is termed dissuasion. "Given the availability of advanced technology and systems to potential adversaries, dissuasion will also require the United States to experiment with revolutionary operational concepts, capabilities, and organizational arrangements and to encourage the development of a culture within the military that embraces innovation and risk-taking."[62] The prevention of what might happen, a principle to be resignified as preemption a year later (in Bush's National Security Document of September 2002), treats distance in time and space as fungible—that is, as something that can be moved forward. In practice, deterring forward realizes that future by acting on the conceivable opportunity presented by the seemingly infinite capacity for intervention. Now if transformation can convert all these disparate tactics into a unified strategy, then that is beginning to sound quite grand indeed.

Visions of grandeur have been tempered by close observers of RMA and force transformation since long before these gleaming schemes crashed on the rocks of Iraq. For many within military circles, the merits of the claims were weak before they ever had a chance to be falsified in practice, with some doubting whether the changes have been anything but incremental in the first place.[63] Writing in the Army War College journal *Parameters*, John Gentry worried about the narrow applicability of Joint Vision 2020. He noted that the document centers long-term planning on medium-intensity conventional conflicts against weak opponents with vulnerable infrastructures. He also echoed concerns that information technologies either don't work, don't apply to actual combat situations, or are easily countered. What emerges is a long-range master plan based on a kind of

Gulf War exceptionalism, with a flat battlefield that can accommodate all the heavy motorized equipment lying about on American bases, and an already compromised, incompetent enemy.[64]

If the solution to the military's regret that it is always planning for the last war is to make that one the next war, then Gentry's critique confirmed that the revolution was more backward-looking than forward-thinking. The military was being tooled to refight the first Iraqi war, already among the most lopsided in history, and to improve on that mark. Military planning was driven by largely continuous ideas, despite changing administrations which claimed that the schemes of their predecessors had failed. Theory and practice finally united with Gulf I as political efficacy quickly dissipated, a lesson that the elder Bush paid dearly to learn. While decisive, military assertiveness became an end in itself. This was the target that shock and awe sought to improve upon, by assuming that an auspicious beginning would generate its own end.

Robert M. Cassidy, writing in the same issue of *Parameters*, lamented that with Vietnam, the military "lost a generation's worth of technological modernization there while gaining a generation's worth of nearly irrelevant combat experience."[65] The doctrine of decisive force promulgated in the run-up to the first Gulf War by Colin Powell (then chairman of the Joint Chiefs of Staff) was based on a clear understanding of the political legacy of Vietnam: "long conflicts would cause public dissatisfaction with the military."[66] Powell's morphing from military advisor to Caspar Weinberger (Reagan's defense secretary, 1981–87) to secretary of state in George W. Bush's first term (2001–January 2005) represents the insinuation of the military's self-concern into foreign policy, and helps account for what might otherwise look like a dove amid the hawks.

The military's own knowledge implies that even in an all-volunteer force dead bodies make wars domestically unsustainable and therefore erode public support for procurement. The aversion to casualties effectively means that the principle if not the practice of antiwar movements is built into transformation, mobilization, and deployment. As a corrective, the military planning undertaken by Weinberger to cure the Vietnam syndrome would allow the "military to prescribe to the civilian elite what kind of wars the military does and does not fight."[67] Hence while only the president might decide when to go to war, the die would already be cast by years of preparation as to which war would be fought and under what conditions. But if there was some sense of inevitability to the second Gulf

War, there was equally a concern that despite successful prosecution of war, victory might never come.

Developing a different implication of postmodern war, the military sociologists Charles C. Moskos and James Burk argue that objective factors of technological superiority matter little when both sides claim victory, because there are no clear standards by which to judge who won. Postmodern relativism meant that Saddam Hussein also declared victory in 1991.[68] This blank appropriation of the postmodern turn makes Hussein the logical cognate of the terrorist, one who refuses to grasp the reason of force and makes a virtue out of being but a derivative discourse. Yet this blankness admits a certain slyness as well, the postmodern emphasis on rupture or break, and the shift from grand to small historical accounts—elevated to a still grander, universalist account of the way things now stand—winds up being not such a bad approximation of the RMA's production of derivative wars.

There is of course a far more rigorous engagement with the philosophical entailments of postmodernism than the more prosaic use of the term in military literature. Influenced by poststructuralism, which critically interrogates the operations and exclusions of cultural representation, theorists such as Paul Virilio, Jean Baudrillard, and James der Derian have perceptively examined how the informational aspects of contemporary war have made their own truths. Virilio observed that "war has moved from the geographic *field of battle* to the multimedia *field of vision*."[69] With zero casualties, war becomes inhuman or transhuman, and with the development of techno-science, war moves from the material to the immaterial.

Clearly the idea of war without casualties is a military planner's fantasy. These arguments are not to be seen as empirical claims for those visited by war, who especially among the civilian population in Iraq have been killed in large numbers and denied the techno-scientific accouterments of health care, drinking water, and infrastructure. The materiality of war-induced scarcity is for these millions unavoidable. Virilio's interest is in speed, and force transformation certainly intends to decrease the turnaround time of deployment and engagement. Jean Baudrillard has explored the consequences of the saturation of war images, whose semblance overwhelms the war as such. For Baudrillard, the principal asymmetry of the first Gulf War meant that victory was assured before the combat began, effectively nullifying any actual political outcome to the war: "Since this war was won in advance, we will never know what it would have been like if it had existed."[70] This virtualization of the decisive win met its parallel notion in a prescribed defeat, because the war effectively insulated the combatants from one another: "The fact that the Americans *never saw* the Iraqis is compensated for by the fact that the Iraqis never fought them."[71]

The "military-industrial-media-entertainment" effect of war, as der Derian has articulated it, is a move away from seeing what war does where it lands to seeing it as a virtuous means "to effect ethical change through technological and martial means."[72] Der Derian's point is that the virtual makes possible the virtuous, and he provides a framework for understanding the messianic tones of the present terror war. He also imagines that "virtual theory" "opens up the naive black/white, good/bad, doomed/saved binaries of technoscientific discourse," presenting the prospect of a move from a closed system where nation-states are locked into a condition "as *being-between* wars" to a global politics "constituted as *becoming-different* from war."[73]

As both Bushes have found out, the temporality of virtue is fleeting, for it did not take long for the virtuous effects to dissipate. More troubling, when fast wars are not fast enough they seem to lose their virtuality as well, and in short order virtue also loses its shroud. Another thing that tends to drop out in the study of war's simulations and virtual effects is the labor that continues to be needed to fight. Labor is what actualizes or realizes warfare, and the military's self-reflection cannot ignore the question of how to keep its million-plus employees productive. Like good managerial science, force transformation remembers that soldiers must become part of the managerial circuit. More than this, however, soldiers who have undergone appropriate transformation are not simply killing machines, their bodies gone primitive. They have become warriors.

: WARRIORS IN THE MIDST

The question of how to make a perfect soldier could only be a historical one. The appropriate relation between techniques of weaponry and those of the body is a problem that has recurred since Greek and Roman times. The emphasis of the Greek tradition, as expressed in the writings of Ailianos in the second century, is on centralized command and drill formations for coordinating the deployment of weapons. The Roman approach, evident in the late-fourth-century work of Flavius Vegetius Renatus, provides a decentralized exercise regimen to advance the physical prowess of individual infantry. The roots of modern western military training in the sixteenth century bring together bodily comportment, martial states of mind, and fighting techniques and formations that permitted the individual soldier to be subjected to institutionalized command structures.

The formalization continues in the seventeenth century under the influence of the Dutch noble Maurice of Orange, with drills consisting of precise choreographic sequences that are to be applied literally in battle. The organization of camps, the emphasis on the visual coherence of military formations in battle, suggests a confidence in the reason of planning and command at a time when individual conscripts are seen as lacking the capacities of rational decision making. The drills are to lead to a tactical machinery of battle that integrates constituent elements into a smoothly functioning and naturalized whole.

Recognizing the contradictions of technological advance, the military historian Harald Kleinschmidt has observed that treating soldiers as readily replaceable cannon fodder by emphasizing ideal formations resulted in high casualty rates (up to 50 percent of regular combatants died in sixteenth-century battles). Yet as elaborate tactics required better-trained soldiers, high mortality threatened the machine with collapse. By the eighteenth century the formations became more mobile, more discretion was devolved to soldiers themselves, and casualties dropped to 10 percent.[74] At the end of the eighteenth century drill shifted from the machine analogy to "general principles of bodily behavior which were observed in humankind as a whole."[75] The proliferation of poorly functioning firearms that jeopardized soldiers' lives, Kleinschmidt suggests, helped support an "ethics of self-constraint and non-mechanistic aesthetics."[76] As mass armies increased in scale over the nineteenth and twentieth centuries, the professionalization of training had to take ever more costly human assets into consideration. Proper training would need to attend to the antinomies of an individual's bodily truth and the appropriate articulation of highly specialized soldiers with the general machinery of war.

Attention to these longstanding problems of training was most recently paid in January 2004. The Army committed itself to inculcating a set of values "across the force," from basic training to strategic initiatives. A counterpoint to the high-tech rhetoric of transformation, the approach, called the "warrior ethos," has a kind of neoprimitivist ring to it.[77] According to the army's Center for Training Doctrine (TRADOC), "Warrior Ethos is the foundation for the American Soldier's total commitment to victory in peace and war. While always exemplifying Army values, Soldiers who live Warrior Ethos put the mission first, refuse to accept defeat, never quit and never leave behind a fallen comrade. They have absolute faith in themselves and their team. They are trained and equipped to engage and destroy the enemies of the United States in close combat."[78]

A patina of net-centricity washes through this approach to training and mixes with the concerns of ancient Greek and Roman drill doctrine. To kill others one needs to have the right attitude—faith in oneself and immediate solidarity through the corporate-borrowed team concept. Fighters are part of a managerial scheme called a quality circle, in which employees get together to share ideas about increasing productivity, offering up their own initiative for the good of the firm. Self-confidence is vital because of the intimacies of combat. Freedom in the field and initiative in decision making are achieved by trained standardization. While victory may be difficult to define in strategic terms, the function of the soldier's labor is to make winning unambiguous—to reduce it to a zero degree of agonistic, interpersonal encounter: "I beat you." Face-to-face absolutism trumps the abstract relativism of nation-states unsure whether to count themselves winners or losers.

Training is not simply physical preparation for battle, but an intricate alignment of tactic and strategy, self and society. Recruits who may have lived a marginal existence in civilian life will have their place fixed in the world by psychic self-transformation. To start down this path, all soldiers are required to memorize and recite the following creed:

> I am an American Soldier.
> I am a Warrior and a member of a team. I serve the people of the United States and live the Army Values.
> I will always place the mission first. I will never accept defeat. I will never quit. I will never leave a fallen comrade.
> I am disciplined, physically and mentally tough, trained and proficient in my warrior tasks and drills.
> I always maintain my arms, my equipment and myself.
> I am an expert and I am a professional.
> I stand ready to deploy, engage, and destroy the enemies of the United States of America in close combat.
> I am a guardian of freedom and the American way of life.
> I am an American Soldier.[79]

Life and death is equated with getting the job done, such that the command of business and war are made equivalent. So too are the maintenance of self and self-maintenance of the machines that extend the self. Despite being but one cog in a long line of logistical supporters, the soldier is an auto-mechanic. At the same time, in an army where more soldiers are likely to be mechanics than combatants, being hailed as a warrior is a different kind of address. Clearly the creed means to assimilate identity to action. I am and I will. It begins and ends with the adhesion of nation and occupation. The iteration of self washes away all doubt, even as it leaves undefined the who, what, where, when, and why of the enemy, which is to be the source of all this clarity of purpose and certainty of will. The actuality of closeness can be a menace to all virtue.

The affirmation of this generalizable identity is in response to the perils of the Iraq War, where noncombatants have been brought into the fray, and to a longer-standing tendency toward military specialization. The need to address this role strain was well appreciated by senior officers. "This is the thinking of Army Chief of Staff Gen. Peter J. Schoomaker, who, after the war with Iraq started, noted that Soldiers need to refocus their attention on what it means to be a warrior instead of focusing as much on their military specialty."[80] Studies on motivation to fight going back to the Second World War and affirmed by the sociologists Edward Shils and Morris Janowitz found that commitment to colleagues—the buddy ethos— was the most potent factor in a soldier's ability to place his or her life on the line.[81] A more recent study conducted toward the end of the American infiltration of Iraq ties propinquity to affect. "That person means more to you than anybody. You will die if he dies. That is why I think that we protect each other in any situation. I know that if he dies, and it was my fault, it would be worse than death to me."[82] The challenge of training doctrine is to turn this immediacy of feeling into a network of national fidelity.

The warrior ethos intends a seamless transition along a networked chain of moral obligation from buddy to team to Army to American Way of Life. The interpersonal in combat, the refusal to quit or accept defeat, ascends to a managerial principle. Writing for the Naval War College, David Buckingham defines the excellent warrior as one who does what he is supposed to do "even when the boss is not watching."[83] He notes that small isolated units which characterize self-managed deployments require high degrees of unit cohesion and attention to detail, especially when high-tech hardware is used to fight. But it is equally important that soldiers never lose sight of how awful death is, as an indifference to death increases the possibility for atrocities to take place.

Inner strength is the capacity to sustain feeling rather than sublimate it to a decision-making machine. Far from monochromatic machismo, what the warrior has is an ability to channel intelligence and affect. The other correlate of a high-tech military is that more and more labor will be deployed moving and maintaining war matériel. Indeed, it has been argued that the RMA is predicated on a total shift in logistical operations that focuses on managing information about supplies rather than inventory, outsourcing to private firms what a warrior ethos would call "non-core competencies."[84] Wars could be fought out of inventory, but the warehouses would be privately owned.

Before Vietnam removed the front lines that separated combat and logistics, the structure of military occupations had been dramatically altered. Buckingham notes that during the Civil War, over 90 percent of soldiers were in combat occupations. By Korea that percentage had fallen below 30.[85] Now the people filling over four thousand military occupations —80 percent of military personnel—serve in noncombat occupations.[86] These facts are featured on the Army's recruitment home page and are given positive spin with trademarked slogans like "Today's Military: See It for What It Really Is," and "Qualities Acquired While in the Military Stay with You Forever." Here one doesn't see fancy weapons, but smiling faces. The web site copy asserts that the Army is safer than one might think and its training is readily transferable to civilian employment. Peel back the cover, get into boot camp, and the warrior ethos implies that something must compensate for these shifts.

Part of what the new ethos compensates for is prior training doctrines that made multiculturalism into something of a national doctrine, albeit a highly assimilationist one.[87] The 1990s had opened with an African American leading the United States into battle, women getting closer to combat, and gays acknowledged as existing in the military. When it appeared that cultural differences might unseat established hierarchies, backlash was constant. One critic of the "kinder, gentler military" complained that in the 1990s, "a doddering kind of hypochondria filled the land."[88] Women were becoming base commanders and not allowing the boys to be boys. One, Captain Cornelia de Groot Whitehead, changed training in light of evidence that 40 percent of recruits were abused and 26 percent had contemplated suicide.[89] Consequently obstacle courses were being retooled as "confidence courses" and recruits were losing discipline as well as their competitive spirit by receiving training that wasn't tough enough.

New Army doctrine challenged the notion that the self had to be broken down to be reconstituted as disciplined. If selfhood lay at the core of combat, the army would need to replace constructivist concepts of person-making with its own version of strategic essentialism. Army training would undertake a kind of restitutive justice that would actualize the battered selves kept down by discrimination inside and outside military life. As affirmative action was being dismissed and civil rights and feminism were conventionally portrayed as being in decline, the Army would work where the labor market could not. Once the scars of discrimination were removed through confidence building, historical identities based on race, gender, sexuality, religion, and poverty would be shed in favor of the originary and somehow precultural warrior ethos. The warrior weaves the noble savage into the neoprimitive, an immediacy of response that shares intimacy with kindred beings and technologies. Rather than specific cultural difference, it was the American way of life—what the soldier was sworn to uphold—that would need to be shed if the warrior would be properly embodied.

By the time American troops were occupying Iraq, this cultural critique of America-the-decadent was written into the Army's "Standardized Physical Training Guide." The manual begins with the observation that "the softer influences of our modern society make the challenge of conditioning soldiers more important than ever before."[90] Toughening becomes a means of reconditioning the body from its soft, civilian form. Continuous improvement must be shown. Fitness needs to meet measurable targets: thirteen push-ups, seventeen sit-ups, a mile in eight minutes and thirty seconds (markers which for a warrior would appear remarkably modest).[91] Concerned with attrition as well as the anxieties of failure that pose challenges to recruitment, the hardening process must also control injuries, all the while working toward corporeal standardization.[92] For all of the high-tech hardware, it is curious that the twenty-first-century military body is to be achieved by applying late-nineteenth- and early-twentieth-century body mechanics,[93] defined as "posture in motion."[94]

Army training seems to be crafted against the carefully calibrated cybernetics of contemporary fitness regimens that meticulously isolate muscle groups, emphasize internal motions of the body to maintain low impact, and create complex counterpoints of strengthening and stretching. In contrast, to judge by the book, army drills appear to eschew the diligent attention to physical appearance as a softener that only an embrace of the "mechanized bodies" of First World War vintage might correct.[95] Soldiers are to inhabit these postures. "When soldiers live in good postures, the results are better performance, fewer injuries, and a confidence borne of grace, balance, and power."[96] Commands are to be given on rhythmic counts, the exercises taught as a sequence of positions, executed with tense firmness. The imagery affirms an externally oriented body consciousness: "imagine drawing the gut straight inward as if preparing for a blow to the mid-section or trying to appear slimmer than you really are."[97]

The manual is richly illustrated. The model for the photos holds the prescribed positions with what might be taken as signs of bad posture—tension in the back of the neck, hyperextension of the lumbar region, splayed knees, and the like. This body may be a machine, but it is not an ergonomically enlightened one. Were one to accept an evolutionary analogy for the shift from machine age to automation to information, training recidivism in the form of a return to earlier mechanical bodies itself has a primitivizing effect. Army training may unseat a civilian body that is in some ways more advanced and better able to to affect the more pristine state of the warrior.

It would be too easy to say that the military's hostility toward the presumed physical decadence of civilian life has left it without the opportunities to learn from elaborations in fitness training beyond what has been undertaken in its revised approach. The functions of basic training as a rite of passage that separates the soldier from civilian life, and the holdovers of prior drill regimes, jostle with the need to assimilate newer approaches. Certainly the last thirty years have seen a veritable revolution in fitness affairs. In 1973, with the end of the draft, the Army did indeed revamp its training concept from the "Army Training Program" in effect since the First World War. A "systems approach to training" based on skills evaluation and inculcation in core army values evolved over the next twenty-five years.[98]

But like the RMA itself, basic training chased developments in the civilian sector. Force transformation in the bodily dimension has extended to all manner of attention to alignment, preventive health, stretching, breathing, low-impact movement, enhanced aerobic capacity, and so on—none of which seems to be reflected in the standard training manual. On the other hand, soldiers themselves will likely have been exposed to these more sophisticated physical regimens through sports and fitness training and will be importing these very corporeal knowledges from the civilian world into their work. Gyms and free weights are now standard accessories of military bases: the training manual offers a warning on (but no pro-hibition of) the use of "dietary supplements" and "injury risk" due to overexercise.[99]

The warrior ethos transfers responsibility for managing the dangers of combat from commanders to the individual soldier. The training doctrine would seem to have as much to do with managing the divide between individualized risk and reward, professional training and corporal experi-ence, as it does with negotiating the distance from the civilian realm that would both subvert and supersede it. In actuality the training doctrine does not uniformly extend down to every body, but covers the gap between the proliferation of noncombatants and their exposure to the risk of harm in the course of soldiering. A refusal or inability to revolutionize military training as a standard across the board speaks volumes about the military's more general conception of labor. The body lag is especially poignant in the face of a corporeal intelligence whose advances could be considered as dramatic as the technological ones that have occurred over the same pe-riod. This effective mind-body split creates the kind of intelligence gap that is so programmatic in information warfare. All will be responsible, few will be in the know. The few, the special, will be trained and hardened to become "the point of the spear." The rest will be left with an ethos of self-managed risk.

: SPECIALISTS WITHOUT EXIT

Before the warrior ethos sought appropriate risk distribution throughout the force, Special Operations was its model. Customization is the rubric for Special Operations, and it defines itself by the capacity to continuously assimilate multiple kinds of training (physical, psychological, linguistic, scientific, technical). Whereas the generic warrior is organized around an ethos, the specialized operative hails to "truths," listed as follows:

> *Humans* are more important than *Hardware.*
> *Quality* is better than *Quantity.*
> Special Operations Forces cannot be mass produced.
> Competent Special Operations Forces cannot be created after emergencies occur.[100]

Despite deep cuts to conventional force strength, these élite forces have retained their force structure of twelve active combat groups across the services, with some recent calls for substantial expansion.[101] Rather than being extraordinary, they are the soldiers most likely to be deployed, their extensive use the result of planning and heavy investment. While their equipment may be among the most sophisticated, it is their own labor and its use value that takes precedence. The Fordist protocols of mass production do not apply to these units, which include the 2,500 members of Delta Force, the 2,200 Navy Seals, the 5,000 Green Berets, and the 1,800 Rangers, in addition to specialized groups like psychological operations, communications, and aviation.[102] According to the Special Operations Command, these soldiers are committed to act "against strategic or tactical targets in pursuit of national military, political, economic or psychological objectives. These operations may be conducted during periods of peace or hostilities. They may support conventional operations, or they may be undertaken independently when the use of conventional forces is either inappropriate or infeasible."[103] The pervasive deployment of the special as the general presents a moment when the derivative has become primary.

These are the forces that can put jointness and interoperability into practice. It is not simply that these forces are flexible: their existence and primacy in deployment effaces the very delineations between defense and offense that were captured in the movement from security to securitization. Peace and war, strategy and tactics, military and psychological objectives occupy the same space and time. The mission of these forces is "unconventional" by definition. Their very deployment engages in innovation by thwarting whatever is taken as convention. To this end, the soldiers are to absorb a series of principles which apply whenever they take up an assignment. These are called "Imperatives:"

Understand the operational environment
Recognize political implications
Facilitate interagency activities
Engage the threat discriminately
Consider long-term effects
Ensure legitimacy and credibility of Special Operations
Anticipate and control psychological effects
Apply capabilities indirectly
Develop multiple options
Ensure long-term sustainment
Provide sufficient intelligence
Balance security and synchronization[104]

Here the integration between the strategic and the tactical becomes clearer. The dream of command-and-control schemes is realized because the individual soldier is fundamentally an analytic entity. It is not simply that the small war which has evolved over centuries of colonial rule is normalized. Special Operations do not engage an enemy in its entirety but rather discriminately and indirectly. Each action is to be considered for its long-term consequences, which range from the political to the psychological.

Rangers, Navy Seals, and their kin exist in a state of forward deployment. It is among these élite forces from various services and their cognates from other nations (such as Britain's 14th Intelligence Unit, Pathfinders, and Special Air Services) that jointness and interoperability become practicable features of deployment—an international of the small and the unconventional. Under various guises unconventional forces conducting the equivalent of special operations have a long and tangled history, with references going as far back as the *Iliad* and the Bible. Later examples include Robert Rogers's Rangers, who ambushed the French from the thickets of the Hudson River valley in the 1750s, and Francis Marion, "the Swamp Fox," who used the lowland marshes of South Carolina to drive the British out in 1781.[105] The Office of Strategic Services (oss) was established during the Second World War (the first Ranger battalion was activated in 1942), followed by a Special Warfare School in 1956. Special forces were fully professionalized in the 1980s as an occupational specialty and consolidated as a separate command in 1989 after the Berlin Wall fell.[106] In this genealogy, the spy has become a soldier, intelligence has become interventionist, and the ability to circulate in and out of terrain rather than hold it has become paramount to achieving successful missions. It should now be apparent that all this specialness also fits with the logic of the derivative, since an intervention is designed to allow a small force to make all the difference. Like the derivative as well, special forces proliferate the terms and conditions of their application. No longer stuck in a state standoff or in two simultaneous medium theaters, special forces can be put into play everywhere.[107]

Starting with the Green Berets that John Wayne made famous and culminating in current special operatives who undertake the most crucial tasks of combat (as in Afghanistan), the specialist warrior has truly become a mainstay. If so, the new way of life is a way without exit even if it always comes to an end. When the daring of the mission becomes its measure of success, a virtue is made of the strategic failures of exit strategies. From Vietnam to Iraq the problem of how to get out of the mess created by interventionist prowess has been the military's persistent problem—especially when the mission has changed over the course of intervention.[108] In a version of the frontier theses where only beginnings matter, war has been made a cultural expression in which "endings run counter to the grain of American thought."[109]

Exit strategy, a notion applied to the contemporary dilemmas of war, was originally a business term used to denote a company's response to the exhaustion of a product cycle.[110] It seems there was a time not so long ago when the death of people and things was clearer than it is now. A product could be put to rest when continuing investment in it yielded diminishing returns. But when money can be made just as well on gains as on losses, volatility itself is what enables risk to be rewarding. Force transformation would aspire to this opportunity by allowing small investments and deployments of assets to move through larger fields of effects. Forward deterrence becomes the anticipation of all available difference.

What the RMA teaches us is that long before there was a terror war, the military was preparing to make asymmetry its own principle of advance. Low-intensity conflicts, specialized operations where a modest sprinkling of brains and brawn matter most, would change into high-extensity effects. The loss of a center would make any minor difference absolute. Strategy would become a matter of tactical execution, as cold war containment, deterrence, and defense would surrender to an opportunistically oriented risk management. Outsourcing would keep peeling value off the military machinery, allowing it to refocus on its core competencies. Slicing off pieces of ham would have a purgative effect on the whole pig.

The military as a whole might acquire the autonomy that would free it from self-made conditions of necessity. The derivative war would trade the defined benefit of national development for a defined contribution that would allow war itself to order the world. The goal was not achieved, but not for want of planning or clarity of intent. As the military came to be able to control its own future, as wars to come were made into an immediate present, the military lost control of its destiny. That paradox becomes evident when we examine what came to pass in Afghanistan and Iraq.

With the war on terror, liberation has been the operative term. Military intervention liberates insofar as it establishes an equivalence between hitherto unrelated values so that they may be placed into a universe of exchange. Dispossessed capitalists and dictators past their expiration date can be tossed into the same terror hole. By assembling the world into gradations of risk, an anti-productive network of missed opportunities can animate those choice moments that yield effective gain. Even if terrorists are not caught, weapons of mass destruction are not found, or regimes end but don't change, freedom will be achieved by installing representative self-government. That ongoing wars in Afghanistan, Iraq, and various "sheriff"[1] operations around the world have stretched military forces to the limit is not necessarily an endgame of imperial overreach. Rather, derivative wars indicate how the world's peoples are to be sorted into those who merit discretionary attention and those who can be ignored.

The question is what this liberation consists of and how it resembles the freedom of capital to circulate in financial markets. Iraqis are to be liberated from their oil, no doubt, but it would seem as well that many people have been emancipated from the economy as such. That the invasion force was not designed to police national development is less a planning oversight than a statement of intent for the resources applied for the return to civilian rule. Similarly, Paul Wolfowitz, architect of the Iraq war, made a promise to Congress and the world that national reconstruction for the imperially vanquished would be self-financing. He meant this as a matter of policy, not a forecast of oil production targets (which would go unmet). For the "coalition of the willing," whether in Afghanistan or in Iraq, tactical success did not readily translate into strategic value. Regime change was effected without realizing the political objectives (stability, security, democracy, free markets) that the regime in question was said to harbor.[2]

Fighting terror unleashed it elsewhere, just as a well-placed put or call (sell or buy) of stock would send ripples of price volatility through the market. Drops in price can be hedged against, turned into derivatives, and sold for gain. The terror war converts both wins and losses into self-perpetuating gain. Risk rules and all must pay the price. The war without end is its own triumph, just as is the confidence that any social security is best off privatized to the glory of self-management. For the analogy to hold anything, however, international politics must be as seamless a medium of exchange as the market means to be. Unlike the al-Qaeda or Baathist leadership, risk must not be allowed to slip away. But only through opportunity lost may it return, now with others in tow.

The prosecution of the war on terror has had this effect, to socialize politics by making opposition to objectifying rule impossible in principle (if not certainly in practice). After the conquest of Afghanistan, Defense Secretary Rumsfeld insisted that his soldiers not stick around to clean up the mess, a task better left to others. In Iraq, the United States has been even more mischievous in its inconsistency. While military intervention was highly destructive for Afghanistan, it was modest in relation to total capacity. The Iraqi operation, while at a larger scale, allowed the United States to keep one eye on its prey and let the other roam from Syria to North Korea to Iran. Both interventions were treated as but limited moments of a larger conflict from which they derived and to whose economy they would add. Each followed the logic of a derivative war.

: SELF-MANAGING TO GET BY

In terms of both domestic solidarity—the production of an America in the world—and international alignment, the problem of what is called distributed or dispersed warfare extended a politics of securitization in the name of global security. Relative to the massive deployments in space and time of a Second World War or even a Vietnam, Afghanistan and now Iraq are targeted investments to create spheres of participation where non-American governments can respond to the threat of being "with us or against us." Hence even while the initial goals of intervention can become obscured by means of their realization, the installation of new regimes of self-management maintains the nervous system of the imperium.

As we have learned at home, bad risk is denied movement, isolated, incarcerated. The terror at Abu Ghraib is not simply a scandal of command and control in which responsibility is distributed downward (like the recurrent intelligence failures that provided the foundation for war). The tactics of humiliation are familiar to those who follow carceral developments in the United States, and are in this regard but another export of civilian life back into the military. The lessons learned from the various domestic wars that end in the maximum security of prison is that whole populations can be managed by moving minorities through the system. Suspects can be picked up in Afghanistan, held at Guantánamo, released in Australia. The small prison packets can be bundled together for greater effect.

The strategic point of securitization in financial terms is to delocalize risk so that it can become a general feature of activity. Risk, like money itself, is both means and end of exchange, medium and store of value. Through securitization one is not indebted to a person in a place but to the generalized other of the market. A successful war on terror, a specter of ongoing intervention actualized through severely limited and selective engagement, would have to manage itself. Networks and nations alike would find themselves equally treated. Liberation would allow them to continue, colonial cauldrons unto themselves, connected to the world at the point at which they would matter most—where risk, for better or worse, could be embraced. Afghanistan and Iraq are the twin peaks in the terror war but they are twins that were made, not born. Each needs to be examined to disclose the underlying value from which the relationship derives.

"We have no credible evidence that Iraq and al-Qaeda cooperated on attacks against the United States."[3] This finding by the commission charged by the Bush administration with giving a factual account of the circumstances surrounding the September 11 attacks was widely construed as formally giving the lie to justifications for the war against Iraq. Vice President Dick Cheney disavowed his own statements about the linkage, and voiced outrage at *The New York Times*, originally a conspirator in the fable, for publishing the commission's findings.[4] Certainly the disclosure of misrepresentation in expressions of the rationale for invading Iraq was one more nail in the already deflated tire of public support for the war.

By the middle of 2004, when the commission's report was published, a year's worth of provisional administration was leaching back onto the once impermeable popularity of Bush's presidency, fomenting a mix of policy-induced foreign-domestic insecurity.[5] By the time of the preemptive departure of the American proconsul L. Paul Bremer two days early on 28 June 2004, the occupation only seemed capable of shocking itself with the element of surprise. Each with its decisively dissatisfying elections, Afghanistan, Iraq, and the United States looked like three sides of a Bermuda triangle into which sovereignty had fallen. Amid all the efforts at reconstruction, people were left to fend for themselves.

Whatever pleasures might attach to exposing the Bush administration's malfeasance in going to war without the benefit of truth to explain its unbounded belligerence, another point was missed. While Afghanistan and Iraq were falsely linked to the assaults of 9/11, they became genuinely connected through Bush's war on terror. Deposing the governments of Mullah Omar and Saddam Hussein fatefully entangled two countries that hitherto had the most tenuous of ties. The war on terror had established its own truths. An underlying asset could be detached from the value (in this case sovereignty) of which it was part and bundled together or securitized to establish benefits from newly assumed risks. The new class of warfare, from which Afghanistan and Iraq found themselves unwitting graduates, made of disparate evils an axis. Not only would the bad be banished, but the derivative war would leave liberation in its wake. It would not be enough to contain bad influences, nor would security be a basis for reconstruction. Rather, occupation would provide a cover for self-management.

The war on terror creates what it seeks to destroy. By the dead weight of numbers and casualties, terrorism as tabulated by the State Department was on the rise once the United States launched its offensive.[6] Escalating terror turns out to be the perfect medium for force transformation where armed conflict has an effect that is revolutionary. To appreciate what the embrace of risk in foreign affairs has wrought, it is important to dwell in the domain of effects. In short, the link between al-Qaeda and Iraq does not lie in their common cause, but in the realm of consequences that they have now been forced to share. The shadowy network of assets meant to compose the grand strategy of the American imperium—if there is such a thing—is detectable in the prosecution of these two wars and their aftermaths. The derivative war, that most distinctive of American exports, aspires to be the generative force of a world order in the making.

These recent conquests display all the hubris of prior colonial incursions. But for all their immediate military success, they lack their clarity of interest. It is not difficult to pronounce the attacks against terror a failure in their own terms, a failure to make the world more secure or put an end to terror. Nor do liberation and national reconstruction look particularly appealing if Afghanistan and Iraq are the poster children of the new imperial project. Given the harm done by the Taliban and Hussein to their own populations it is difficult to rue their passing. The efficacy of present governments introduced under conditions of occupation is difficult to assess, given the mixed condition of civil war and selective political openings. Military occupation did not produce a sovereignty that could be handed over to a new government, any more than a country in the grip of a foreign power can hope to rule itself. Two nations thoroughly ravaged by colonial and cold war attentions have struggled to realize whatever benefits reconstruction might have to offer.[7] Physical degradation of already compromised infrastructure. Economic deterioration, increased unemployment, corruption, and swelling of illicit trade. Terrorist attacks up worldwide, with seemingly increased numbers of recruits and operations in places where terrorism was previously thought absent. An unrivaled superpower manufacturing its rivals everywhere.

Far more conceptually challenging than a recounting of the terror war's failures would be a consideration of what might be implied by success. A revolution in military affairs affirmed? Regime change? Liberation? These victories remain tremulous. Derivative. Securitization. Risk. How might these keywords of finance be seen as the fruits of battle? Our small wars of late have been tied to big ideas. A highly interventionist privatizing state. Deliberately restricted applications of resources intended to be leveraged to larger effects. The breakup of fixed values, the dispossession of populations from their productive capacities in search of new opportunities.

Before September 11 Donald Rumsfeld already grasped the shift. At the Senate hearings to confirm his appointment as secretary of defense, he proclaimed that the United States could not wait for another Pearl Harbor but would "have to be more forward-looking."[8] In its 1999 report the Defense Intelligence Agency had already anticipated the source of the threat that Rumsfeld would use to channel his aspirations of force transformation from a staid defensive posture to an opportunistic one: "State failure will be more common in the developing world."[9] The attentive embrace of risk yields productive returns whether prices rise or fall, and whether states succeed or fail. The world's volatility would launch a thousand ships. Military intervention for liberation would become the means and end of politics, and force would become the kind of change agent once reserved for the idea of development. Aid would remain a promise, forever falling short of expectations. While positioned to go anywhere, intervention would remain highly selective, hoping that a couple of well-placed calls might ripple throughout the world. All this under the sign of an evangelical capitalism. All this pressing its limitations and counter-prospects to the fore. The elements of this design for better opportunities through war were already in place with homeland security. Now let us search for them among occupations' ruins.

The revolution in military affairs carried the corpse of the cold war with it. Released from an arms race without application, opportunities for the uses of weaponry would now abound, as a forward-deploying logic of leveraged investment would replace the old savings plan of mutually assured destruction. The terror war too retained its debts and absent causes to a missing communism.[10] Small wars were always considered the hot spots of the world; now they were supposed to light the way as well. For a foreign policy as content with freedom fighters as with internal purges of political parties, anti-communism was the pre-linkage of Osama bin Laden and Saddam Hussein, once useful assets allied by what they opposed. Evidently the measure of communism's monstrosity could be found in what would oppose it.[11]

The governments of Afghanistan and Iraq combated alien ideologies and attained their global notoriety by hosting their own foreign agents. In Afghanistan there was financial and military patronage enabled by bin Laden. In Iraq the foreign agents were chemical and biological, sent by the United States during the 1980s to its then ally to use against Iran. The anthrax, botulism, and E. coli bacillus provided by American firms were later recovered by UN inspectors and given imaginary life by American invaders.[12] The U.S. Defense Intelligence Agency helped Iraq plan its use of chemical weapons against Iran, considering their deployment "inevitable in the Iraqi struggle for survival.[13] Both al-Qaeda and the Iraqi weapons of mass destruction turned out to have a phantasmic aspect that gave momentary coherence to American intervention. It is not that the threats were absent, but rather, like a hedge fund, they dispersed and placed their interconnected assets into wide circulation.

: INTO AFGHANISTAN

Bin Laden went to Afghanistan in the 1980s and helped finance a recruitment network for Muslims from around the world called the Maktab al Khidmat (Bureau of Services). At this time he also established training camps for regional warlords engaged in the battle against the Soviets.[14] His own combat experience was probably limited to a rout by the Soviet army in April 1987 in which many of his recruits died.[15] When the Soviets with-drew, bin Laden sought to maintain the international network of fighters. Al-Qaeda, an Arabic term that means at once base, camp, foundation, pedestal, precept, and method, was used in the 1980s to refer to the associa-tion of anti-communist militants and subsequently adopted by bin Laden himself in the early 1990s.

Abdullah Azzam, a Saudi professor and bin Laden's mentor, defined al-Qaeda ideologically rather than organizationally. "This vanguard consti-tutes the strong foundation of the expected society."[16] Norman Friedman, an anti-terrorism analyst for the Navy, characterizes al-Qaeda as a "holding company for numerous local movements" that collects money indirectly through a network of charitable Muslim organizations patterned after the CIA's money laundering through the Bank of Commerce and Credit Inter-national (BCCI), which collapsed in 1991.[17] Another observer, Jason Burke, likens it to a "venture capitalist firm, sponsoring projects submitted by a variety of groups or individuals in the hopes that they will be profitable."[18]

Since being cut out of his family's inheritance (and his million-dollar-a-year expense account) in 1994, bin Laden has served more as a manager and trainer than as a financier.[19] He has sought to broker relationships, but al-Qaeda's overtures have often been rebuffed by movements or govern-ments with a different political or ideological itinerary, such as the Al-gerian Groupe Islamique Armée, the Indonesian Lashkar Jihad group, or Iraq itself. On the other hand, at a moment when al-Qaeda was said to reach everywhere, tenuous links could very profitably be declared solid to provide cover for other political purposes. Two such examples are the Islamic Movement of Uzbekistan, which netted aid for the government in Tashkent, and Abu Sayyaf in the Philippines, whose purported ties to al-Qaeda were used as a pretext by the United States to send in troops.[20] While not the only group being sponsored, the Taliban were al-Qaeda's most successful deal.

Ruled by a monarchy that received backing from the British and then the United States until 1973, Afghanistan saw the People's Democratic Party take power in 1978, supported by the Soviets a year later. After years of counterinsurgency by a range of groups from the Islamist Mujaheddin to the secular Revolutionary Association of Women of Afghanistan, sup-ported by billions in aid from Washington, the Soviet Union withdrew in 1989. Najibullah became president of the communist government in 1986 and he himself survived a coup attempt in 1990 before agreeing to step down in 1992. He took refuge at the UN compound in Kabul until 1996, when he was dragged out by the Taliban and hanged from a traffic light post. The Mujaheddin, who had taken over in 1992, in turn wrecked themselves in internecine conflict. Over the next several years the Taliban stepped into the vacuum left by great-power abandonment of the country and in 1996 overthrew the government of Burhanuddin Rabbani.[21] The Taliban came to power and subverted the modernization project that had included the education of women, extension of health care, and incorporation of minority cultures. While the Taliban opposed foreign infidels, they owed their capacity to govern to subventions from Pakistan and al-Qaeda that were used to pay off local leaders. These funds allowed the Taliban government to sustain a measure of popularity because, unlike previous administrations, it did not have to resort to extorting money from the population to maintain its army.

When Pakistan threatened to withdraw support if the Taliban could not end the civil war by late 2001, al-Qaeda stepped in and formed the 055 brigade—a kind of praetorian guard that both defended the government and killed Afghans who tried to abandon their posts. It was this brigade of non-Afghan fighters that successfully assassinated the Taliban's chief rival, Ahmed Shah Mahsood, on 7 September 2001.[22] With the promise of an oil pipeline through the country looming, the United States returned to the scene in 1998 as the Taliban's main source of cash, through its program to pay for suppressing the poppy crop from which opium is produced.[23] Needless to say, such a heavily indebted government is also a highly volatile one, and the Taliban could no more give up bin Laden than they could surrender themselves. The irony in al-Qaeda's offing of Mahsood, besides accomplishing what the Pakistanis had demanded, was to provide cover for CIA and Special Forces infiltration of individual Northern Alliance Groups (of which Mahsood was the putative unifier).

On 7 October 2001—three and a half weeks after September 11, a period deemed sufficient to prepare for war and negotiate bin Laden's surrender and al-Qaeda's departure—carpet bombing of Afghanistan began. Dropping fifteen-thousand-pound bombs was meant to have a demonstration effect both to the Taliban and to the Northern Alliance, while at the same time the seemingly indiscriminate reach of the mass munitions was meant to conceal the specific targets that American operatives were designating for precision-guided assault.[24] Dumb bombs were a cover for intelligence. A little over a month later, on 9 November 2001, the major northern city of

Mazar-i-Sharif fell to the Northern Alliance, whose forces entered Kabul just four days later. Kandahar was given up to the Southern Alliance on 6 December. The fall of the last major city left the two largest offensives that would involve American troops, Tora Bora and the Shah-i-Kot valley (Operation Anaconda), for the aftermath of the fallen regime in the winter of 2002. In a landlocked country, a thousand marines established a beach-head one hundred miles from Kandahar called Camp Rhino, supported by carrier groups in the Arabian Sea four hundred miles away.[25] With 7,500 American troops in Afghanistan (over half of the 14,000 contributed by the twenty nations in the coalition) and another 47,500 military personnel in the region as part of the war effort, direct occupation was never part of the scheme.[26]

Much has been made of the spectacular aspect of the war against Iraq in 1991.[27] Not only was a formidable opponent conjured through vivid graphics, but crystalline images of intelligent ballistics stood for the deadly inert of more mundane munitions. In contrast, the Afghanistan bombing was prosecuted as a kind of "don't touch me" intervention—dusty and remote, a series of dull glows on night-vision screens. Smart bombs rocketed to 60 percent of all bombs deployed, with 90 percent accuracy, while use of ground troops in small dispersed packets could best be described as speculative.[28] The account that follows rests upon a reading of the work of the military analyst Anthony Cordesman. Cordesman is a consummate Washington insider, having worked as an advisor for the Senate Armed Services Committee, the secretary of defense, and the departments of energy and state. As a state intellectual his work is treated here as representing foreign policy's internal analytic and reflective moment, a kind of governmental foundationalism. He is a fellow at the Center for Strategic and International Studies, a think tank that is contracted to conduct studies for the Army and the Coalition Provisional Authority. Cordesman has a long history of writing on the Middle East and has conducted work on both Afghanistan and Iraq, before and after the interventions. He considers this speculative aspect of the attack on Afghanistan one of the "problems of distributed warfare":

> The United States and its allies won the battle in spite of the problems of fighting against forces in nearly 200 well-positioned caves and fire points in the mountains. The United States and its allies also seem to have inflicted at least several hundred casualties. Nevertheless, the Al-Qaeda forces largely

escaped—often because Afghan troops either took payment to let them, simply chose not to fight, or let factional rivalries paralyze effective coordination and action.

Nothing that U.S. and allied forces did in Operation Anaconda or in independent search-and-destroy missions, however, has shown that the United States and its Western allies have a solution to the problems of dispersed warfare against an enemy that is fluid and unwilling to fight. Al-Qaeda has shown that it can disperse without a trace in spite of the best efforts of U.S., British, and Australian Special Forces; use caves and other hiding places to keep arms and ammunition in spite of massive search efforts; move into neighboring countries like Pakistan; and disperse into countries outside the immediate area of combat operations.[29]

When we move from the ideology of the war on terror to its applications, virile unilateralism and overwhelming force with high yields and near total accuracy give way to a delicate leveraging of engagement. The principal ground fight of the war—lasting eighteen days at Tora Bora—deployed two hundred American troops against an enemy considered uncountable and invisible. The logic of the body count—outperforming the enemy at killing became the measure of success—was a key symptom of the Vietnam syndrome. In both Afghanistan and Iraq, faith that productivity at killing would deliver victory was itself being buried. The wars affected what Martin Shaw refers to as risk transfer from soldiers to civilians—generating a series of attendant risks now in evidence.[30] One of bin Laden's development projects was to use his construction company to enlarge the caves around Tora Bora. At the battle some three hundred of his combatants were seen dead, with another two hundred estimated to have been entombed—perhaps half of the al-Qaeda fighters gathered there.[31]

The Vietnam era's dull arithmetic of the dead was out of sync with the new strategics of minimal expenditure of blood for maximum gain that reflected a more complex approach to mortal accumulation. While the dead would be thoroughly planned for, casualties would be considered more as threshold points that would trigger political consequences than as discrete bodily items that would demonstrate a specific productivity. Enemy dead were uncountable and fallen coalition troops unviewable. The unwillingness to count bodies—on either side—betrayed an indifference to the human costs of the war but also gestured toward the missing calculus for the intervention's strategic success. Through December 2001, before any American soldiers were killed in combat, estimates for Taliban and al-Qaeda kills ranged from fifteen hundred to three thousand, and estimates of collateral civilian deaths ranged from five hundred to six thousand.[32] For the revolutionized military there was no forensic interest in the enemy and the numbers were free to fluctuate wildly.

Despite the celebratory seamlessness or "jointness" among CIA, special forces, and the branches of the armed services, competition for credit prevailed. From a narrow, tactical perspective, the largest massing of American troops (one thousand soldiers from the Army's 10th Mountain and 101st Airborne Divisions) at Shah-i-Kot could be considered unnecessary. According to Norman Friedman: "There was also speculation that the U.S. Army leadership badly wanted to demonstrate its relevance to the Afghan War. Until Anaconda, the only large U.S. units on the ground had been Marine Expeditionary Units. To critics, the grandiose name of the operation reflected the Army's need for credit. There was talk that some U.S. Army units had to be withdrawn because they had proven unsuited to guerilla warfare."[33] The commanding officer, Major General Franklin C. Hagenbeck, decided to forgo air support to achieve an element of surprise. Instead, al-Qaeda fighters "anticipated the assault, took up the high ground and fired down on advancing troops, leaving nearly a hundred dead or wounded."[34]

The reconnaissance efforts greatly reduced practical horizons of the actual battlefield, leaving out of its penetrating gaze nearly half of the al-Qaeda positions. Similarly, the highly touted Predator unmanned surveillance plane provided pinpoint focus that tended to distract from the larger picture. Friedman notes that "a photo exists of the entire 10th Mountain Division staff staring at a Predator's footage of a fleeing truck, which might have been carrying Osama bin Laden—and not thinking at all about the wider battle they were supposed to be directing."[35] On the ground, American forces unsuccessfully attempted to force al-Qaeda into traps, imagining a topography with which the enemy was unwilling to comply. The focal precision of surveillance technology had closeted its prey, abetting an underground existence.

The pinpoint accuracy, full-spectrum dominance, speed, and agility imagined by the revolution in military affairs were all in evidence in Afghanistan. The war had not solved the problem of dispersion: rather, the far-flung network of effects that goes by the name of terror had been advanced by this leveraged intervention. While the carpet bombing that had concealed the belligerents' knowledge of one another moved on to make dust in Iraq, the day-to-day tactics of special operations combat and challenges to national reconstruction remain. Writing two years after his initial appraisal, Anthony Cordesman concluded:

> Afghanistan has become the not-quite-forgotten war. Americans and America's allies die there, but not as regularly as in Iraq. Nation building is in crisis in Afghanistan but at less cost and largely without high-profile media examination.
>
> Victory, however, has proved to be as relative in Afghanistan—its second current war—as in Iraq. The Taliban has mutated and is again fighting; Al Qaida has lost many of its leaders but also has mutated and relocated some operations in Pakistan; internal tensions in Afghanistan threaten to make its central government the government of only a Kabulstan; and the spillover of Islamic extremism into Central and South Asia continues.[36]

The operations are just as quick, but speed has become dissociated from progress. The terms and the temporality of the derivative war were transferred to the occupation; 2004 was not the future of 2002, but its perpetual present. As the terror war continued, the passage of time did not suggest forward-moving progress but seemed stuck in a replay of the same scenario.

Reconstruction would seem to connote making things as they were, without specifying the golden moment to which we seek to return. In actuality the ambitions for post-invasion Afghanistan are far more circumscribed. The World Bank scheme for "Transitional Support" is to "place primary emphasis on the role of the private sector," and to move the laboring masses from "food-for-work to cash-for-work."[37] Aid workers face an increasingly dangerous environment, one that has shifted emphasis from building a nation to constructing a class. According to testimony to the Senate Foreign Relations Committee on the progress of reconstruction after occupation, risk had become intertwined with development. Goals were stated succinctly: "Encourage the development of an entrepreneurial class of people at USAID and reward wise risk taking."[38] The United States has undertaken what one development scholar has termed a "minimalist position" on reconstruction, focusing on the elimination of terrorists to enhance security over concrete support for development.[39]

For the years 2002 and 2003 Afghanistan achieved the dubious distinction of being the most minimally supported post-intervention country—

having received a tenth of what Kosovo had after its intervention and less than Haiti and Rwanda after theirs. "Financial aid to Afghanistan, measured per capita, has been far lower than for any other nation recently during a period of rebuilding after a conflict."[40] Outside of military expenditure, less than a billion dollars of aid money from the United States was spent in those two years, most of it on emergency food and shelter and the rest on "small-scale, quick impact projects" with no long-term plan for development in place until June 2003.[41] The modest investment was intended to be leveraged to national reconstruction, and not merely symbolic of studied indifference—although the distinction might be difficult to sustain.

In the absence of aid, the market has been decisive in its typical cruelty. In 2003, after prices for a kilo of flowers soared, poppy production again became the dominant economic activity, accounting for a quarter of the country's GDP. By early 2004 prices had collapsed because of overproduction, and many of the nearly two million small farmers found themselves overwhelmed by debt.[42] Itself an enclave protected by a detachment of marines, the government of Hamid Karzai, installed in June 2002 and inaugurated on 7 December 2004 (after winning 55 percent of the vote in the elections of 9 October 2004) has been relegated to administering these dwindling promises. Much of the new Afghan Constitution seems to have fallen between the cracks of state ownership and market investment, without much consideration of how the resulting wealth might benefit the Afghan people. Article 9, for example, states that "minerals and other underground resources are properties of the state" while Article 10 mandates that this same "State encourages and protects private capital investments and enterprises based on the market economy."[43]

In the 1970s, before the terror war wrought its imposed isolationism on the land, tourism was a major source of foreign currency, with ninety thousand visitors a year—many traipsing along what was then the poppy-strewn "hippie trail."[44] Tourism might be considered the archetype of self-managed "recovery," with the state and local entrepreneurs hosting fresh dribbles of foreign capital. Afghanistan after communism has been subject to all manner of travel. Some, like nomadism or pilgrimage, as Hakim Bey has observed, offers meaning to the landscape, while war and terror take it away. Where the state no longer treads, terror and tourism become entwined: "Even the most subtle propaganda of the State never approached this ultimate edge—after all, it always evoked its own opposition—while tourism represents the end of all dialectic—since the only negative gesture it evokes is terrorism, which is its own suppressed content, its 'evil twin.' The tourist, seduced by the utopian trace in its most poignant aspect—the image of difference—becomes a molecule of pollution, bears the virus of sameness, and the burden of disappointment, into a world that once lived for itself."[45] For Afghanistan, the desire to return to that world is poised between a nostalgically impossible localism and an attachment to a world where living for itself would be a radical departure from life as we know it.

: DISPERSING IRAQ

In the first week of the Iraqi invasion, there was much muttering from military analysts and lobbyists about low troop levels and insufficient force. Conventional criticism—that the basket of hardware is not bountiful enough and that all the goodies that lie within need upgrading—is typically aimed at higher military appropriations. The most prominent voice among those questioning the soundness of the war plan was the chief of the Army, General Eric Shinseki. He estimated before the bombing began that "several hundred thousand soldiers" would be needed to occupy Iraq after the government was deposed.[46] We should recall Deputy Defense Secretary Paul Wolfowitz's promise, made at the same time: like a successful hostile takeover in the business world, Iraq would in short order "finance its own reconstruction," by selling off its assets.[47] The debate over which road best led to slaughter turned out to be moot. The troop levels were already maxed out for what the regular and reserve force structure could bear. The reserve was no longer a haven from military service but was now subordinate to the logic of outsourcing. Short of further recruitment or a draft, the Army largely went with what it had. Military critics were finding a technocratic way to disagree with the civilian hijacking of their machinery. Even when the war began, generals on the front lines were making requests for additional troops that were denied further up the chain of command.[48]

By declaring himself a "war president," Bush was assuring that war making would be the art of politics. Diplomacy and financial incentives would take a back seat to intelligence, which for the information war seemed always doomed to fail.[49] The strategic inevitability of invasion (in terms of the many years that went into planning for it) was tempered by tactical surprise—what was termed either the "rolling" or the "running" start. In actuality, the second war against Iraq started already in motion, because the first one had never stopped. If anything, it's the end that has continued to roll on. It had been rolling since American troops stopped at the Kuwaiti border in 1991, and it continued through the embargos and inspection regimes of the 1990s that were more strident versions of the domestic wars against youth, drugs, and education (and children suffered disproportionately from the eradication of clean drinking water and medicine).

At its most reductive, the revolution in military affairs was a scheme to make the war against Iraq the next war. Well before 17 March 2003, when Bush gave Saddam Hussein forty-eight hours to get out of town, the invasion was well under way. The aerial attacks to destroy the remnants of the Iraqi anti-aircraft capacity under cover of enforcing the no-flight zone had already begun at the end of 2002, and in the months leading to the land invasion the CIA bribed Iraqi officers in the North to discourage them from fighting, while Special Forces operatives scoured the countryside looking for the ever-AWOL weapons of mass destruction.[50] While the Turkish Parliament withheld permission to use its bases as a staging ground for a northern front, American bases in Kuwait had years of preparation for this task. Major General Henry Stratman, deputy commander for the 3d Army stationed in Kuwait, admitted that September 11 was understood as the trigger for the Iraqi war, and the question "was not whether but when."[51] The running start was meant to bring together the foreign policy of preemption with the military doctrine of rapid dominance. Given that the Iraqi forces at 350,000 would not likely be overwhelmed by an invading force a third their size, the Army opted for operational surprise and an "overmatched" deployment of state-of-the-art systems against Iraq's severely compromised war matériel.[52]

The land invasion began on 19 March 2003, before full troop strength and logistical support (especially spare parts) had been delivered. The Army called this defined-contribution mobilization "just-in-time operations" and called it more efficient than the stockpiling of people and equipment that had taken place in 1991, when Saudi Arabia was the staging area. This time it was the Kuwaitis rather than the Saudis who provided the free gas, and their national oil company spent two years laying a pipeline right up to the Iraqi border.[53] In addition, the Army would take what it considered a "systems approach" based on Saddam's means of political control over the city of Baghdad. By seizing "key nodes" of repression and consent —from the secret police to sewerage—the invasion would assault the "critical vulnerabilities of centers of gravity" so as to collapse the regime and save the city. The coalition forces assumed that they would be treated to a repeat of the earlier Gulf War, in which conventional Iraqi forces did not resist and surrendered en masse.[54]

The plan was to get to the capital as quickly as possible and to deploy soldiers as if they were precision-guided missiles on selected targets. The reliance on systems logics, which creates equivalence between different kinds of resources, political processes, and social activities, combines readily with the post-Fordist managerial approach that makes equipment and labor interchangeable inputs. The anxiety that labor will work like a machine and the worry that machines will work with the reliability of a good soldier are the wobbly pillars supporting the revolution in military affairs and the criteria by which the war was planned and evaluated. The soldiers in today's army are expensive, with a "median lifetime cost" of some $4 million each and future debts of $653 billion in retirement benefits that the Pentagon does not have. The high value of human assets supports the logic of machine replacement—a shooting robot costs less than a quarter-million dollars. Robots may come without the need for a reenlistment bonus, but they are as likely to concentrate labor costs as replace them. Recently the Pentagon put up a million-dollar prize for a 142-mile robot race across the Mojave Desert. None of the entrants made it to the finish line.[55] The race to Baghdad was far more effective—but the finish line has proved equally elusive.

To fulfill their civilizing missions, wars must teach. But since the lessons that they teach the vanquished can lead to further barbarism or terror, the military takes on a commitment to lifelong learning, forming vehicles for outcomes assessment like the Center for Army Lessons Learned, on whose findings this account of the war draws. Among the various narratives of the war, the Army's is instructive because it represents the perspective of labor as it attempts to assert itself in a setting at once thoroughly mediated by technology and conceived of as integral to a system, part of a fighting machine. The official Army assessment of its performance in the invasion of Iraq and assault on Baghdad is called "On Point." It is the few weeks between 19 March and 9 April 2003 that the Army sees as holding lessons for its future—rather than the actual future, the downward spiral of occupation. Before the assessment is an assertion of the Army's essence, the small band of infantry whose position of honor and greatest responsibility is that of the team member leading the way, a position known as being on point.

Being on point is a metaphor for the team concept of the warrior ethos, functioning both interpersonally among comrades in the squad, and more abstractly in the division of labor among the services. The Army's claim to continued relevance in a high-tech world rests upon an ethos based on affect, according to which "humans, not high tech sensors remain indispensable. . . . Every values-based institution has an image of itself at its purest most basic level. It is a single mental snapshot—a distillation of all that is good and right. Reaching back to the institution's foundation, it evokes a visceral emotional response from the members."[56] The Army's institutional apologia as fundamentally humanistic stands in for the absent values of freedom by invasion and occupation, as labor's assertion against dehumanizing "sensors" provides the heroism that might otherwise be converted into more reflective values of liberation.

The remote-controlled ballistics of shock and awe were underwritten by the intimate contact of infantry brawn. While long-distance bombing raids may give cover to those issuing orders, the open theater distributes risk among all military occupations and applies to bombs and bullets, whether released near or far, the shared logic of leveraged force—less is more. Rather than form a broad front with steady advance, the intervention was calibrated to maximize turnover time. Ribbons of troops traversed highways and pierced cities. Yet while the Army was performing according to its own mandates, achieving speed, agility, and surprise, the enemy was not behaving as forecast. To American observers, Iraqi forces had "melted away" like an approaching mirage in the desert. Absent was any insight into their disappearance. Explanations for the absent opposition ranged from strategic orders to preserve the force, to the success of psychological operations (some forty million pamphlets were dropped on the Iraqis telling them that liberation was nigh), to the efficacy of bombs, to fear or inability to surrender.[57]

Equally surprising to the Americans was the fierce presence of unconventional forces that lacked the prudence to protect themselves from hostile fire and armor. These paramilitary forces' "tactics were suicidal in that they literally ran and drove to their deaths" rather than use the "cover" of the urban environment. The battlefield was declared "noncontiguous," "non-linear," and occupied by an enemy prepared to fight "asymmetrically." While drawing fire away from homes rather than making targets of them might be taken as evidence of reason, the combatants were already being constructed as proto-terrorists willing to embrace risk and opportunity—purportedly what the transformed army was itself prepared to do.[58]

In the minds of some commanders, unpredictability, irrationality, and evil easily slid into one another: "We overrated this army but we underrated the irregulars. They were fierce, but not too bright. They were evil men who deserved to die. They didn't adapt to our forces. They would continue to impale themselves on our BIFV [Bradley Infantry Fighting Vehicle, an armored troop carrier] and tanks."[59] Further down the chain of command, exuberance for technology and an enemy stripped of characteristics altogether is reported. Sergeant First Class Jason Christian of Charlie Troop 3-7 Cavalry gushed about the surveillance and targeting abilities of the sixty-ton Abrams tank and the digitally linked Bradley armored carrier: "The hunter-killer team concept works fantastic . . . The M1/M3 combination is outstanding. What you get when they work together is lots and lots of dead folks." Troops shut inside these vehicles communicated with one another through global positioning technology called Blue Force Tracking. The more sophisticated Army Battle Command system was not distributed to all forces in the coalition. The simpler system reduced fratricide and allowed commanders to keep track of their own troops spread across many miles. Locked inside their thinking tanks, the invaders used a technology that did not allow them to see the enemy. In a manner consonant with the Americans' lack of interest in body counts, the enemy other, so meticulously imagined by the cold war surveillance system known as Red Force tracking, was now being disappeared.[60]

Despite the larger scale of operations, the primacy of Special Forces to identify targets and call in strikes joined Iraq with the leveraged logic of the smaller war in Afghanistan. With Iraq for the first time, conventional forces were actually assigned to Special Forces, the mass applied to support the special effect. While separated physically and culturally from conventional forces, the specialists were normalized by constant deployment and reintegration with regular units from the Balkan intervention onwards. Special Forces called in strikes from air, land, and sea—serving as the hinge to achieve the vaunted "jointness" which the military sought.[61]

A third of all the bombing sorties were called in by Special Forces in the North; at the height of combat four-fifths of the bombs were directed at

Iraqi ground troops; and all told, two-thirds of the munitions were precision guided.[62] In Iraq as well, Special Forces worked closely with the internal opposition, especially the Kurdish Peshmerga, earning them the praise of Lieutenant General David D. McKiernan as a "huge combat multiplier."[63] The precision afforded by strikes directed by Special Forces made it possible to isolate a particular threat (or risk) from its physical, political, or military environment. In terms of deployment, the Special Forces lost their specialness and had become the norm, but their function was to concentrate risk effects that would ripple throughout the warscape.

The resulting approach is not limited to ground troops but also applies to aerial attack and is called "effects-based" bombing. As explained by Colonel Gary Crowder, chief of strategy, concepts, and doctrine of the Air Combat Command, "If we understood what the effect we desired on the battlefield, we could then figure out ways of creating that effect more efficiently, more effectively, striking less targets, using less weapons and, quite frankly, mitigating or easing potential concerns for collateral damage and civilian casualties." This greater efficiency is then distributed throughout a range of "target systems, creating a greater effect on each individual system, and that, in turn, started to collapse the system from the inside."[64] Crowder makes a distinction between collateral damage, which can be planned for and anticipated as a "reasonable occurrence" resulting from a targeted attack, and "unintended damage," which is "when something goes wrong" and is therefore beyond calculation.[65]

The distinction is consistent with that made in finance between risk (a calculated departure from expectation) and uncertainty (the prospect of the unknown occurrence which eludes any calculus). While bodies may never be counted, collateral damage presents a risk opportunity that drives the planning process. But confidence in the planning process may be undermined by a look at the numbers. In one estimate, between 9,436 and 11,317 Iraqi civilians were killed (nearly twice the estimated 5–6,000 Iraqi combatants) and another 40,000 wounded by the time the Provisional Authority dissolved in June 2004.[66] On the other hand, by this time the coalition had incurred over 6,000 casualties, a number approaching the 9,000 they had planned for before the conflict in a worst-case scenario.[67] And even these figures are arrived at by the most conservative statistical approaches available. By the end of 2005, when Bush was willing to refer publicly to 30,000 casualties, more comprehensive epidemiological approaches that counted deaths due to the failure of reconstruction to restore public health estimated 200,000–500,000 dead "as a direct result of the Anglo-American invasion and occupation."[68] What political system was being installed when collateral damage had double the effect of military targets? If the civilian population of Iraq is held as collateral, what is going to count as a security?

Baghdad during the initial forays into it was made to resemble more the caves of Tora Bora than the conventional proscenium theater of war. The drive to Baghdad that began with armored columns crossing the Kuwaiti border on 20 March 2003 had taken but two weeks (roughly the same amount of time as it took to get to the principal battle with al-Qaeda). By the time coalition forces had reached their prize, whole Iraqi divisions had dispersed and slipped away. Combined with the looting and dismantling of infrastructure, the invasion looked like the work of a time-release capsule for a poison-pill merger, or of a corporate raider on speed. The assault on the city consisted of a series of small incursions and souped-up drive-by shootings, called "thunder runs," that disappeared the government within another week. By 4 April, when coalition forces had surrounded Baghdad, "all major systems within the city had been dissected, studied and targeted. Every section and building in the city was mapped and numbered."[69]

The transformation of Baghdad into a targetable system of systems reflected twelve years of aerial surveillance and reconnaissance—for the army "preparations for Operation Iraqi Freedom begin March 1, 1991—the day after the first Gulf War ended."[70] Yet aerial bombardment was also formative in the creation of Iraq as a country by the British in 1921 (with the aid of a mandate from the League of Nations). After betraying promises for independence if Arabs fought with Britain during the First World War, the Royal Air Force proved instrumental in suppressing a nationalist uprising in Iraq in 1920. British military planners of the day understood that "the attack with bombs and machine guns must be relentless and unremitting and carried on continuously by day and night, on houses, inhabitants, crops and cattle."[71]

The hostile space would be pacified by numeracy, transformed into a decapitated body. Baghdad was also refamiliarized along the lines of American popular culture. American troops first occupied Baghdad's suburbs as a staging ground to take the city. These captured objectives were named after favorite football teams (Saints, Lions, Titans), cartoon characters like Woody of Pixar's *Toy Story*, and Curly, Larry, and Moe of the Three Stooges. Before the war, the expectation of military planners had been that divisions of the Republican Guard would retreat from the perimeter and engage in urban warfare throughout the city. The utter devastation of those divisions and the detritus of abandoned bodies and equipment suggested that the final siege would not correspond to expectations. "It was unclear whether Baghdad was a trap, a clever ruse, or a hollow shell."[72] The thunder runs were devised in response to this ambiguity as a kind of "armed reconnaissance": diagnostic probes into the city.

The first, on 4 April, consisted of several hundred soldiers aboard twenty-nine tanks and fourteen Bradleys that took a fourteen-mile drive lasting two hours and twenty minutes right through the center of the city to the airport. This armored column drew small-arms fire from Iraqi fighters, killing one American soldier and wounding several others, with one tank destroyed. While the mission was considered a military success in its own terms, since it demonstrated that Iraqi defenses could be violated at will with acceptable losses, it was recognized as politically counterproductive. The Iraqi information minister, Mohammed Saeed al-Sahhaf, broadcast word that American forces had been repulsed. For the conquering army, the phoenix of postmodern relativism had reared its ugly head.

Major General Buford Blount III and Lieutenant Generals William Wallace and David McKiernan, in charge of ground forces, ordered Colonel David Perkins to conduct another run into the city on the 7th. Perkins proposed to undertake the riskier operation of seizing a psychologically strategic objective in the center of the city and staying overnight. The commanders supported their subordinate's embrace of greater risk: "all intuitively understood the opportunities—and risks—and reached similar conclusions."[73] This was a larger operation with an entire army division, but with similar time constraints, as the gargantuan Abrams tanks can only run for four hours before needing to refuel. Objectives were seized and attacks and counterattacks joined over the next two days and nights. Once again, the operation was considered a military success that foreshortened hostilities by perhaps two weeks. The message that Iraq was without government, clear as intended, was decidedly more mixed.

The waves of appropriation by Iraqis that went under the generic name of looting seemed to follow the vapor trail left by the attacks on the system of systems. The "nodes" in the system consisted of government facilities of every stripe, including schools, hospitals, and the national museum, as well as links in the supply chain of basic foodstuffs, which had been part of the state rationing system. It was not simply that coalition forces were unable to secure and protect the civilian infrastructure. Combat power was drained by treating soldiers as an extension of the intelligence network. Eager to establish the truth of the war, units were deployed to investigate some nine hundred sites purported to hold weapons of mass destruction.[74]

The speed of operations generated substantial logistical problems that created their own political demonstration effects to Iraqis. Despite the revolution in logistical affairs that had moved an entire army base worth of parts to Kuwait in three weeks and a digital global parts network, "almost none [of the spare parts] reached intended customers during the fighting," because the requisition process required numerous approvals and elaborate processing through the complex system. Field units were constantly "cannibalizing broken down equipment and towing what they could not repair."[75] Twenty days into combat, the coalition forces consumed forty million gallons of fuel, as much as was used during all four years of the First World War. By the army's own assessment, the two weeks saved on major combat may have been crucial, as the war machine might have consumed itself by then. "Fortunately, major combat operations ended before the failure of the parts distribution system affected operations in a meaningful way."[76] Speed is not self-sustaining.

The fragility of supply lines and the expediency of speed to deflect attention from it would not be lost on military planners, who during the next intervention might be considering a neighboring country to serve as their gas station or a local Wal-Mart to provide parts. The military was far from self-sufficient even in a war of such limited duration, and had to rely on the enemy for provisions. The shortages meant that "units used what they captured from Iraqi forces or improvised. . . . Units resorted to using Iraqi lubricants acquired by foraging parties."[77] For some Iraqis, these "parties" may have resembled more a license to loot. If coalition soldiers were helping themselves to the Iraqi army's stuff, the local population might be doing the same. It was, after all, dog eat dog, liberate or die.

Saddam Hussein had of course been preparing for this "mother of all battles" for as long as the Americans. The resistance he was able to mount during the drive to Baghdad was but a trace of what he had hoped for. He was able to create what the Americans could not—a local network of munitions to arm the people, who rallied not to defend his government but to repulse the occupation. According to Anthony Cordesman, "Iraq sought to create a massive Popular Army with the capability to draw on a mobilization base of some 7 million and the goal of actually arming up to

1 million men."[78] The invaders offered Iraqis what their former leader only dreamed of. Iraqi defenses were pierced while the arms caches distributed around the country were preserved intact. Weapons for the masses were strewn about by the invasion, whereas weapons of mass destruction had long been spirited away. Smaller bundles of these massive stockpiles could subsequently be placed in circulation to leveraged effects, as the thousands involved in the resistance laid claim to their own version of the nation.

Further, the efforts to build a coalition and achieve interoperability seem to have been more gifts to the vanquished than assets of a military global leader. The United States remains one of few nations in the world with "wide and diverse combat experience"; as for Europe, old or new, most of its land forces lack "the capability either to act as independent expeditionary forces or to be fully interoperable with the US."[79] With the exception of Special Forces, even the closely allied British were assigned responsibility only for Basra. Not only did this defrock interoperability, but it disclosed a historical irony. Basra was a former province of the Ottoman Empire originally ceded to the United Kingdom in 1916 by the Sykes-Picot Treaty that had carved up the Middle East among Britain, France, and Czarist Russia.[80] Interoperability may work better at the point of purchase than at the point of expenditure. Left to their own command structures, the British had to take their lumps in some of the most sustained combat of the war.

⋮ PROVISIONING AUTHORITY

Fourteen months of rule by the Coalition Provisional Authority (April 2003 to June 2004) cannot forecast what Iraq will become, but it does disclose what derivative war and discretionary reconstruction imagine for their world. While Osama bin Laden and Saddam Hussein had earned their credentials as staunch anti-communists, each wound up taking communism's place as the abject other while continuing the anti-communism of population management according to financial perquisites. Whether through faith-based mutual aid societies that supported an anti-colonial international or centralized government food rationing to compensate for limited employment, the market was being subverted by other logics of distribution. While Afghanistan could scarcely be considered to have a functioning national economy, Iraq under the embargo assumed all of the marks of a centrally planned one.

If the Pentagon's new way of war turned out to be Iraq redux, twelve years in the making, the plan for reconstructing Iraq's economy was lifted from the blueprints of the World Bank and the International Monetary Fund for making the transition from communism to the market.[81] After twenty years of war and sanctions, 60 percent of the Iraqi population depended on government food rations to survive, and as much as a third of the workforce was government employed, with many more working in the informal sector.[82] CPA economists thought "disheartening" the finding of a poll conducted by the International Republican Institute about what Iraqis sought in a political party. Nearly half reported favoring "more government jobs" and only 5 percent "more private sector jobs."[83]

Iraq is among the world's most indebted nations, with debt six times the GDP, and the CPA has put unemployment at nearly 30 percent (although other studies found rates more than double that—largely a result of the CPA's disbanding of the state sector under de-Ba'athification).[84] While the CPA has said that its economic policies were modeled on those of the transition economies of Eastern Europe and Central Asia, the heady brew of liberalized interest rates, increased foreign ownership of banks, and micro-credit to establish small businesses is the familiar recipe of post–cold war fiscal policy for development the world over. To assure that currency speculation takes official form, the Ministry of Finance sells oil dollars to the Central Bank, which then sells dollars at a currency auction. A year after Baghdad fell, the CPA had managed to create a perception among nearly 90 percent of the populace that it was a force of occupation rather than liberation.[85] A year's occupation had not been too good for the American military's support of the CPA either. Over half of all troops reported to the Army that their morale was low and three-quarters said they were poorly led.[86]

When Bush finally made a public appearance to justify the year's occupation of Iraq, he was sharply rebutted by our man in Washington, Anthony Cordesman: "An Iraqi middle class has effectively profiteered from the opening up of Iraq, the flow of coalition aid and oil revenues and a lack of tariffs. The CPA has made virtually no progress, however, in carrying out broad structural reforms of Iraq's command economy and state industries. Moreover, it has failed to work out any meaningful mid and long term plan for the energy sector and has left the agricultural sector in virtually the same command dominated mess it was in when the U.S. arrived. . . . The President left the Iraqi economy and the critical area of jobs a virtual black box with no signs of a plan to really fix critical problems."[87]

A week before, Cordesman had testified before the Senate Foreign Relations Committee that "Iraq now has a "bubble" economy, not real reconstruction, and Iraqis know this."[88] Even if for Cordesman the project of making Iraq into "a successful free market democracy was never practical," the success in creating a bubble economy of benefit to a few did have a familiar ring. The CPA seemed to treat reconstruction money the way the Bush administration had used tax cuts. The cronyism and corruption that had shadowed executive offices from Enron to Halliburton were manifest in Iraq, where the government's own studies were revealing "a company and a contracting environment that has run amok."[89]

On the eve of their departure, the CPA had given away nearly all the funds in the form of commitments to American multinationals.[90] While half of the $18.4 billion appropriated by Congress in the fall of 2003 has been allocated to contractors, fewer than 140 of the 2,300 planned projects had actually got under way by 30 June 2004, the day that the new ambassador, John Negroponte, presented his credentials to the interim Iraqi government.[91] Negroponte, seasoned anti-communist and supporter of dictatorship in Central America during his tenure as ambassador to Honduras, would appreciate the first act of state of Prime Minister Iyad Allawi, himself a former CIA employee: arrogating to his governing authority the powers of martial law.

The CPA's early decision to disband Iraqi forces was one vehicle for the dispersion of conflict. Both the insurgency and the Allawi government sought to derive their forces from the remnants of the defeated army that had been placed in circulation. In this regard, Allawi's national reconstruction efforts, following on his sponsor's, replaced securitization as a priority over development.[92] With development funds diverted for their own administration, the Iraqi government of occupation was unable to move the nation forward along any measurable index of education, health care, economic opportunity, services, governance, or even security itself.[93]

Although the planners of the invasion of Iraq in March 2003 imagined that they could occupy the country intact, the counterinsurgency war in the twenty months that followed resulted in the evacuation of whole cities, as in "Operation Phantom Fury," the assault against Fallujah on 8 November 2004. Establishing zones of exclusion in this fashion had the predictable effect of sorting out populations, constituting the Sunni areas as outside the reconstruction project and subsequently outside the drive to self-management through elections. The war would have more insidious and deferred sorting effects as well. The depleted uranium munitions favored as targets by American forces to increase target penetration and kill range generated lasting hazards, especially for children, who are far more susceptible to radiation's pathogenic effects. After the first Gulf War, when this sort of targeting was done, congenital illness and stillbirths increased precipitously. Rob Nixon writes about the derivative effects of ballistic brilliance: " 'Smart wars' become wars of ecological folly when we turn soil, air, and water into slow weapons of mass destruction, wielded unremittingly against ourselves."[94] Expendable populations are the prejudgment of these deployments.

In the race to a new colonial reconstruction, who could do the managing and what would be managed were left unspecified, as if any set of political values would do the trick of realizing the goals of liberation. Ironically, Allawi could ride his incumbency and his American connections to only a distant third-place showing in the elections of 30 January 2005, his Iraqi list polling only 14 percent of the eight and a half million votes cast. The United Iraqi Alliance came in first with nearly half the vote, followed by the Kurdistan Alliance, at just over a quarter, and the remaining 11 percent spread over more than one hundred parties.[95] The turnout of 58 percent, while greater than that of any recent election in the United States, nonetheless largely excluded the disenfranchised Sunnis, who make up roughly a third of the population.

Insofar as elections themselves are equated with liberty, Iraq could be seen as having had its liberation delivered. With or without the continued presence of tens of thousands of American troops, the exit of what was strategic in Iraq could now be placed on the table. The United States had succeeded in advancing an insurgency against itself, one on which it could now turn its back. Iraq and Afghanistan presented problems that could not be fixed by a dispersing intervention. The military entered the war concerned about sufficient levels of troop deployment, and after three years could no longer meet its recruitment goals, placing the sustainability of military labor itself at risk.[96] The derivative wars had yielded whole new product lines of difficulty, but the elections would gain credit for mandating the new management.

Parallel developments were on offer in the United States, where a president purportedly reelected on his terror war claimed a moral imperative to fix Social Security without a popular sense that it was broken. Salvation would be achieved by excluding a demographic group (the postwar generation of baby boomers) from privatizing reform that would convert state pensioners into private portfolio owners. Similarly, education would be fixed by killing off Perkins loans for low-income students to fund modest and belated increases to Pell Grants. The poor students once benefited by the Perkins loans would no longer be recognized for their extraordinary needs, which would disappear in the general pool of applicants for Pell Grants. In the name of eliminating redundancy, money was shifted from one program to another without actually giving more to support education.[97]

Shaving off a portion of the population from the body of an electorate or citizenry is certainly a venerable form of divide and rule. But the fluidity with which one entity or another may become the excluded other speaks to a more active principle of circulation that now informs self-government, in an ever stranger convergence of foreign and domestic. Afghanistan and Iraq were, at the time of intervention, two countries already wracked by colonial histories. Intervention aimed to demonstrate that the occupiers had transformed themselves and that occupation was itself transformative. Fighting terror, however defined, dispersed not only terrorists but nations as well. Populations that had been forcibly composed into the colonial establishment of nations were decomposed and distributed along varying registers of risk. Reconstruction was presented as a gambit enabling the occupiers to decamp, leaving the recolonized to manage themselves.

Smart wars got clogged with gluts of information and overly narrowed fields of view that produced decisive intelligence failures—leaders who got away, lost first causes, in the absence of plans for stabilization and development. Confidence was left to the conviction that intervention would be leveraged to reconstruction, that nations left with less than they had would still be better off. The decomposed nation would leave a colonial substrate that would spin off endless conflicts and opportunities. The old imperial ambition was to consume the colonial whole; the new aspiration attaches to less, while making more of its partial attentions. It is toward the articulation of this imperium's self-concept that we now must turn.

An Empire of Indifference   ❖   4

The war on terror has been prosecuted in crisp Manichaean terms but has opened empire to deep fissures of paradox. A global vision has been asserted in the name of a national interest, and an indefatigable will to intervene has been assembled on behalf of securitized isolation. The renewed prominence of imperialism as a concept and a topic of discussion is fueled by a confluence of celebratory and critical attention—an unconscious attachment and an extensive speculation. The specific interventions against Afghanistan and Iraq have come to stand for the more general imperial project, articulating a global imaginary by limited and leveraged means. In each case decisive military victory is followed by a long aftermath of failure to make war achieve its stated political ends. Managing economic life and waging war have become entangled in a logic of preemption, the future has been profaned in the present, risk brokers every opportunity, and the foreign and domestic have been pressed into a queasy mix.

This empire is staged as a massive flight from commitment, a wholesale indifference to social attachments that offers liberation in place of a once promised road to development. The official linkage of bin Laden and Saddam took the spontaneity of retributive justice as a mandated response to a surprising attack, and collapsed this urgent reaction with a seemingly discretionary war prepared by military planners years in advance. Much of the examination of American empire has hinged on deciphering the motives for these two incursions—countries seized only to be let go. For all the reasons given, each with its measure of credibility, it has not been easy to adjudicate among them.

A full slate of motives for the empire-making war have been offered. As Slavoj Žižek has observed, "The problem, again, was that there were *too many* reasons for the war."[1] The official reasons—bringing democracy, asserting hegemony, securing oil—are less a contradiction than a parallax view of the truth, with one perspective concealing the others.[2] No doubt all of that could be expected, whether Iraq had been invaded or not. Whether justified by divine right, fearful necessity, or sheer capacity, the celebrants seek the unipolar primacy of the United States over the world as a normative condition of global affairs. Yet for those opposed to American power on the same grounds, the operations of empire can be equally axiomatic. The interests and requisites of nation, state, or capital require an imperial posture. The discussion is bound by a powerful ring of reason worthy of the film character Forrest Gump—empire is as empire does. Such a tautology is best viewed as a political accomplishment, rather than simply a lapse in logic.

Empire is not reducible to a moment of might, an expression of rule, an assertion of order in the service of predetermined interest. Amid the casualties and smoldering ruins, some interconnections are being deepened and others made anew, a world is being forged, and its principles and productivities need to be discerned. Those critical of empire may be far better served by seeing both its fissures and failures as well as what it presents despite itself as opportunities for alternatives, as other worlds in the making. For if we are to see what else lies in the imperial offing, which formations of surplus wealth and emergent society are detectable when we think capital through the medium of war, we will need to attend to the theoretical shifts that occur as well.

⁚ THE FIGURAL AND THE FUNCTIONAL

If one takes for granted the urge or necessity to dominate the world, imperialism requires proper management but little explanation. Conversely, the more closely it is examined, the more complex the enormity of imperialism becomes, the more difficult to see it in its entirety. No less magisterial a thinker than Edward Said humbly offered, "no individual, and certainly not I, can see or fully grasp this whole imperial world."[3] For Said imperialism is a constellation of theory, practice, and attitudes to rule distant territories, but also an enlistment of metropolitan populations to "think of the *imperium* as a protracted almost metaphysical obligation to rule subordinate, inferior, or less advanced peoples."[4] By this reckoning, empire is at once an unseeable totality and an unreflective implication of folks back home in the desire to rule. Between the unseen whole and the unexamined desire lies what could be called the imperial unconscious.

This formulation immediately brings to mind that of Fredric Jameson, whose notion of the political unconscious refers to the vast unfinished plot, the traces of an uninterrupted narrative that restore to the surface a repressed and buried reality of fundamental history. For Jameson history is an absent cause accessible only through narrativization, the interpretive project that he has set forth for Marxism. Orienting analysis toward the unconscious allows a shift from meaning to use, a focus on how politics operates so as to grasp ruptures and difference in terms of underlying continuities.[5] The imperial unconscious operates on the desire for world making and specifies a geopolitical project implicit around us, one whose features need to be surfaced analytically. The urge to world making can be presented as self-fulfilling. To make the prophecy contingent, partial, and changeable requires a rethinking of what can be said about the reasons for rule that we have to hand.

The political economy of imperialism would most properly be the study of how the geopolitical conditions for accumulating capital and the disequilibrating effects of military intervention and defensive isolation allow war to operate productively as a means to generate further social wealth. Since war both depends upon and renders contingent a determinant social surplus (both money to pay for it, and the social forces that must be developed and applied), antiwar movements take on a larger political resonance: beyond the cessation of unnecessary conflict, they raise the prospect of capturing surplus productivity for other ends. Between invasion and withdrawal, intervention and isolation, opposition to war—the most instrumental expression of anti-imperialist movements—displays what the world might be even as contending visions are played out on the national terrain.

Anti-imperialism thus makes manifest the conflicted field, the imperialist dilemma: By what means can accumulation continue while preserving particular geopolitical forms of authority? Intervention exposes an imperial wound, a challenge to the sustainability of global dominance that is best kept a tacit knowledge. Hence that which opposes imperialism is also constitutive of other worlds, not simply because it allows alternatives to be articulated but because it provides a language for what typically remains unspoken. If the imperial unconscious could speak, how would it rationalize itself as forming productive associations amid evident distributions of destructive power?

Unfortunately many of the accounts of the present imperialism that begin with a critique of capital—the various political economies of imperialism—have offered little by way of rethinking. The historical debates around the notion often got boiled down to a single motive, a fatal flaw for which imperialism would be the correction. Development and under-development are treated as either/or conditions of imperialist ambition, as is the need for new markets for consumption or cheap labor for production. When Marxism is treated as a predictive science, any change in social relations becomes a loss to the theory's veracity.[6] The observation that capital must accumulate, made with a kind of ironic twist by Marx himself, can subsequently lose the uncertainty that irony assigns and imputes an almost prescient interest to what is done to advance the conditions of wealth.[7] The resulting impression is of a kind of infallibility and inexorability—capital is as capital does. Wealth just happens.

This interest is said to reign in what Ellen Meiksins Wood terms a "surplus imperialism," a boundless economic domination of capital incommensurate with direct political rule of territories that "requires military action without end, in purpose or time."[8] Wood is sensibly focused on countering the notion that in the era of globalization, nation-states themselves have become obsolete, while at the same time acknowledging that national governance is insufficient to manage the perquisites of capital's global accumulation. But assuming that war "answers to the particular needs of the new imperialism," it remains unclear what military intervention achieves beyond supporting "the universality of capitalist imperatives."[9] While war may attend to the contradiction between competition and cooperation to generate markets and profits, as Wood insists, so too does every other form of state intervention into the "essential logic of this imperial system."[10] Capital retains a kind of transcendent reason that makes it difficult to enter its hidden abodes and contrarian operations, or to consider how war itself might be one of these.

Mirroring this high rationalism is the disappointment that the empire is, in Michael Mann's phrase, "incoherent" and unsustainable because it relies solely on militarism, overestimates economic domination, neglects political authority, and contradicts ideological sources of social power. The result is an imperium weaker and far more uneven in its command than predecessors like Rome, Britain, and Belgium. "The American Empire will turn out to be a military giant, a Back-seat economic driver, a political schizophrenic and an ideological phantom. The result is a disturbed, mis-shapen monster stumbling clumsily across the world. It means well. It intends to spread order and benevolence, but instead it creates more disorder and violence."[11] Mann, himself providing a wealth of detail on the new imperialism, claims to be arguing against realist conceptions of imperial hegemony on the left and right but would seem to share their premises of a rational, rule-governed world. Abandon "commitment to the rules of the game. . . . and the sun will shortly thereafter set on the American Empire."[12]

While Mann is generally hostile to Marxist explanation, there are others in the Marxist tradition who share his approach to pluralizing power while singularizing interest.[13] Taking up the disjuncture between the concentration of "globally effective means of violence" in the United States and dispersion of "universally accepted means of payment" among multinationals and East Asian financial markets, Giovanni Arrighi and Beverly Silver see the present hegemony characterized by a "*fission* of military and financial power,"[14] in contrast to the typical fusion of the two. Yet if finance and war are distinct types of power, the internal relations that might allow them to fuse or fragment will be difficult to detect. Capital will be deprived of a social force that would allow us to see in its critique a constitutive social capacity beyond the realization of economic or national interest.

There are nevertheless political economies of imperialism for which political and social power are immanent to the accumulation of capital. Describing what he terms a new imperialism based upon twin logics of territory and capital, David Harvey asserts that "any hegemon, if it is to maintain its position in relation to endless capital accumulation, must endlessly seek to extend, expand, and intensify its power."[15] Where these logics most centrally intersect is in the use of military power to control the world's oil supply—even if the premises of these neo-Malthusian claims are debatable.[16] "The Bush administration's shift toward unilateralism, towards coercion rather than consent, toward a much more overtly imperial vision, and towards reliance upon its unchallengeable military power, indicates a high-risk approach to sustaining US domination, almost certainly through military command over global oil resources."[17]

The risk to the imperium lies in creating "a geographical landscape to facilitate its activities at one point in time only to have to destroy it and build a wholly different landscape at a later point in time to accommodate its perpetual thirst for endless capital accumulation."[18] This destructive moment, when capital turns on its own basis for social wealth, effectively savages populations, simultaneously forcing open new markets and excluding millions from them. Overaccumulation, a lack of opportunity for profitable investment, creates an outside to any given process of capitalist development to which those cut off from the drive for wealth can be brought back in, as fresh sources of labor, consumption, or debt. Harvey terms this process "accumulation by dispossession," and sees the future of anti-imperialist struggle as sorting out its progressive and regressive aspects. This process amounts to a delineation between commitments to local struggles as ends in themselves and "multiple identifications (based on class, gender, locality, culture, etc.) that exist within populations, the traces of history and tradition that arise from the ways in which they made themselves in response to capitalist incursions."[19]

Rather than see imperialism as a highest stage or latest development of a capitalist beast that knows where it is heading and how to get there (or a system in transition from one state to the next), it may be more useful to recall that imperialism is always "new." Writing over one hundred years ago (1902), J. A. Hobson, whose work is considered the seminal formulation of the matter, defined the "new imperialism" as the "use of national force to secure new markets by annexing fresh tracts of territory."[20] Hobson established a link between interfirm rivalry that would drive down profits and a financial institution's compensatory efforts, a connection that would be picked up by such subsequent writers on imperialism as Hilferding, Lenin, Bukharin, and Luxemburg, and eventually in the contemporary work of Arrighi.[21] Hobson described a politics of taxation with resonance for the present, when tax revolts and tax cuts aspire to a normative relation of state and civil society. "The clearest significance of imperialist finance, however, appears on the side, not of expenditure, but of taxation."[22] Accordingly, capital averts the direct incidence of tax burdens for its expansion onto the shoulders of other classes. Public debt is increased, and war becomes an indirect form of taxation, with free-trade initiatives that overwhelm weaker markets serving as a form of protectionism within the imperial enclave. Even as its geopolitical terms shift, imperialism offers novelty to specific limits to further accumulation, and as such always appears under the guise of the new—an immediate imperative to undertake expansionary initiatives.

Today fresh tracts of territory for capital's grazing may be hard to come by without Harvey's deterritorializing moves. The idea of pristine markets now has less allure than does the capacity to carve out niches customized to taste. Giovanni Arrighi revisited Hobson's categories and distinguished nationalism overflowing its banks (imperialism); expansion of the state without the nation (colonialism); the ancient and medieval hierarchy of states (formal imperialism); and economic interdependence among states (informal empire). Informal relations would promote an anarchy that resulted in war, while formalizations of empire would be channeled into the state spending spree of social surplus that makes for militarism. Writing in the late 1970s, ironically just as financial services and multinationals were becoming intertwined, Arrighi sought to reestablish some autonomy for the powers of finance. He saw in the difference between industrial and finance capitals a schism between anarchic and hierarchical forms, the key fault line for imperialist tensions.[23]

Narratives such as Hobson's, Arrighi's, and Harvey's provide a sense of imperialism as an ongoing conflict between a drive toward capital accumulation and the bounded social units generated in the course of its history. Accumulation takes means as ends, capital applies to the advent of a social base on which it subsequently turns its back. Classes, cities, and nations stand as evidence of social preconditions that capital demands for its development but cannot abide. Imperialism describes at a world scale the moment when circulation at the base (finance) generates conflict (war). It is tempting to get fixed on the reasons provided for any particular intervention, as if a simple evidentiary counterfactual would eliminate an explanation from being considered. In actuality there is oligarchic interest in blood for oil, a militaristic assertion of American power, a rapidly consolidated hegemony of the United States, fear mongering to maintain domestic control, a crisis of overproduction, an arrogance of power, an ascendent class fraction, interimperial rivalry, and more.

Any of these motives for empire could stand as a functionalist account, in which a given logic is somehow demanded by the system's effective operation and continued reproduction. Yet this multiplicity of independent variables is precisely what is employed in the systems approaches favored by financializers and force transformers alike. All variables are merrily accommodated without disturbing the underlying functionalist sensibility that what is being done needs doing. A whole other set of accounts can be distinguished as figural rather than functional. The functionalist form of representation focuses on how a part fits within the whole, when a single factor stands in for an entire explanation. The figural approach operates through a key image which presents a picture of the whole.[24]

The figural might look like a wholesale departure from the functional, were it not for its proximity to the tropes of networks, systems, camps, and other metaphorical niceties. The distance of cyberwar, the bare life of the camp, the psychoanalytics of death, the permeation of society by war, the countering of the multitude also suggest reasons that draw from very different philosophical archives. Ultimately the figural and functional imply one another, or reference the relation between accumulation's drive and boundary, between an imperial unconscious and a political economy of imperialism, between a narrative picture of the world and a reckoning of the formal units, divisions, and partitions that compose it.

Imperialism is here treated most generally as capital's historical contradiction between drive and form. The drive is manifest in the generative movement of human association entailed by expansive social wealth. Form appears as the momentary fixity, the practico-inert of organizational and institutional arrangements expressed as social-spatial units of life (home, community, workplace, city, nation, globe). These units, sites, and formations channel, limit, and place demands on accumulated wealth. Finance can be viewed as a kind of seepage from these drives, an effort by capital to escape social entailments through circulation, an evacuation of capital for its social basis that results in war.

It follows that in at least one aspect functional and figural reason are implicated in one another. For both types of reason imply the mutual incompatibility and attachment of the social units or structures treated as necessity and the movement toward or away from historical possibilities that stand as a kind of liberation (both positively—liberated to; and negatively—liberated from). Liberation will appear as a narrative that references an imperial unconscious. Drive will alternate as intervention and isolation. Boundary will shuttle between units and formations that reference the national and the global. In simpler terms, capital's drive for self-expansion forces people together to create forms of life that encumber social wealth, whose limitations capital subsequently flees. For Marx this is the socialism immanent to capitalism—an immanence that entwines what is and isn't good for capital and for labor, "the entanglement of all peoples in the net of the world market."[25] By this reckoning the functionalist notion of interest turns out to be far more unstable than would be imagined by clearly demonstrable relations between parts and wholes. Interest is not so much inaccurately ascribed to one constituency or another as it is a faith in what is good for oneself that is forever undermined by its pursuit. Similarly, the figure of nation, camp, and multitude is less a false portrait of a disappeared condition than a form whose meanings, feelings, and effects shift from one historical and cultural context to another.

Imperialism has again been forced into consideration, not simply because of unilateralist aggressivity but because interventionist stances shift world risk onto a nation that might have shunned or shielded its population in the name of a secure interest. This imperial attention brings with it neither utter newness nor deadening sameness, rather an obligation to repose the question of how war, power, and capital are related. While these three elements remain irreducible to one another, they are joined by social principles that are most clearly detectable in the movements of capital—less because the economic ultimately determines than because of what capital assembles and discards to invent itself. If we want political economy to again teach the present in the way it once could, we may need to momentarily take leave of it, not to abandon what capital visits upon the world so as to re-enter it afresh. The mutual suspicion between perspectives of political economy and poststructuralism may finally turn out to be productive, if we can learn to read the lapses of one through the other.[26]

: WAR ALL THE WAY DOWN?

For discussions of war, at least, what would seem to be the turning of political economy on its head is Michel Foucault's transfer of the matter from an instrument of state to an entailment of society. Foucault perceptively reverses Clausewitz's thesis that war is an extension of politics and offers a theory that politics is the normalization of war. Even as imperialism marks the moment when war erupts from circulation, the installation of finance as the driving principle of development and of daily life will extend war across the hitherto secure divide of the foreign into domestic. Already in this move from a unitary object to a dispersed process much of the argument pertaining to securitization and derivatives is discernible. But when Foucault is writing, what I am calling financialization is just dawning, and his attentions are focused elsewhere—on what he terms biopolitics.

While certainly not so in Foucault's earlier writing such as *The Order of Things* (1966), in later work the matter of life and money is typically written about as if active consideration of one precluded critical attention to the other. While political economy seems moribund, biopower is money-free. Reimplicating life and money is not just a matter of settling accounts but of spreading the debts around. In *Discipline and Punish* (first published in French in 1975) Foucault introduces his reversal of the Clausewitzian formulation of war as an extension of politics. He states "that 'politics' has been conceived as a continuation, if not exactly and directly of war, at least of the military model as a fundamental means of preventing civil disorder."[27]

Foucault's effort in his lectures at the Collège de France in 1976 (published in English seventeen years later under the title *Society Must Be Defended*) is to come to an understanding of power grounded and operating through something other than law. The organization of war making gives him a different social physics of power, with forces moving relationally rather than held by a sovereign figure like a king. This sovereign model of power "finds its formal model in the process of exchange, in the economy of the circulation of goods."[28] Foucault's pursuit of war as an alternative model for politics is really meant to provide a conceptual differentiation between politics and economics so as to escape the deterministic entrapment of then extant political economy. He identifies his research as the pursuit of a "noneconomic analysis of power":

> First: Is power always secondary to the economy? Are its finality and function always determined by the economy? Is power's raison d'être and purpose essentially to serve the economy? Is it designed to establish, solidify, perpetuate, and reproduce relations that are characteristic of the economy and essential to its working? Second question: Is power modeled on the commodity? Is power something that can be possessed and acquired, that can be surrendered through a contract or by force, that can be alienated or recuperated, that circulates and fertilizes one region but avoids others? Or if we wish to analyze it, do we have to operate—on the contrary—with different instruments, even if power relations are deeply involved in and with economic relations, even if power relations and economic relations always constitute a sort of network or loop? If that is the case, the indissociability of the economy and politics is not a matter of functional subordination, nor of informal isomorphism. It is of a different order, and it is precisely that order that we have to isolate.[29]

The economic here stands for a double determinism. It is at once a first cause that subordinates all other factors and a structure of a fixed and tangible object that can be possessed, like a commodity which organizes and is present in all aspects of human affairs. Foucault does not want to suggest that power and economy are independent of one another, rather that their "indissociability" is predicated upon a dynamic internal differentiation.

It is fair to say that the determinism which concerned Foucault could be found all around him in Marxist political economy generally, and in the conceptions of imperialism more specifically. It's also true that those same conceptions were receiving critical engagement from Marxists as well, most saliently in Nicos Poulantzas's relational notions of class power.[30] Foucault's claim is that the sovereign model of power is based upon an idea of economy in which people and things have the same individuated properties. Instead it seems more accurate to say that his notion of the economy is just the reverse, a mirror of sovereignty. The dynamism of power emerges against an inert and reductive notion of economy, even as power assumes some features of economy. "Power must, I think, be analyzed as something that circulates, or rather as something that functions only when it is part of a chain. It is never localized here or there, it is never in the hands of some, and it is never appropriated in the way that wealth or a commodity can be appropriated."[31]

Certainly the commodity must also be analyzed in circulation; its existence is also realized through the process of exchange as part of a chain. Commodities come to have significance only as part of this universe. Their apparent discreteness and autonomy is the object of Marx's critique of political economy, in which he wants to establish value as an "active factor in a process."[32] Conversely, war would seem to mark precisely a moment when power as a capacity that flows or passes through individuals in the form of an army is appropriated, not by another individual but more diffusely through the activities of the state. Economy admits of all manner of quantification, but its measurement should not be confused with its accomplishment. For example, identifying the way someone is richer than someone else just as thoroughly begs the question of how economies work as identifying one person as more powerful than another elides what power is and does.

One could say as well that the point of analyzing commodities in relation to their whole process of production and circulation, what Marx does in *Capital*, is to show that they are never just things but bear and are borne by all manner of social relations, very much in the manner that Foucault describes. It is because capital cannot simply reproduce itself as part of a closed, self-regulating circuit that politics is indissociably linked to economy. Of course Foucault is not reading Marx in these lectures, but Hobbes, although he is clearly arguing against a particular version of Marxism. He is, as already noted, also writing at the moment when financialization is just beginning to generate the primacy of circulating flows and dispersed, deindividuated, nonsovereign forms of commodity exchange associated with the rise of derivatives.

It is not for Foucault to have forecast this move, but his analytics of power can usefully be applied to understand the social significance of preponderant finance. For what he offers is an account of how difference becomes a problem for social order and institutions, a problem of which war is both the motor and the solution. He first establishes that Clausewitz himself inverted a formula for politics as war that had emerged in the seventeenth and eighteenth centuries and was associated most closely with Hobbes's arguments in *The Leviathan* for the sovereign state. "The primitive war, the war of every man against every man, is born of equality and takes place in the element of that equality. War is the immediate effect of nondifferences, or at least of insufficient differences."[33] Foucault suggests that for Hobbes, it is difference that leads to peace, as the strong and the weak will recognize that accounts have been settled, rather than be constantly on guard against the possibility of attack from potential foes.

The discourse of power to emerge from the seventeenth century rested upon a formalization of difference in the form of race, which now carries with it a biological threat against which society must defend itself by using state policies of purification. This race war which forms the internal dynamic of social order generates an internal cleavage of population. Foucault argues "that the other race is basically not the race that came from elsewhere or that was, for a time, triumphant and dominant, but that it is a race that is permanently, ceaselessly infiltrating the social body, or which is rather, constantly being recreated in and by the social fabric. In other words, what we see as a polarity, as a binary rift within society is not a clash between two distinct races. It is the splitting of a single race into a super-race and a subrace. To put it a different way, it is the reappearance within a single race, of the past of that race. In a word, the obverse and the underside of the race reappears within it."[34] The state elevates this management of bodies to a global strategy of racial conservatism, in effect a condition of perpetual war. War is no longer the medium through which history is made: it now conserves and protects society from threats born of its own body. "The idea of social war makes, if you like, a great retreat from the historical to the biological, from the constituent to the medical."[35]

This new formation, emergent in the nineteenth century, is what Foucault terms biopolitics, an entire disciplinary regime that treats population as a political problem. This new field eclipses the sovereign form, "biopower that is in excess of sovereign right. This excess of biopower appears when it becomes technologically and politically possible for man not only to manage life but to make it proliferate, to create living matter, to build the monster, and, ultimately, to build viruses that cannot be controlled and that are universally destructive."[36] Racism is the governmental protocol for sorting population in response to the threats posed by proliferating forms of life, introducing a regulatory mode that discriminates ultimately between "what must live and what must die," which Foucault terms a "colonizing genocide."[37] This internal cleaving of population is highly mutable, and Foucault traces Marx's and Engels's understanding of class struggle to their use of nineteenth-century French historians of race war such as Augustin Thierry and François Guizot.[38]

As has been keenly observed, Foucault's writings occupy a double register of historical archive and diagnosis of the present.[39] Revolutionary decolonization in the third world, a seemingly endless capacity for expansion of the welfare state at home, concerns over ecological catastrophe, and nascent genetic engineering were all part of the defended society he was diagnosing in the 1970s. Certainly the state's capacity to decide over life and death and to "build the monster" has not abated since Foucault's writing. The question is what the emergence of risk embrace does to the societal conservatism that he observed.

The once defended society has now become opportunistic. The invisible hand is now devoted to stealthy arbitrage. Markets no longer promote equilibrium but asymmetry, as the ideal of unipolarity is realized fleetingly in acts of war. The military controls its future but loses its destiny. Invasion makes governments disappear as it liberates people from state and markets. Looters dance around the fallen monuments of development. Foreign and domestic have become profoundly interwoven in a manner that complicates the sorting function that race could once achieve. Preemption and forward deterrence, securitization and the derivative, have brought the time of the future into the present in a manner that may augur as dramatic a shift for our times as biopower had done for the nineteenth century. Just as race then was the perforated edge upon which society would be cleaved, the binary to have emerged over the past thirty years would separate the risk-capable from those considered at risk.

The domestic wars of the 1980s—against drugs, crime, youth, welfare, and education—retained a significant purgative aspect (like the relatively more constructive war on poverty in the 1960s), but also introduced a demand for self-management under the guise of personal responsibility by which the line could be crossed into risk embrace. In wars still marked by race, gender, sexuality, and other biopolitical divides, victory was presented as a move from a subordinate to a superordinate position by self-managing the difficult passage to risk. Alien bodies, foreign bodies, could with the war on terror travel the same route. Along these lines, Frances Fox Piven has argued that preemptive war "is also a domestic strategy, rooted not only in calculations of America's global power, but in calculations geared to shoring up the Bush regime's domestic power and its ability to pursue its domestic policy agenda."[40]

Foucault had observed that the state had by its own monopoly ended the private wars associated with the nobiliary armies of feudalism, such that "peace is waging a secret war."[41] What happens, however, when the secret is out? When the state reprivatizes war; when economy itself rebinarizes population? In part, the whole history of difference that the various risk categories reference and make equivalent now confronts a governmental regime bent on indifference. Disingenuously, perhaps, but studiously, the neoconservative formation that brought on the derivative wars now presents race as making no difference. The neoconservative assault on affirmative action posits that the need for remedying racial injustice is firmly behind us. Almost by way of substitution, persons who stand for the claim that race makes no difference (Colin Powell, Condoleezza Rice, Clarence Thomas) are appointed to prominent positions of security management and the law. Thus race is to be silenced by its appearance, blanched through its public utterances. Surely these representations do not exhaust the racial imaginary, but they do indicate how binaries of risk and race might interact.

The notion that the nefarious forces which had once threatened the social body could now be converted into productive risks is a significant departure from the idea of economy as homogenizing sovereignty. The bundling together of small packets of debt has a delocalizing effect consistent with nonsovereign forms of power. Shaving bits of these fractured commodities so as to leverage minor volatilities into substantial effects is a self-violating installation of the binary that Foucault proposed. With static conceptions of class difference, the emphasis is on objective relations to the production of surplus value that would locate or position an individual within a given socioeconomic classification. In contrast, Foucault's historicizing binary allows for the active differentiating of population, whose consequence is the production of an antagonism. The internal split of the risk divide marks a political agency in the midst of capital that notions of class struggle, typically prescribed by fixed interest, sought to articulate.[42] The internal cleaving of race had a woeful but stabilizing effect on population. The splitting of population along the lines of risk refuses and disrupts those prior conditions of difference. Race does not disappear, but its effects can be renegotiated. Far from being an end state, death is something that one can hedge against, invest in, benefit from.

Financialization, brought into the realm of the everyday, interconnects all manner of personal credit and debt and makes publicly tradable what was once a domestic matter. This socialization of personal finance would seem to disturb the secret telos of the biological, trampling domestic intimacy and making the smallest decisions seem large and portentous. The local is delocalized, interconnected with far-flung co-investors, subject to renewed state concern. If the ultimate realization of biopower is to bring to life what was once considered inert, then nowhere would this become more apparent than with respect to the economy. Foucault's political genealogy of war moves from the savage exchange of homo economicus (private war) to the historical force of society making (state war) to the biological conservation of population (race war).

The warring ways to have emerged from the systems logics of finance and the revolution in military affairs would now seem to play this genealogy in reverse. Morphing its terms of antagonism from race to state to private life, war now seems to be pressing the limit of the modern order of things. Privatization, the state's internal war on behalf of a capital said to be able to manage itself, savages population, subjecting private matters to the public violence of the market. Privatization is thus a process of securitization, a means of making publics by amalgamating risk. Populations are cleaved by a ruthless state monopolizing of history to effect the privatization of life control that goes by the name of risk. The present imperialism places this genealogical reversal on display for all to see. A "high-risk" presidency crashes and burns in tandem with its asymmetrical opponent, a bad risk well taken.[43] Whereas the divide of the race war was still universal, derivative wars can let a few pass for the many, and still leave open great swathes of population outside the lines of battle.

While the impetus for the Foucauldian schema is to move away from brittle, deterministic conceptions of economy so that it might again be indissociably linked to politics, Foucault seems to accept this notion of the economic at the same time that he replaces it with an equivalent political category, sovereignty. War has spread from state monopoly to domestic affairs under the sign of biopower. Yet if war is everywhere, then there is only politics. The relation between regulation and production, the tension between strategies of force and consent, the antinomy between death and labor all disappear. This is certainly a practical dilemma of the war on terror that spreads risk everywhere, but it is also a conceptual issue of losing the delineation between war and peace, foreign and domestic, state and civil society—all of which devolve into a relation of war and war.

Liberalism of old and the new conservatism are joined by a commitment to democracy—at least of the electoral kind. The cold war victory was taken as democracy's triumph. Instead of being spared war, the world has been scarred by an escalation of violence. Imperial embrace has spread war around, resulting in elections which themselves become predicates of violence. When war is about making risk productive, then the economic returns through the very flows and circulation of power as something intrinsic to the material organization and practices of the political. Civil society, by this reckoning, cannot be the domain outside of state or market, the realm of voluntary associations favored by neoliberal notions of development that seek to unburden human rights from a social economy.[44]

Writing against this notion of civil society and the corollary democratization said to be taking over the world, Achille Mbembe has refigured postcolonial sovereignty as a coercive complex in which violence becomes its own ends. Colonial rule rested upon a normalizing state of exception, in which government routinely broke common law to exercise its authority, administer a regime of privileges and immunities parceled out unevenly, and erase the distinction between ruling and civilizing. The result was to confuse public and private and turn those who refused to accept this form of control into savages, with the native the prototype of the animal. The postcolonial authoritarian regime is a modern, not a recidivist, form. It is built upon this system of command to assert a privatization of public prerogatives and a socialization of arbitrariness.

Violence so permeates society that popular pleasures are organized around an "aesthetics of vulgarity," with the state staging public rituals in which "the masses join in the madness and clothe themselves in cheap imitations of power to reproduce its epistemology, and when power, in its own violent quest for grandeur, makes vulgarity and wrongdoing its main mode of existence."[45] There is a welcome defrocking of the bad faith of state rituals, but also discernible is a disdain for the vulgarized public that borders on the moralistic. This route is open especially if the public is little more than an object of control or abjection. Sovereignty, that closed circuit which Foucault sought to open, now lies at the heart of biopower. This conception of control carries with it the absoluteness of power that Foucault sought to complicate, albeit at the expense of modeling state authority on a mechanical view of economy. The postcolony reclaims this authority and disavows its sources in an economic idea. In a highly influential essay, Mbembe writes that sovereignty exercises "control over mortality and to define life as the deployment and manifestation of power."[46] Politics becomes "death that lives a human life," a necropolitics devoted to the "creation of *death-worlds*, new and unique forms of social existence in which vast populations are subjected to conditions of life conferring upon them the status of *living dead*."[47]

While the state is here stripped of its liberal shroud, it is also free of any problems that the management of labor and regulation of wealth might pose. Curiously, Mbembe subsumes Marx's position as a mirror to his own, which sees overcoming class divisions as a prerequisite to eradicating "human plurality" by means of "revolutionary terror" through a "fight to the death."[48] This is a now familiar cold war reading of Marx: Stalinism is read backwards to its essentialized source, expressed as a metaphor of Russian dolls one inside the other. On the contrary, Marx's *Capital* is more usefully read as an account of labor that produces value through difference, whereas socialism would treat labor rather than capital as society's end, hence a kind of irreducible plurality.[49] Further, Mbembe accuses Marx of conflating labor, "the maintenance of human life," with work, "the creation of lasting artifacts that add to the world of things."[50] Marx's distinction between subsistence and surplus labor is far more robust than this: more than a distinction between people and things, it expands the capacity for living by the ways people engage what they do and create.

Marx saw that expansive wealth would render some part of the population "relatively redundant," and that far from being universal, the process by which capital is drawn to and expunges bodies takes on a form "historically valid within its limits alone."[51] Labor and population circulate through one another, overlapping and transforming the relation between what is productive and what is reproductive. Redundancies are never absolute because of the draw of what was excluded as a fresh source of productivity. Relative surplus in population marks the capacity for making difference from which capital seeks to free itself by cleaving labor and population. War is one machinery for setting relative surplus population in motion. Crucially for Marx, what is excluded is always poised to return in the form of some further productivity. Capital's indifference to the human associations that it amasses suggests the potential of a population whose own surplus, whose own excess body, is a thing for itself.

Without discounting the scope of repression by which the state operates, or the ever more elaborate production of relative surplus populations, consolidating all politics around the figure of death is also a tremendous narrowing of the whole range of social contestations over forms of life and the shape of society. Necropolitics would suggest that the state itself affects this reduction, but this conception of the political is, at the very least, complicit. The same caveat would apply to risk as well—by identifying an emergent politics we may leave the impression of exclusivity, as if risk trumped all other possible political expressions.

The separation between life as such and any particular way of life imagines that the state's ability to kill legally, the state of exception by which a person is placed outside the restitutive framework of liberal law, is the most salient feature of politics. With social regulation taking the shape of war, killing would seem to be modeled everywhere. Giorgio Agamben's notion of bare life treats this capacity as the basis for rule. Accordingly, bare life is transformed into a way of life, and exceptional measures—in his case the concentration camp—are the structure in which sovereignty "is realized *normally*."[52] The normalization of the camp allows the mind to race in affirmation from Guantánamo to Abu Ghraib. Yet these are also highly unstable forms, and if imperial sovereignty is vested in them, then the figure of the camp may prove to be its own exception. Here the figural and the functional share limitations for thinking through imperial effects.

Both Mbembe and Agamben will give pause to any who would seek to minimize the stakes of the war on terror. The capacity to suddenly make anyone part of a populus non gratus is readily generalized into a coded emergency. At the same time, it is tempting to overconsolidate the authority of the state to exercise its war on terror. Terror evinces a politics of fear as well as vulgarity, but we should not cede to the state the affective mono-tone that would be most conducive to its effective rule.[53] Sovereignty may project emotional monotheism, but that doesn't mean it can secure the faith. The move from uncertainty to risk is a shift from the fear of the unknown to the thrill of the unexpected. While fear remains a dull if undulating constant, the excitable acts of speculation only fuel further volatility as well as the capacity to sustain it. As in Afghanistan and Iraq, the limitations are at once practical and political. If one is committed to opposing the state of emergency, it may be more useful to recognize these limitations than to affirm the omnipotence of the sovereign form.

Not all political analysis that takes up sovereignty avoids Marxist con-cepts of political economy or the analysis of labor. Combining questions of rule and value affords the fullest engagement with the current imperium. A "global form of sovereignty" as a "series of national and supranational organisms united under a single logic of rule" is what Michael Hardt and Antonio Negri understand as Empire.[54] Writing before the present terror war was formally joined, they declare that imperialism is over, and that there can no longer be a single world leader or center of power. At the same time, the United States is distinctive in that it has a constitutionally based juridical structure that can adapt to challenges to the state's legitimate authority. The United States has also assimilated diverse populations, con-stituting the alien as native. Constitution as legal framework and social process composes the formal and informal basis of sovereignty. While sovereignty is an account of domination, resistances are to be found in the realm of production, something that Foucault himself "fails to grasp."[55] Hardt and Negri reinterpret Foucault's account of the ascent of biopower and align it with Marx's analysis of the shift in the way of dominating labor from formal to real subsumption: "The analysis of the real subsumption, when this is understood as investing not only the economic or only the cultural dimension of society but rather the social *bios* itself, and when it is attentive to the modalities of disciplinarity and/or control, disrupts the linear and totalitarian figure of capitalist development. Civil society is absorbed in the state, but the consequence of this is an explosion of the elements that were previously coordinated and mediated in civil society. Resistances are no longer marginal but active in the center of society that opens up in networks; the individual points are singularized in a thousand plateaus."[56]

"A thousand plateaus" is a reference to the work of Gilles Deleuze and

Félix Guattari, who expand the generative effects of labor from the workplace where products are made to the "productivity of social reproduction," where determinant forms of life and labor are created. Hence the realm of affect and aspiration once relegated to the superstructure and thus the creative—but insufficiently so, since the radical potential of their move remains "insubstantial and impotent."[57] In contrast, Hardt and Negri use what they see as more politically serviceable concepts—intellectual labor and mass intellectuality. Immaterial labor issues from symbolic, intellectual, and communication activities, becoming commodified and organized occupationally through the service sector. Mass intellectuality considers the critical forms of subjectivity that emerge with the industrialization of knowledge production. Transnational corporations now do what states once did in terms of organizing labor and populations. Shifts in capital investment can incite mass migrations and corporations can engage bilaterally in financial transactions from around the world. Since the geopolitical field is "permeated by money," "every biopolitical figure appears dressed in monetary garb."[58]

Even as empire refers to the ravenous subsumption of all forms of life to further accumulation, it also composes new figures of resistance, collectively known as the multitude. Not merely negative or oppositional, "they also express, nourish and develop positively their own constituent projects; they work toward the liberation of living labor, creating constellations of powerful singularities."[59] Singularity is a term drawn from the work of the seventeenth-century philosopher Baruch Spinoza. For Hardt and Negri, it refers to a recognition of the distinctiveness and fulsomeness of subjects and events, a communication based on differences rather than resemblances, a form of immanence in which being and becoming, power and substance, subject and nature are one. Singularity is meant as a philosophical alternative to dialectical dualisms, while maintaining a materialist stance. But this escape from the dialectic only detaches its most mechanical formulation (the inevitable forward motion of thesis, antithesis, synthesis) and leaves singularity susceptible to its own reductionist temptation to isolate matter from the process that has set it in motion.

Surprisingly for the authors of an avowedly Marxist book, Hardt and Negri attracted considerable attention from the popular media as well as academic circles, along with intense criticism. Written between the first Gulf War and the NATO intervention in Kosovo of 1999, *Empire* reflected a seemingly more benign United States and a debate around multilateralist armed humanitarians and just wars.[60] The virulent nationalism and pre-emptive militarism of Bush's administration trouble the idea that a glob-ally sovereign empire had usurped a warmongering imperialism. The de-mographics of immaterial labor proved unsupportable, more a fable of new economy encomiums than a supportable shift away from the grit and grease of material production (even if now the grease would likely be hydrogenated fat at McDonald's and the grit something from the stock-rooms of Wal-Mart).

Confidence in the U.S. Constitution as an open-ended framework for new principles of rule seemed quickly misplaced when the Patriot Act drew upon considerable legislative precedent to reduce the conditions of consti-tutionally based sovereignty. The philosophical encumbrances of Spinoza freighted the multitude with a difficult passage to actual social move-ments.[61] For the purposes of this argument, it is important to note that while Hardt and Negri effect a turn to production, and insist on a place for finance, it is after all but a "garb" for the biopolitical. There is no imma-nence applied to the critique of capital itself so as to allow an examination of how the multitude is cleaved within and against empire. The term "singularity" recognizes autonomy as a value of very disparate political entities without insisting that they assume a shared organizational form like a party. By not insisting that people disengage from their primary political activism to come together around some overarching movement or organization, singularity effectively avoids a divisive politics of unity. But it also renders challenging the evaluation of political difference and organizational strategy as presented by varieties of movements, to say the least.

These critical attentions were in no way wasted on Hardt and Negri. Four years after the publication of their book they responded to the shift in circumstances and opportunities and published a sequel that offered a popular political philosophy—a rarity on American bookshelves. The new book, *Multitude: War and Democracy in the Age of Empire*, clarifies the significance of sovereignty as a radical democratic project against a "gen-eral global state of war."[62] *Multitude* is really about the primacy of networks as simultaneously an ontological figure (a material being), an organiza-tional form (self-expanding association), and a societal end (reflexive in-terconnections). The elaboration of production beyond the workplace generates a medium of communication, cooperation, and collaboration known as the common, whereby the multitude is drawn together without becoming the same. The model for the multitude is the internet, "because, first, the various nodes remain different but are connected in the Web, and, second, the external boundaries of the network are open such that new nodes and relationships can always be added."[63]

While offering an appealingly synthetic view of transformative form and drive, this figural privileging of networks is not without problems. Networks are not so much proxies for social life but portraits of what it is and ought to be. The internet is as much a technology of exclusion as of linkage. It both colonizes and decolonizes labor and consumption, and invests the immaterial, symbolic, and expressive activity with a materiality hitherto unknown to it. Hardt and Negri aim to displace the fixed geometry of a complex or structured totality constituted through mediations among various institutional sites, which appears as functionalist reason, with a more open, unbounded, unmediated figuration. Ironically, however, the network is less an alternative to the functional logic of part and whole than it is a purer geometric figure. In the words of the social movement theorist Manuel Castells, it is "a set of interconnected nodes," where a "node is the point at which a curve intersects itself."[64] But as has been suggested already, function and figure are not so readily disentangled from one another. Network implies a very specific entanglement.

The democracy immanent to empire comes to pass because networks are unbounded and open, therefore inherently expansive so as to spread the generative capacities of resistance that enlarge deliberative capacities. The network unleashes a "profound desire for democracy—a real democracy of the rule of all by all based on relationships of equality and freedom."[65] Hardt and Negri have slyly inverted Hobbesian savage war as peace, and done so by preserving difference in the body politic. Yet beyond the conviction that networks spread and with them democratic desire increases, it is not easy to know how to substantiate the claim that what people, movements, or the multitude seeks is more rule.

If rule is an extension of war it is understandable that many should be disenchanted. So too, the work of networking may be disdained by many. Surely Hardt and Negri are correct in seeing the sheer mass of activities that are the object of constitution or transformation as expanding, but it is not apparent that rule per se is what drives the expansion. The figure of politics as rule is consistent with that of an activist or organizer who has endless time and energy for meetings and deliberation. The generalization of this desire is far more problematic and can lead to the disappointment that those who inhabit the common lack political desire—a very difficult position from which to organize.[66] If "real democracy" needs to resemble endless meetings or e-mailing, it may turn out to be a far more restrictive figure, a vanguardism without the organizational supports of a vanguard that Hardt and Negri so carefully position themselves against.

At this point one wants to hear more about the politics of social production borne by the dispersion of labor everywhere, one that makes labor the end of deliberation and not merely its means. Doing so might demand an engagement with the difficult histories of socialism. For Hardt and Negri this is a failed tradition, because "socialism did not succeed in constructing independent and original ideas or practices of political representation."[67] While transcendence was admittedly not available to socialist governance, it would be more helpful to assess the differences that were made available, not least to see what more than democracy the multitude might yield. Were socialism nothing other than a practice of representation, its success or failure would still need to be assessed in terms of a connection between participation, the spread of social production, and the constitution of a social economy.[68]

If the multitude could be articulated in these terms and not simply in the register of rule, we might come much closer to a means of evaluating the immanent accomplishments of this empire that Hardt and Negri so productively seek. Hardt and Negri have taken us as far as anyone in mining what could be meant by an imperial unconscious, in which what is repressed returns as an irrepressible project. Such a project needs to consider the interplay of form and figure, drive and boundary, socialism and democracy, the historical and the biopolitical, as these operate in the mutually constitutive imperial space of nation and world. If finance is treated as more than a cloak or an iron cage, but as the medium for circulating risk, and risk itself portends a shift in what we imagine the world to be, we may be able to rewrite the books that govern the imperial accounts.

⠒ DREAMING THE IMPERIAL UNCONSCIOUS

The imperial field has become rather crowded, a thicket of contrary arguments and ideological crosscurrents. It is not enough to choose sides, to achieve a proper political alignment, so as to combat the world that this imperialism imagines and replace it with a more habitable one. A way needs to be found to link those perspectives typically treated as outside one another. We need to map these various positions as a way of getting to those other worlds that may lie within reach but that we have yet to grasp. Dreaming the imperial unconscious, we may awaken elsewhere. More precisely, the positions can be charted along two pairs of fragile binaries, each describing a dimension of difference. One can be described as that of isolationism and interventionism. The other is that of the national and the global.

Imperialism, taken most generally as the geopolitical contradiction between the drive to accumulation and the forms of social life, is itself described in this double relation. The twin binaries allow us to read simultaneously the discourse of foreign policy that makes use of a prosaic meaning of imperialism, and a problem for expanded wealth that makes evident the inner workings of capital. Isolation and intervention are less mutually exclusive policy options taken by a hegemon than an imperial dilemma to which both responses are the solution. Invasion and abandonment, leaving dispersed warfare in its wake, is but one expression of this dilemma.

Giving boundaries and taking them away, possessing and dispossessing, isolating and intervening are two moments in the uneasy alignment between war, capital, and the state. For capital, isolation and intervention relate to the forced association imposed on populations to create conditions for further accumulation. Colonization, our prime example here, assigns people to places under the authority of an installed state and makes of their labor a means of extracting wealth. But wealth making is also a historical resource. People want it back, not just to return what was lost but also to further the novel ways of life that they envision. When the tab is rung up on what that would take in terms of social investments, governance abilities, real wages, and the like, the result for capital is an expensive proposition. Thus the urge for capital to cut and run, even if it means postponing the return for some new business opportunity. Imperialism expresses territorially the flight from or rejection of the practical encumbrances that come from the socialization or mutual interdependence of hitherto disconnected peoples, a flight inherent even in coercive settlement.

As sociohistorical forms the national and the global are at once mutually dependent and disruptive. Capital is not simply impatient to turn profits in shorter order—to speed up the plant—but restless about the created spaces that others might call home. Hence the reckless movement into and out of territory where national borders sound like doors slamming while capital catches its breath in its global abode. Nations are formed and ruined out of global seizures, implicating enemies without and within along lines of race, nationality, religion, sexuality, and now risk. Risk transforms the danger of returning to the scene of the crime into a calculable opportunity. Imperial risk isolates some subset of volatilities without having to attend to the whole of the colonial corpse. Afghanistan and Iraq, as scenes of many prior imperial intrigues, fit this problem well.

At the same time, the global is itself a historical form. As the term "globalization" implies, making global space is a process that produces its own institutional densities and pathways of exchange. Invasions may be launched from a military base or securities exchange marked as a global space (even as it is in someone's nation). Once the mess is made, the invaders can return to their launch pads. But globalization is at the same time a process of associating peoples, creating interdependencies by which they too can claim the world as their own. This old dream of an international cannot be killed off by the extinction of a political party or social movement. Rather it is the recurrence of internationalisms under so many guises that must be explained. People have forever been on the move; capital and its regimes of property take the sorting and cleaving of populations across geopolitical space and time as their historical project. The social units, their momentary boundaries crafted in the course of intervention and isolation, are also consistent with the framework of territorialization and deterritorialization, now part of the poststructuralist reading of Marx that Hardt and Negri exemplify. Since there is nothing to guarantee the preservation of the national form, and the drive to accumulation would conspire to disperse it, the tremendous oscillation of intervention and isolation renders the global highly contingent.

At first glance, the resulting combinations of national and global would appear to sort into distinct ideological positions. In practice, the two binaries cut into one another. But because they are constituted through risk, they are also destabilized by it. Bush's national security statement of 2002, like the troubles visited upon Afghanistan and Iraq, is at once isolationist and interventionist, national and global. Security, specifically defense, is the prime function of national government and serves to keep America safe or isolated from its enemies. National self-determination in the Wilsonian vision was a kind of protective isolation associated with decolonization (from the American Revolution on), until neoconservative liberation misappropriated this ideal. To liberate, to set free, allows a messianic future to figure in the present. Those morally fit for liberation can abide it, while others will be laid to waste. Judgment day usurps the long road to development. Regimes can change, nations can be reconstructed, but the resources needed to consolidate an entire population will be held in abeyance, mobilizing the excluded against the agents of exclusion. Indifference is forever shocked to discover that the dispossessed would notice.

Interventionism can also have a national inflection, especially when the terror war is defined in terms of retribution for a national wound. Accordingly, the United States was entitled to invade Afghanistan to restore its own breached security. Invasion would seem to undo the slippage between foreign and domestic effected less by terrorist attacks than by securitization. This intervention could operate nostalgically to produce an isolationist affect—a national "we" that is once again insular and safe at home. Reconstruction, the weak promise that accompanied liberation in Afghanistan and Iraq, is also a form of intervention by one nation to return another violated territory to some originary national wholeness. These examples of intervention that affirms a national principle can be contrasted with interventions meant to be world-making. The doctrine of preemption, both preventing rivals from forming and attacking those considered a menace, certainly treats the world as a field for exercising national prerogatives and is a global idea with isolationist effects. The global correlate of preemption would be the principle of nonintervention of states in the internal affairs of other sovereign entities. Ironically, nonintervention —once an equally global and heretofore progressive notion—is now seemingly reserved for the United States alone.

The combinations of drive (here the double movement of isolation-intervention) and form (the mutually constitutive relation of national-global) each generate an ideological spectrum that gives the present discussion of imperialism its odd imbrication of left and right. These couplings can be stated very succinctly and are presented schematically in the accompanying table.

A national isolationist position is divided between self-determination and security. Nations should be left alone to decide their own fate—a response to their having been bothered (and often formed) by the same colonial master. Security, the reaffirmation of borders, is typically invoked to keep others out or repress them at home. A national interventionist stance divides between reconstruction and retribution. Like self-determination, reconstruction assumes a prior imperial power breaker and assumes also that international aid and military humanitarianism will help to reassemble the pieces. Retribution likewise effaces the history of harm to isolate the

Drive Form	Isolationist	Interventionist
National	(L) self-determination (R) security	(L) reconstruction (R) retribution
Global	(L) non-intervention (R) preemption	(L) development/socialism (R) primacy/grand strategy

predicating act of terror and render imperial aggression innocent. Non-intervention assumes that national sovereignty is a practical universal available to all. Preemption treats the world as a hostile terrain that must be kept at bay to maintain the isolation of the hegemon. Global isolationism would generate an ideological split between nonintervention and preemption.

The fourth combination, global-interventionist, is the potent absence that animates the other three. For what stands as "left" in each combination is largely ameliorative of imperial history. Proponents of imperialism outside government articulate the reason of state in terms of a grand strategy that would claim primacy as either a right or a civilizing burden. Historically, the left project tied to globalizing intervention is social development in the name of an international socialism. Military assistance to revolutionary movements was invariably met by imperially assisted counterinsurgency long before (and, if even partially successful, long after) the social development piece could be put into place. And as is now evident, anti-imperialism can be attached to any number of political projects.

Radical democratic politics tend to want to liberate themselves rather than complicate these traditions. Missing the socialism of a globalizing capital, concern with rule and right displaces an expansive wealth of social interdependencies that lead toward a society that subtends polity. Not all internationalism based in human rights or civil society is as ambitious as radical democracy, but insofar as there is no critique of capital to conjoin state and market, civil society becomes a dangerously liberated zone, where voluntary association does the work required of mutually associated labor. Most saliently, there is no shortage of international solidarities, global interdependencies, or sheer politicization of what might be entitled to assume the mantle of the global. Some socialism is discernible among these. The question for imperialism, then as now, is how this project might resurface.

The embrace of an overtly imperialist project, a rightist globalizing interventionism, could be said to reside in the uneasy ligature of neoliberalism and neoconservatism. Recall that financialization has come to prominence in the context of these often contradictory rightist moods. The neoliberal conceit is that the market is self-sufficient for regulating society, that the state should abdicate its role in promoting social security in favor of promoting risk. Neoconservatism is in many ways a narrower and more fragile formulation.[69] Briefly, it treats liberalism rather than socialism as its antagonist. Liberalism was the siren from which the newly born conservatives have turned away, having been mugged by reality. The corrupting influence of dependency on government is also its target, but it is not anti-statist. Rather it is concerned that state intervention and reform should have a moral dimension. According to Irving Kristol, among the movement's elder statesmen, it is essential for political life to ensure a "capitalist future" by renewing faith in the market, and to reverse the spiritual poverty caused by a "cultural nihilism" which strips life of meaning.[70] Religion and art are to be the counterpoints to the atheist philosophy taught in universities and the hedonism in music and television driven by modernist secularisms such as "frank female sexuality."[71]

The combination into an interventionist state project of risk and moralism, freedom of choice and reconsolidated cultural form, aims to return lost boundaries at the same time that it erects new lines of fissure. As Kristol makes clear, the neoconservative impulse is toward a kind of evangelical and even messianic capitalism that Bush made his own. The matter of securing nations would therefore include de-distributive tax policies as called for by Bush's national security document. Where neoliberalism would have preferred to maintain a leveraged hegemony through financial protocols established by the International Monetary Fund, the neoconservative hubris is that market truths must be affirmed by might. As was observed in chapter 1, the privatizing state and interventionist markets sit uneasily with neoliberal nostrums of government lite and market reasonableness.

The dry air of market calculation can give to imperial conviction the ring of objectivity. Max Boot, former editor at the *Wall Street Journal*, grew up at a time (the 1980s) when "conservatism was cool."[72] In his phrase, borrowed from Kipling, "the savage wars of peace" are unapologetically imperial wars, small interventions for punishment, protection, pacification, or profit that underwrite Pax Americana. He elegantly takes the neoconservative imperial hubris of a Cheney, Rumsfeld, or Wolfowitz and gives it an economic logic along the lines of a yield curve. After the cold war, the hidden costs of intervention have been reduced. "The perceived cost grew dramatically during the cold war, when every use of American force risked provoking a clash of superpowers. But in the post–cold war world, the price of exercising power appears low once again."[73] Even the pragmatic, if wary, acceptance of American Empire evident in Andrew Bacevich's realist view is cast as an economic logic of "scaling imperial ambitions to fit imperial assets," so that Americans can figure out "what sort of empire they want theirs to be."[74] The implication is that for imperialism to succeed, it needs to be widely embraced by the subjects and not simply the rulers. It is not enough to exercise world domination. That domination must be popular as well. In this light imperialism is not a civilizing burden but a choice, a risk worth taking.

Whatever is novel to imperialism of late, the justification for it as a civilizing mission casts the new in the sepia tones of old certainties. Niall Ferguson gives a pep talk to Americans, urging them to overcome their reticent will to power and undertake what he terms liberal empire. He sees two choices for the present if, as he seeks, capitalism and democracy are to become practical universals. One choice is continued national independence and a mounting disorder of monstrously failed states, as in Africa. The other is imperial governance that would suspend national sovereignty in part or whole for decades to come. To decide, "we need to compare the costs and benefits of both empire and independence in the modern period."[75] Indeed, the subtitle of his book *Colossus* is *The Price of America's Empire*. Ferguson means this literally: his point is that the United States has got empire on the cheap, and that pursuit of global assets through military intervention is therefore a good business decision. "Like Britain's liberal empire a century ago, America's nascent liberal empire is surprisingly inexpensive to run."[76] Further, the military budget and foreign aid that fund imperial activity have declined since America became the hegemon on the block, and present reconstruction efforts pale by comparison with those following the Second World War.

Ferguson concedes that imperial successes have been outnumbered by failures. There has been overstretch, but not because of the costs that the United States pays to maintain its global prominence. Rather, overstretch is a domestic ill, driven by domestic debt, dependence on foreign credit, and overconsumption. Equally grave has been the failure to produce the legions of experts required to bring the imperial word to the world. "Unlike their British counterparts of a century ago, who left the elite British Universities with an overtly imperial mindset, the letters ambitious young Americans would like to see after their names are CEO, not CBE [Commander of the British Empire]."[77] As in combating the cultural failure that concerned Kristol, universities are key to reproducing imperium—and they have not been pulling their weight. The third failure—most fatal for Ferguson—is "attention deficit," the hit-and-run approach to intervention that attempts "economic and political transformation in an unrealistically short time frame."[78]

In a manner consistent with neoconservative cant, Ferguson wants to blame the deficit on the decadence of American culture. Particularly pressing is the failure of that culture to engender an appropriate masculinity. American men are overweight and unwilling to die in foreign adventures—leaving the nation "a kind of strategic couch potato."[79] The deeper crisis may lie in reconciling the undemonstrable value of imperialism to a stubbornly escalating price. This rift between price and value is a feature of the speculative environment that Ferguson would have us embrace. If commitments to empire cannot be assured as a titled birthright but must be demonstrated as an investment whose returns are superior to others, then imperial fidelity will be difficult to sustain. Further, if few can afford to participate in imperial speculation, patriotism will not be a sufficient lure and democracy at home may have to be curtailed. None of these are consequences that Ferguson is willing to imagine. Far from being an incentive to imperial bravado, the risk calculus that he advises us to employ has become constitutive of culture. Consequently, value may leave the realm of shared beliefs and norms that attach to a nostalgic view of old empire and enter the volatile temporality of incessant exchange. Opportunities crowd the field and must be seized, even if that means discarding some older and slower performers in the portfolio. Here the simple import of older imperial visions breaks down. Attention deficit is, in the end, the product of imperial reach rather than its limitation.

The imperial accounts discussed here share the perspective that war has become the principal means of American rule. Consequently, we need to see what the power of war produces and distributes when capital itself forms the military corps.[80] Cheap, fast, small, and devastatingly dirty wars have long been instruments for acquiring and maintaining imperial assets. Territories have been grabbed only to be discarded. Fresh populations for labor have been captured only to be dispossessed. War today offers different capital services and discloses other logics of accumulation. Not just a release for underconsumption or overproduction, an outlet for surplus expenditure or profit, war is now an elaboration of the apparatus for producing risk. Derivative wars create the risk environment that they would treat as their opportunity. Imperialism is no longer fixed into the architecture of center and periphery, sovereign and subject, self and other. The present imperium absorbs credit from without as it emanates the cleavage of population from within to the farthest points of forward deterrence. Money from abroad pours in to finance U.S. currency account deficits (the dollar-denominated gap between imports and exports), while the sorting of the citizenry into the risk-capable and the at-risk is the principal export of war-inspired rule.

As with biopower, nothing of the older imperialist logics disappears. Rather, now that biopower is itself absorbed into the life of capital, the proliferation of derivatives converts threats to life into opportunities for living as capital. If the self is composed of risk, it can be differentiated along gradients of opportunity and volatility, the most promising of which can be put forward as investments. One learns to isolate liabilities or job performance to advance "core competencies" or hedge against unwanted exchanges by screening out unknown callers or electronic correspondents. The derivative is not simply a product on the shelves of the financial services industry but stands, along with securitization, as a pervasive principle of socialization, a refinement of the drive to accumulate that expands the realm of social interdependencies as it advances the terms of wealth.

Derivatives parcel the body of value, multiply the means by which interconnection is possible, deepen the density and intensity of mutual contingency, and increase the scale of transaction devoted to interdependencies. Failure can ripple past quickly, success can pass unnoticed. The derivative has become a vast machinery that converts difference into indifference, insofar as specific qualities of life become exchangeable attributes of risk (whether one's salary will double in ten years, whether one will get cancer). Value is disassembled and reassembled in pursuit of further circulation by creating not just faster movement but different pathways to travel. Bounded unities of value are dispossessed of their local integrity and intercalated with an anonymous and tentacular social body.

The social body is not an organic whole, an analogue with a human body. Nor is it a system that maintains or strays from equilibrium as if it were analogous to a machine. Capital generates a body by assembling capacities to make life together, labor that yields more wealth, certainly, but also generates more capacities for the social as such. This is not to say that capital's socialization of labor is progressive in the older sense that a subject—the proletariat—has primacy and is guaranteed to win politically and achieve a felicitous outcome historically. Greater indebtedness, greater entanglement, and an enlarged view of what counts as social life guarantee neither victory nor happiness. Instead, the claim for an expansive social militates against the sense that there is a scarcity of political opportunity or that the dominance of capital translates simply into its triumph.

Multitude, or any other term for naming the generative force of the social, should be treated as a whole field of difference, the living legacy of what capital's virulent real subsumption produces. The creative capacity of this intricate mass lies not simply in other principles of rule or order but in the mobilization of difference at the discretion of what can be made of the very surplus capacity collected in such discretionary discharges of wealth as war and securities markets. When the markets head south, where the wars are most forcefully joined, not just destruction but the immediacy of what else wealth's expenditure might bring heaves into view. Perversely, under the sign of liberation and democracy, the Bush administration seeks to take credit for and contain this surplus of the social unleashed by intervention, just as it prepares to abandon what it had captured in a fit of indifference.

Apologists and critics of imperialism alike understand contemporary social movements as driven by and toward democracy. Electronic communication networks, global meetings of activists, or elections may indeed be practical instances of democracy that the world is demonstrably seeing more and more. At the same time, electronic surveillance, centralized decision making, and electoral corruption and cooptation suggest that it is the contesting of participation and decision-making that is expanding. A similar argument could be made with respect to socialism. It is not that more and more movements understand themselves as socialist, but that together they constitute a challenge to the discretion over dispensing wealth and organizing society. What is at stake is how the efficacy of global movements —both in their specific intervention and in their interconnection—is to be assessed and valued. Surely that value will be diminished if the politics of participation are traded off against the question of social wealth. Democracy and socialism name movements and histories but are also abstractions, evaluative criteria by which we can make sense of the politics in our midst.

We should be careful, therefore, not to present an overly literal characterization of how our theoretical means of valuing politics fit with the fact of their presence or persistence in the world. As capital's drives thicken interdependencies, as people are forced into new arrangements of cooperation and debt, the mounting complexities and contingencies that constitute life make for greater differentiation along mutually recognizable lines. Repertories for managing debt, supplementing the lives of adults and children with discretionary activities, and strategizing work enlarge the spheres of difference by which we live together. But a difference is forged that can have many actual political inflections and affiliations. For example, suburban sprawl enhances both the construction and credit industries at the same time that it makes strangers near and far more interlinked for the provision of food, fuel, or information and provides spatial sorting for racial, gendered, and socioeconomic divides.

These elaborate solidarities and fields of difference do not fix political tendencies or patterns of participation.[81] Both a functional and a figural privileging of specific movements can prescribe either the mediations or the aspirations of opportunities for action that can be joined. The functionalist account can assume that capital always knows what is good for it, missing the self-destruction that lies in what happens when, for instance, a speculative bubble is burst. The figural perspective can invite generalization from an image, site, or metaphor that may turn out to be genuinely exceptional. Torture in legally self-exempted military prison camps does disclose the heinous idea of rule that lies in the hearts of liberators. But the government has not been able to keep cases out of its own courts—where its record of defending its actions has been abysmal.[82]

Theoretical reflection is better suited to making more of mobilizations than they can, in their immediacy, make for themselves. It is easy to dismiss protest as unsuccessful tactically (in bringing an immediate end to the war) and ineffective strategically (in generating organizational capacities to assume governing powers or programmatic clarity in offering alternate societal designs). But such instrumental approaches to assessing what opposition produces miss what mass mobilizations make legible about the political present. It is the proliferation and not the scarcity of politics that makes a place for theory. A conceptual understanding bridges the valuing of the concrete particular to its contextualization so as to avoid divisive calls for unity that emerge when we assume that our politics are insufficient to the times. Still, the anti-imperial impulse has material and organization effects that are worth mapping. Antiwar events have been striking for their spatial dispersion and internal diversity. Most notable was the demonstration on 15 February 2003 that gathered millions across dozens of cities. Such demonstrations disclose a surplus of mobilization at a time when the military has had difficulty obtaining recruits. They challenge the privatizing mandates of the terror war and the discretionary aspects of the derivative war while adopting certain properties of leveraging and securitizing of their own. These dispersed demonstrations need to be assessed not simply in the causal terms of their success in bringing an immediate end to war, even if this is their immediate goal and occasion. They must also be appraised in terms of the mobilization they accomplish.

Like other large-scale demonstrations, anti-imperial marches provide a momentary occasion for a vast array of organizational entities (trade unions, community organizations, social service groups, etc.) to mingle with a more general and apparently unaffiliated opposition.[83] The packaging of small bundles for aggregate effect, the movement of movements, is well understood in the context of securitization. Like the assemblage of credit card debt or mortgages into exchangeable securities, the securitized demonstration has both an immediate instrumental occasion and a series of immeasurable social effects by which people are rendered mutually interdependent.

But these protests disclose global affinities to all those placed at risk by war and challenge imperial discretion when direct solidarities are not necessarily available (as with political opposition in Iraq, such as the Mahdi Army). The rallies demonstrate a global difference that securitization has visited upon us. Further, they do not await war but anticipate it, shaping and limiting how the subsequent war can be fought. The "Vietnam syndrome," the specter of quagmire, still haunts despite the revolution in military affairs, which is why thousands of smart bombs were launched to assure rapid dominance. In this regard, the American war against Vietnam signaled not simply a problem of troop deployment but the politicizing of military occupation at a global scale. The antiwar mobilizations caution against eternal war and compromise the political viability of mass mobilizations on behalf of the war machine. Further, the peace movement is an ongoing opposition to military might such that protests now precede war rather than forming in response to it.

The resistance to imperial war is already a mobilization for what else wealth might be, beyond an interest in private gain. Under the sign of war so much is assembled of human need and interest and the capacity to organize people around a collective will. The organizational capacities occasioned by war—whether for or against—suddenly become legible and public during a mass demonstration, so as to make all the surplus wealth expended in war appear contingent and discretionary rather than the natural outcome of intrinsic hostilities. The myriad constituencies that compose the demonstration bring a double consciousness. They are linked in opposition to the war (even if on different grounds) but at the same time remain dispersed by virtue of retaining their particular identities and banners that together compose an inventory of how the social surplus might be allocated. They march as a kind of alternative budget, with education, health care, day care, and dozens of better ideas of what to do with public money on display. Against the dulling literal-mindedness of the official electoral campaign, the political theater on offer speaks to a mass creativity, a mingling of performance and audience that momentarily frees political speech of the reductive terms of decision. The global marches linked to the Iraq war are a tiny body derived from a larger population that lives by and through the world's volatility.

Demonstrations do not stand in for the many; rather they make palpable the capacity to assemble across difference otherwise tacit in daily life. The presence of the demonstrations—however fleeting—needs to be set in relation to the nonpresence of polled opinion. The number that stands for the people in standard survey samples (500–2,000) is also subject to the volatility of the market. Consider, for example, just one opinion measure: those agreeing with the statement that "it was worth going to war," fell from 76 percent on 9 April 2003 to 44 percent on 9 May 2004 (vacillating as well at every point in between).[84] In this sliding (declining) polled support for war occupation, intervention is the attention-deficit-making effect of this culture of measurement. Despite a hastily declared conclusion to combat, occupation would become a kind of time bomb for public opinion. War success only sets into relief imperial failure. The scheme for self-managed colonialism abroad was also mismanaged at home. Supporting troops could not be reconciled with exposing them to risk. Hardly sedentary, the inability to orient a view of life through war is deeply embedded in the prosecution of force-transformed intervention. The idea that the war is won before it is joined undermines the steady state of support needed to continue to endorse a war without end. Planning as represented by the revolution in military affairs so as to avoid a sustained conflict winds up helping to make war unsustainable.

The revolution in military affairs was meant to cure the Vietnam syndrome of unsustainable imperial intervention by shortening the turnover time of war. Low contact, low casualties, low duration would replace the quagmire of escalating investment and slow accrual of interest with a self-liquidating intervention ever ready for the next opportunity. The success of force transformation would be carried over from the prosecution of derivative wars to the very public support that it sought to manage. What took nearly a decade in Vietnam was compressed to a year in Iraq. Opposition to war mobilized before the war began, and public support could not survive the transition from invasion to occupation. Casualties were collateralized, forming a kind of escrow account that would hold support in check. While damage to strategic military targets was minimized, the collateral damage came knocking at each Iraqi's door, turning the knob against occupation. For all the advertised distance of shock and awe, it was the dull intimacy of collateral damage to ways of life there and here that killed support. When support for the terror war is the measure of security, the staff of life, success is denied its sustainable moment. Intelligence failures generate security lapses. The utopian futurity of liberation, the promise that freedom waits for those willing to take the risk is mockingly profaned by an insistence upon measuring the occupation's success. Indicators of public support or effective reconstruction slide mercilessly downward.

In the economy of the new imperialism, war is central to sorting the risk-capable from those at risk. But war itself is too volatile to sustain itself or its vaunted sorting operation renders it unsustainable. The paradox of the derivative war is the extreme disjuncture between its aspirations to link all value, all difference to a single investment, and the severely particularistic and circumscribed conditions of the intervention as such. Afghanistan and Iraq are the proper names elided by the terror war, which denies even enemies their reference. The terror war allows intervention to remain indiscriminate, a blow to Iraq that can ripple everywhere. The creation of derivatives is a process by which the body of a commodity is sliced up to hedge risk, increase the turnover time of exchange, and expand collateral. Iraq cannot be repeated everywhere, but its collateral damage—planned but ultimately unconfinable—is to be felt as much abroad as at home.

Its two wars brought the isolation of Iraq to an end. In the twelve years between them Iraq was contained by low-intensity conflict, a guerilla war from the air. Intervention delocalized risk, bundling it back home as securitization is wont to do. Selling Iraq as an imperial accomplishment would make Americans feel safe again. But the failure to realize its value as an imperial asset would only make Americans feel at risk. Since Iraq was tapped to be the site of the next war no matter what, the urgency of waging war had to be manufactured if Iraq was to stand for the first strike in the interminable war. In practice, the only thing that turned out to be discretionary in the Iraq war was its timing: when to begin something that had already begun and end something that could not be stopped. Derivatives are instruments of asymmetry, and wars fought by their logic would enter volatility decisively only to make more of it. Domestically, on other topics, in other arenas, war disenchantment was readily displaced as a symptom of the economy. People were feeling too insecure about the jobless recovery to appreciate the feat pulled off by military forces. It was as if the mismanagement of Iraq's reconstruction was clouded by the disorienting effect of domestic tax cuts on laboring populations. Success was to hand, the economy was moving, there were profits to be made but no joy to be had. Imperial desire was missing its pleasure principle.

The preemptive empire of indifference consumes its own futurity, expending its assets in advance, delivering its promises before they are made, announcing its successes before its failures can catch up with it. Widespread death and destruction have long been part of the imperial repertoire, as has the callow impunity of price-gouging privateers contracted to supply reconstruction and the confidence that torture could yield truth. Yet there are signs of a massive indifference that marks a departure from prior imperial projects. Among these are the lack of expertise applied to imperial management, the selection of corrupt expatriates without local followings as proxies, the dismissal of government infrastructure tout court, the conviction that Iraq could be ruled as a system still far from reaching equilibrium, and a plotting of coordinates without history.[85] Liberation is far from a civilizing mission, self-managed colonialism a faint echo of its administrative forebears. Looting Iraq, stripping it of assets, refusing to count deaths, claiming billions for reconstruction that are never delivered are the disenchantments of risk management that are by now all too familiar. Freed from itself, Iraq was to be disenchanted. Liberation, for all its messianic promise, aimed at the reenchantment of a world profaned by self-management. Self-rule would be organized as supervised civil war, with a desire for order and a cynicism toward its possibilities.

Arbitrage, the opportunistic disposition to volatility, is the hinge on which the oscillation between neoliberal disenchantment and neoconservative reenchantment would totter. The arbitrageur is a kind of financial bricoleur, making events out of what can be found lying about. Wealth expands without any of the forward movement associated with growth and progress. Booms are nonexpansive and busts refuse to recover even as indices improve. What was once excluded, cast away as insufficiently promising for investment, can always be returned to with renewed interest. Iraq can be allowed to fester with minimal attention until the proper moment arises. Beating the market is all about timing.

Arbitrage, the exploitation of differences in the price of a good or commodity, shares its root with the arbitrary, the unmotivated quality of the sign, the context-driven association of image and concept by which linguistic value is achieved. The value of a commodity bears an equivalent structure to that of the sign. Economic value is made in the encounter of exchange for profit and the use of a material property realized in consumption, not an a priori attribute of the commodity in production. Value lies at the nexus between production for others and the practical activity occasioned by use.

In the geopolitical terms of imperialism, possession and dispossession of people from places, of productive capacities from specific sites, leaves behind a social will where production and consumption have been joined. The landless occupy land held in escrow. The jobless demand not simply work but a share of the social surplus. The invaded demand not simply self-determination but self-development. The landless, the jobless, and the occupied forcibly bring people together and produce not simply demands for participation but ways of making use of being together. Hence empire's unmaking of worlds returns in the form of sheer sociality, production in the service of societal possibility. The opposition to empire asserts other prospects for social wealth (demands until now unmet for development aid) and social cooperation (real flows of persons to projects). The terror against which empire forms itself becomes a means that makes known the secret of war. Rather than unnameable, shadowy networks, war is prosecuted against the very idea of society. As the rule over foreign and domestic spaces is modeled on war, local opposition raises similar stakes. Protests out the secret: war is the thought that society is impossible. Instead, society lurks at every opportunity.

What exactly accounts for this dynamic of accumulation-driven and reactive indifference? Why do the forces of difference so persistently abandoned in the march to wealth return bearing a social wealth of their own? As has been noted, one residue of Marxist considerations of imperialism was the notion that capital accumulation had a progressive aspect. Much ink was spilled seeking to understand progress in the double sense of fulfilling the interest of capital and expanding the means for social development. Ultimately, progress entailed creating a heroic historical actor, the proletariat, whose very preponderance and interest would assure that history took the proper course toward its glorious end. The interest of capital and labor mirrored one another. They were singular, knowable in advance, readily translatable into clear, unified courses of action. But history proved an uncooperative partner to this conception of interest-driven progress, both for capital and for labor. Interest tends to betray itself. Cutting wages and taxes drives companies out of business as much as it generates new wealth. Grabbing land for oil or water or imposing price controls sets rebellions in motion and can destabilize prices. The mass of labor can increase but so can its internal divisions along lines of race, nationality, gender, and age.

Is there something progressive to the movement of capital beyond there being ever more of it? If so, any idea of progress would need to be qualified as arising in the shuttling between the dispossession that David Harvey described and the repossession that Marx understood as mutual interdependence, or socialization.[86] What is progressive for capital is its intensive reach into forms of life possession, its extensive grasp of what is taken over or dispossessed, its clawing into the fabrics that bundle people together in order to open up new markets. There is today demonstrably more interconnection, more intricate association in the world. Rather than being reduced to a struggle for bare life, struggle for existence poses elaborate prospects for how we might live together. There is recognition that race, gender, sexuality, religion, ecology, and nationality cannot be reduced or sacrificed to one another. That is surely a more complex elaboration of the political than has been available hitherto—an embrace of this whole field of difference and a treasuring of the value in being able to expand the field, a sociophilia to combat indifference's sociophobia. Not only is life subsumed but production is expanded in this process. The progress of the social is admittedly far more difficult to measure, but at the very least its value can be established.

The accumulation at a global scale to which imperialism is the means is the elaboration of capital through particular social forms that assumes the boundaries of race, nation, gender, sexuality, socioeconomic stratum, urbanism, and religiosity—in short what can be taken as the material forms that momentarily appear as the bounded units of social life. Socialization (of which securitization is but the most recent tendency) bundles and unbundles productivities, assembling and dismantling the boundaries around which various histories of difference affiliate and clash. To say that imperialism is now animated by financialization says more than that finance is once again prominent in the passage from one imperium to another, as Arrighi's *Long Twentieth Century* so sweepingly suggested.[87] With each turn, finance conquers new social horizons, enclosing in its turn geography, labor, and culture. The expansion of territory to capture raw materials, the subsumption of populations to intensified regimes of labor, colonizing the future so as to make risk productive—each addresses historically novel problems of accumulation that have presented themselves from the fifteenth century to the present.

Finance now moves into the personal; it possesses labor as well as capital, it becomes a practical feature of life—establishing a moral code for the household, integrating it with work, incorporating the future into the present. Effacing the foreign and domestic, finance invites those who can to live by the protocols of risk and those who cannot to accept themselves as beings at risk. At the same time, financialization demands labor for running its apparatuses, whether in the form of investment clubs whose members do their own research, self-help recipes to keep money in motion, or defined-contribution pensions and other schemes that have labor doing the work of finance as well as the work of securing the future which once belonged to the state.[88] For capital, financialization is delocalizing—it bundles and repackages debt for global marketing and reparticularizes those packages in an elaborate array of possibilities, but whose most searing expression is captured by the term "derivative."

Financialization emerges at the nexus of the socialization of capital and the socialization of labor. Set into global terms, the American power that has arisen under the sign of financialization does to the national form what was done to the domestic sphere. Neither the nation nor its domesticity disappears—rather they become a scene of risk by means of an effacement of a foundational binary, what bounded and divided inside and outside. In the terms employed here securitization effaces the isolationist-interventionist binary, as the national interest is divested of its stability and war pulls it both away and into the world. If the domestic is violated, colonized, terrorized by risk, isolation will be a recurrent desire but also an achievable state. Similarly, if intervention pursues risk it will need to withdraw as soon as the volatile opportunity dissipates. By this light, intervention will be recurrent and unsustainable.

The derivative names the formal process that effaces the national-global binary, insofar as the state acts to generate privatizing zones and regions at home and abroad. Contracts for security or supply of material, or for reconstruction or foreign-government services, will be forged that carve out some piece of the national body (in this case a sliver of the Iraqi population that is invited to participate in this speculative investment) and then destabilize that body. The rest of the population is destabilized either by corruption or by the inability to succeed at its assigned task, thereby jeopardizing the good American name borne by occupation. Surely this is also true of the military personnel who form the coalition of the willing— those who perform their duties without appropriate equipment like armor for their bodies and vehicles, or without a strategy for occupation, reconstruction, or exit, or a means to integrate various national forces, all shortcomings that have made the coalition itself so unstable. The military itself is parsed between the Special Forces, handsomely rewarded with incentives to stay on, and the general infantry, who cannot be drawn in sufficient numbers from the general population. The various derivatives divide the nation between support for the troops and for country, between a warring way that affirms the nation and one that tears it asunder. Support for the troops yields a concern to bring them home; defense of the nation generates worry that it not be overexposed to risk. The military's own concerns about politicizing the procurement process on the eve of war come back as real problems of corruption in procurement and the jeopardizing of force levels (through new recruitment and retention). There is no route into war that does not generate its own derived opposition. Other applications of the derivative are still more insidious to the national/global. Hedging against the dollar while living by it (as the dollar has declined against other major currencies since the occupation) can weaken the national position while enlarging the gap between dollar-denominated exports and escalating imports from other nations.

These scenes of risk rebinarize the biopolitical wars of race, so that population is recleaved in the register of capital. Financial securities are made of retirements and homes—literally the future and domestic spaces as well as the medical bills and loans that constitute what we know of life. The internal divide between subrace and superrace now is organized between the blanched public figures for whom race makes no difference, or who have redeemed themselves from race, and the racializing apparatus of terror. The war on terror allows nations and populations to be marked with the occult motives and shadowy intention that have long characterized racial loathing. But terror is also a method, an operation, a cunning calculus, a risk embrace. In this the war on terror channels the anxieties of financial reason gone awry onto categories that look racial or biopolitical. To mark a population as terrorist is to racialize it as the bad other or object of risk—risks to freedom, liberty, ways of life, and identity. It is the calculus of risk that translates the biopolitical into the machinery of capital accumulation. Translation assumes that there was some prior biopolitical marking. The indecipherable utterances of an inscrutable bin Laden, the hooded torture victims of Abu Ghraib, the savaged Saddam cowering in his cave are very much offerings of racialized bodies. Further, that the torture is emasculating references a potent trope of the racial other as a sexual menace.[89] The menace is calibrated to an assessment of forward deterrence, the intimations of pleasure in beating the accused terrorist to the punch.

Military intervention rebrands the nation—an evangelical Americanization without history—forced now to realize itself in the disjoint opportunities of fleeting victory amid a lost calculus of gain. The derivative war is an instrument of volatility that regionalizes national spaces without being able to maintain the boundaries around its fresh kills. Empire flares around new rivalries, promising freedom but leaving alone the question of development. America bothers Iraq and Afghanistan so as to leave them alone, just as it would hold and release—without apparent cause or reason—those uneasy within the vigilance of homeland. Risk destabilizes its own boundaries. It undermines the solidity of threat so as to overcome its internal opposite of being at risk by submitting to measurement or furthering organization.[90] Imperial intervention seeks to isolate risk but winds up organizing populations. Since those populations are to be found already in a state of war, the issue they confront is not how they would come to politics but how they would come to value and evaluate an already politicized situation.

If there is a political crisis of the present, it does not lie in the scarcity of mobilization or the sufficiency of politics to the scope of domination. The extremities of war across the tattered divide that once separated foreign and domestic landscapes disburse the political excessively. The skepticism toward such politics as we have is a problem of theory to which a certain excessiveness is always ascribed but which in actuality is always marked by scarcity, as explanation falls short of accounting for all that is possible in our midst. The present celebration of empire that is hostile to theorizing its own deficits also returns theoretical consideration to the political scene. So many reasons in search of an explanation. Reason chasing interest. Appeals to figuration when calculations can't add up. The apology for empire winds up imagining the society that it would flee—one with insufficient will and excessive culture, where some risks are left untaken while others are pursued to incalculable gain. When war is the ultimate expression of sovereign exception—who can live and who must die—it becomes possible to treat the power of decision as its own productivity.

Those "at risk" do not simply die or only suffer social death—although they may be subjected to death, they are also mined, managed, and materialized as a factor of production, just as Marx imagined for surplus populations that allow new social productivities to form. Public requisites are reprivatized, as Lisa Duggan has noted in the case of constitutional pushes for marriage (whether these be gay or straight).[91] Shifting boundaries do not simply sunder old norms: they occasion fresh demands for normative obedience. Populations are both desocialized labor (through capital abandonment, state violence, immigrants without destination) and the basis for further socialization (how are the people assembled, for what ends, to solve which problems?). As social principles displayed in the products and mechanisms of finance, securitization and derivatives are volatile but also fickle about their own delineations and boundaries. Bundling and parsing, assembling and dissembling, capital moves constantly propose and reconfigure the social body that population takes on as its own ends. What will enable accumulation one moment will be jettisoned the next. That detritus can be picked up and recycled as the most profitable junk bonds. The shadowy terrorist and the imminently at-risk share this prospect of suddenly being made productive again. Population stands for that surplus difference that capital makes its noisy neighbor. The empire of indifference speaks to the queasy mix of endless ambition and limited means, in which capital's ability to imagine its future is stymied by arbitrage as the social imaginary is exploding all around.

Mobility has these principles and refinements of assemblage as its ends, precisely at the moment when the instrumentality of labor is denied. Against the state of exception that comes from sovereignty's focus on rule, we are wise to adopt the perspective of socialization, accumulation, population. Each of these terms generates a kind of excess, but only from all three can a genuine surplus be derived. Rule would seem to forever favor the rulers. When even the state is approached from the productivities that it embraces and avoids, the surpluses of sociality that it resists, and the lost wealth that it pursues, then the challenge to war which now consistently precedes warfare is magnified beyond those who might assemble.

Each assemblage presents to its own body of difference an assortment of possibilities for the future available now. The protest against the war affirmatively displays all that might attach to the same disbursement of social wealth. While protestors enter willingly into a category of the at-risk (whether they are arrested and criminalized or simply demonized as unpatriotic), they simultaneously oppose the domestic war with a different narrative of what mass mobilization can yield that violates the secrets of the imperial unconscious. The desire for dominance, the vast scene of the global that exceeds the grasp of anyone, is confronted with a counternarrative and an oppositional will. Life has been politicized to the point where it is dense with apparatuses and assemblages. What now lies beyond life is not death but the infinitude of the social, a socialism after socialization. This is no longer a prospect to which we can remain indifferent.

Notes ⚭

INTRODUCTION

1 Among the features of the concept of globalization is the difficulty of containing it within anything like a literature or discipline, as the attention paid to it has produced something of a riot across the humanities and social sciences without the benefit of clear intellectual or philosophical foundations. Nonetheless, quite interesting commentary can be found in Fredric Jameson and Masao Miyoshi, eds., *The Cultures of Globalization* (Durham: Duke University Press, 1998). Jameson notes in the collection that when seen by the lights of globalization, imperialism appears to be equally an old formula and an eccentric one, especially given the intimate articulation of culture and economy. William K. Tabb has expressed the concern that globalization would distract from the larger critique of capital, and that it should be understood as the "imperialism of finance," itself a comment on the amnesia accounting for a failure to recognize the earlier imperialism as exactly that. See William K. Tabb, "Globalization Is *an* Issue; The Power of Capital Is *the* Issue," *Monthly Review* 49, no. 2 (June 1997); and William K. Tabb, *The Amoral Elephant: Globalization and the Struggle for Social Justice in the Twenty-first Century* (New York: Monthly Review, 2002), especially chapter 4, "Globalization as the Imperialism of Finance."

2 The popular formulation of a flattened world is Thomas Friedman's. Even he acknowledges factors that make for an "unflat world" and sees himself as a technological determinist but not a historical determinist. The mechanisms of homogenization will spread, but there is no guarantee of their use. Thomas Friedman, *The World Is Flat* (New York: Farrar, Straus and Giroux, 2005), 374. Carl Boggs states that globalization theorists ignore the expansion of American power and militarism on the premise that the nation-state has become obsolete. See Carl Boggs, *Imperial Delusions: American Militarism and Endless War* (Lanham, Md.: Rowman and Littlefield, 2005). For more nuanced reflections on the relation between globalization and violence see Arjun Appadurai, ed., *Globalization* (Durham: Duke University Press, 2001), which explores the relationship between new forms of sovereignty and internal violence, as well as Appadurai's own recent study *Fear of Small Numbers: An Essay on the Geography of Anger* (Durham: Duke University Press, 2006), and Lisa Lowe and David Lloyd, eds., *The Politics of Culture in the Shadow of Capital* (Durham: Duke University Press, 1997), which complicates the binaries of global/local and economy/culture. Jan Nederveen Pieterse examines the conceptual and political stakes of framing the world in terms of globalization or empire. He treats empire as but a moment of globalization, and observes, "In promoting the interests of American corporations worldwide, the United States actively promotes globalization yet it views the risks this entails only from the standpoint of national interest." See his *Globalization or Empire?* (New York: Routlege, 2004), 80.

3 This is not to say that the economic views tending to inform mainstream representations have been univariate. Books presented as defining the poles of debate share much by way of assumptions, especially in linking globalizing markets and democracy. See for example Alfred Stiglitz, *Globalization and Its Discontents* (New York: W. W. Norton, 2003); Jadish Bhagwati, *In Defense of Globalization* (New York: Oxford University Press, 2004); and Martin Wolf, *Why Globalization Works* (New Haven: Yale University Press, 2004).

4 Rudolf Hilferding, *Finance Capital: A Study of the Latest Phase of Capitalist Development* (London: Routledge and Kegan Paul, 1985), 335. Hilferding completed most of the work on the manuscript in 1906 and the book was first published in 1910, as Tom Bottomore recounts in his introduction (5).

5 Nikolai Bukharin, *Imperialism and World Economy* (New York: International, 1929).

6 V. I. Lenin, *Imperialism, The Highest Stage of Capitalism: A Popular Outline* (New York: International, 1969). Rosa Luxemburg, who examined the creation of an agrarian hinterland as a means to resolve a crisis of underconsumption where insufficient buyers exist for metropolitan goods, also forms part of this classical tradition. Her discussion of an outside to accumulation becomes more interesting today in light of a lack of interest on the part of imperial powers in growth on the periphery. See Rosa Luxemburg, *The Accumulation of Capital* (New York: Monthly Review, 1964).

7 The argument that the United States was in its foundation an imperial project is made by Richard W. Van Alstyne, *The Rising American Empire* (New York: W. W. Norton, 1974). Neil Smith tracks the turns in geopolitical domination that take place during the twentieth century in terms of the rise and fall of liberalism in his *American Empire: Roosevelt's Geographer and the Prelude to Globalization* (Berkeley: University of California Press, 2003). The religious inflection of American expansionism is incisively analyzed in Anders Stephanson, *Manifest Destiny: American Expansion and the Empire of Right* (New York: Hill and Wang, 1995). Stephanson suggests a longer arc to the evangelical impulse's sense of time. "Divine omnipotence notwithstanding, apocalyptic expectation is thus a call for serried *intervention in the here and now*" (10).

8 The sheer venality of Bush's and Cheney's world is amply documented in Mark Crispin Miller's *Cruel and Unusual: Bush/Cheney's New World Order* (New York: W. W. Norton, 2004).

9 Synoptically it could be said that this critical engagement of Marx and Saussure is the basis of poststructuralism. Interesting markers could be found in Ferrucio Rossi-Landi, *Language as Work and Trade: A Semiotic Homology for Linguistics and Economics* (South Hadley, Mass.: Bergin and Garvey, 1983); and Gayatri Chakravorty Spivak, "Scattered Speculations on the Question of Value," *In Other Worlds: Essays in Cultural Politics* (New York: Routledge, 1988), 154–75.

10 Giovanni Arrighi, *The Long Twentieth Century: Money, Power and the Origins of Our Times* (London: Verso, 1994).

11 For some examples see Bertell Ollman, *Dance of the Dialectic: Steps in Marx's Method* (Urbana: University of Illinois Press, 2003); Kevin Brien, *Marx, Reason, and the Art of Freedom* (Philadelphia: Temple University Press, 1987); G. A. Cohen, *History, Labor and Freedom: Themes From Marx* (New York: Oxford University Press, 1988); Arun Bose, *Marx on Exploitation and Inequality: An Essay in Marxian Analytical Economics* (Delhi: Oxford University Press, 1980); Edward Martin and Rodolfo D. Torres, *Savage State: Welfare Capitalism and Inequality* (Lanham, Md.: Rowman and Littlefield, 2004).

12 See Michael E. Brown, *The Production of Society: A Marxian Foundation for Social Theory* (Totowa, N.J.: Allen and Littlefield, 1986). Brown reads Marx's three volumes of *Capital* for their account of "the society of producers," the generative principle of labor that is immanent to capitalist production.

13 "On Top of the World: In Its Taste for Risk, the World's Leading Investment Bank Epitomizes the Modern Financial System," *Economist*, 29 April 2006, 11–12.

14 See Erik Eckholm, "Rethinking Occupation: Grand US Plan Fractures Again," *New York Times*, 17 April 2005, §A, 24. The article notes that the "Bush administration has redrafted its project to rebuild Iraq" for the third time in nine months and that $4.8 billion of the $18.4 billion approved by Congress is being redirected to security costs.

15 James Glanz, "Former US Official in Iraq to Plead Guilty to Corruption," *New York Times*, 1 February 2006, §A, 1.

16 See the book assembled by the collective Retort, *Afflicted Powers: Capital and Spectacle in a New Age of War* (New York: Verso, 2005), especially chapter 2, "Blood for Oil?"

17 For a synoptic discussion of this thesis see Neil Smith, *The Endgame of Globalization* (New York: Routledge, 2005).

18 The endemic aspect of a kind of contempt of knowledge is documented in Seymour M. Hersh's *Chain of Command: The Road from 9/11 to Abu Ghraib* (New York: Harper Collins, 2004).

CHAPTER 1 : FROM SECURITY TO SECURITIZATION

1 The historical shifts in the meanings of the words "investment" and "security" are traced in the *Oxford English Dictionary*.

2 Marieke de Goode, *Virtue, Fortune and Faith: A Genealogy of Finance* (Minneapolis: University of Minnesota Press, 2005).

3 This is the definition given by Bruce Schneier, *Beyond Fear: Thinking Sensibly about Security in an Uncertain World* (New York: Copernicus, 2003), 11. Schneier applies a utilitarian logic to speak of security "tradeoffs" in which rational calculation comes to define both what security is and its management.

4 For a succinct account see Leon T. Kendall and Michael J. Fishman, eds., *A Primer on Securitization* (Cambridge: MIT Press, 1996), especially chapter 1, Leon T. Kendall, "Securitization: A New Era in American Finance," 1–16.

5 The key work here is Giovanni Arrighi, *The Long Twentieth Century: Money, Power, and the Origins of Our Times* (London: Verso, 1994).

6 Wendy Brown, "Neo-liberalism and the End of Liberal Democracy," *Theory and Event* 7, no. 1 (2003), para. 38.

7 Ibid., para. 9.

8 Doug Henwood, "Neoliberalism, RIP?," *Left Business Observer* 106 (24 January 2004): 1. Henwood here is defining neoliberalism in terms of economic policy: fiscal discipline, flat taxes, financial deregulation, free trade, privatization.

9 This dialectic of object-subject, reason-unreason, cognitive-somatic as constitutive of the whole ensemble of practices that finance calls to order is developed in my previous book, *Financialization of Daily Life* (Philadelphia: Temple University Press, 2002).

10 Joyce Oldham Appleby, *Economic Thought and Ideology in Seventeenth Century England* (Princeton: Princeton University Press, 1978), 52.

11 Michael J. Shapiro, *Reading "Adam Smith": Desire, History, and Value* (Lanham, Md.: Rowman and Littlefield, 2002), xxxi. Shapiro has done extensive work on the philosophical elaboration of how meaning relates to value, moral economy to political economy. See also Michael J. Shapiro, *For Moral Ambiguity: National Culture and the Politics of the Family* (Minneapolis: University of Minnesota Press, 2001); David Campbell and Michael J. Shapiro, eds., *Moral Spaces: Rethinking Ethics and World Politics* (Minneapolis: University of Minnesota Press, 1999); and Jane Bennett and Michael J. Shapiro, eds., *The Politics of Moralizing* (New York: Routledge, 2002).

12 This point has been argued by Andrew Sayer in a paper entitled "Moral

Economy," http://www.comp.lancs.ac.uk/sociology/papers/sayer moral economy.pdf, visited January 2005.

13 Goux establishes this general condition through a reading of André Gide's "radical subject" in his novel *The Counterfeiters* (1925). Jean-Joseph Goux, *The Coiners of Language* (Norman: University of Oklahoma Press, 1994), 32.

14 For a survey of these recent changes in financial structures and monetary geographies see Robert Solomon, *Money on the Move: The Revolution in International Finance since 1980* (Princeton: Princeton University Press, 1999), and Benjamin J. Cohen, *The Geography of Money* (Ithaca: Cornell University Press, 1998).

15 For an accessible account of the impact of finance's ascent on the world, and specific figures on the circulation of financial capital, see William Greider, *One World, Ready or Not: The Manic Logic of Global Capitalism* (New York: Simon and Schuster, 1997), especially 21–24.

16 For various accounts of Pax Americana see Giovanni Arrighi and Beverly Silver, *Chaos and Governance in the Modern World System* (Minneapolis: University of Minnesota Press, 1999); Michael A. Bernstein and David E. Adler, *Understanding American Economic Decline* (Cambridge: Cambridge University Press, 1994); and Michael J. Webber and David L. Rigby, *The Golden Age Illusion: Rethinking Postwar Capitalism* (New York: Guilford, 1996).

17 For useful discussions on this topic see the essays collected by David C. Engerman et al., *Staging Growth: Modernization, Development, and the Global Cold War* (Amherst: University of Massachusetts Press, 2003).

18 Charles R. Geisst, *Visionary Capitalism: Financial Markets and the American Dream in the Twentieth Century* (New York: Praeger, 1990), 144.

19 Joseph Nocera, *A Piece of the Action: How the Middle Class Joined the Money Class* (New York: Simon and Schuster, 1994).

20 Ibid., 148–49.

21 On the emergence of these new regulatory frameworks see Cynthia Glassman, James L. Pierce, Roberta S. Karmel, and John J. La Falce, *Regulating the New Financial Services Industry* (Washington: Center for National Policy Press, 1988), and Clifford E. Kirsch, ed., *The Financial Services Revolution: Understanding the Changing Role of Banks, Mutual Funds, and Insurance Companies* (Chicago: Irwin Professional, 1997).

22 Richard Duncan, *The Dollar Crisis: Causes, Consequences, Cures* (Singapore: John Wiley and Sons, 2003), 21. Duncan's perspective is that the system disequilibrium will lead, if left unchecked, to the dollar's collapse.

23 Robert Guttmann, *How Credit Money Shapes the Economy: The United States in a Global System* (Armonk, N.Y.: M. E. Sharpe, 1994), 226.

24 Ibid., 236.

25 Ibid., 7.

26 See Philip Mirowski, *The Effortless Economy of Science?* (Durham: Duke University Press, 2004).

27 Two reviews of the state of organizational sociology written nearly thirty years apart by W. Richard Scott are especially instructive in marking these shifts. See "Organizational Structure," *Annual Review of Sociology 1975*; and "Reflections on a Half-Century of Organizational Sociology," *Annual Review of Sociology 2004*.

28 Duncan, *The Dollar Crisis*, viii.

29 The term is from Chalmers Johnson's *Blowback: The Costs and Consequences of American Empire* (New York: Metropolitan, 2000).

30 Edward LiPuma and Benjamin Lee, *Financial Derivatives and the Globalization of Risk* (Durham: Duke University Press, 2004), 173.

31 P. Vijaya Bhaskar and B. Mahapatra, *Derivatives Simplified: An Introduction to Risk Management* (New Delhi: Response, 2003), 11.

32 Ibid., 12; "On Top of the World: In Its Taste for Risk, the World's Leading Investment Bank Epitomizes the Modern Financial System," *Economist*, 29 April 2006, 11.

33 Michael Hudson, *Merchants of Misery: How Corporate America Profits from Poverty* (Monroe, Minn.: Common Courage, 1996), 12.

34 On micro-credit see Aminur Rahman, *Women and Microcredit in Rural Bangladesh: Anthropological Study of the Rhetoric and Realities of Grameen Bank Lending* (Boulder: Westview, 1999), and Maria Otero and Elisabeth Rhyne, *The New World of Microenterprise Finance: Building Financial Institutions for the Poor* (West Hartford: Kumarian, 1994); and on the Microcredit Summit Campaign see http://www.microcreditsummit.org/.

35 Otero and Rhyne, *The New World of Microenterprise Finance*, 145.

36 Paul W. Feeney, *Securitization: Redefining the Bank* (New York: St. Martin's, 1995), 20.

37 Geisst, *Visionary Capitalism*, 144.

38 Robert Guttmann, *Cybercash: The Coming Era of Electronic Money* (New York: Palgrave Macmillan, 2003), 40.

39 See Robin Blackburn, *Banking on Death; or, Investing in Life: The History and Future of Pensions* (London: Verso, 2002), 107.

40 See Roger Lowenstein, *The Origins of the Crash: The Great Bubble and Its Undoing* (New York: Penguin, 2004), for the transformation in financial culture on either end of the boom.

41 This argument is made by Andrew A. Samwick and Jonathan Skinner, "How Will Defined Contribution Pension Plans Affect Retirement Income?," NBER Working Paper no. 6645, July 1998, JEL nos. J32, J14, D31. Figures cited from page 3. For a recent synopsis of these changes see Mary Williams Walsh, "More Companies Ending Promises for Retirement," *New York Times*, 9 January 2006, §A, 1. Data are collected by the Employee Benefit Research Institute, accessible online at www.ebri.org.

42   Blackburn's is undoubtedly the most exhaustive left treatment of the pension question. Blackburn contrasts his views with those of the business consultant and writer Drucker. Blackburn, *Banking on Death*, 12–13. For an argument on the inextricability of public and private social insurance functions see Nicholas Barr, *The Welfare State as Piggy Bank: Information, Risk, Uncertainty, and the Role of the State* (Oxford: Oxford University Press, 2001).

43   Home ownership also articulates with other normative categories. Native citizens are more than twice as likely to own as noncitizens (70.3 percent versus 34.9 percent) and married-couple families have twice the ownership rates of "two or more person non-family households" (86.3 percent versus 42 percent). U.S. Census Bureau Current Housing Reports, *Moving to America, Moving to Homeownership: 1994 to 2002* (H121/03-1).

44   In 1983 the National Commission on Excellence in Education published *A Nation at Risk: The Imperative for Educational Reform: A Report to the Nation and the Secretary of Education, United States Department of Education* (Washington: U.S. Government Printing Office, 1983). Twenty years later the question still frames educational policy discussions. See for example David T. Gordon, ed., *A Nation Reformed? American Education 20 Years after "A Nation at Risk"* (Cambridge: Harvard Education Press, 2003).

45   For a summary of the law and its applications see www.ricoact.com, visited 12 April 2005. Of particular interest is the manner in which the object of prosecution is rendered transitive by the law, under the rubric of association-in-fact enterprises:

> Association-in-fact enterprises are probably the must useful and abundant forms of RICO enterprises, but they are also the most difficult to grasp on an analytical level. When Congress passed the RICO Act, the phrase "association-in-fact" enterprise was probably intended to apply directly to the Mafia, because a Mafia family is not a formal legal entity nor is it an individual, rather it is a "union or group of individuals associated in fact although not a legal entity." *Id.* Corporate parents and their subsidiaries allegedly engaged in criminal activities have also been named as association-in-fact enterprises. Most courts will accept any informal group as an association-in-fact enterprise so long as the group possesses three characteristics: (a) some continuity of structure and personnel; (b) a common or shared purpose; and (c) an ascertainable structure distinct from that inherent in the pattern of racketeering.

http://www.ricoact.com/ricoact/nutshell.asp#constitutes. Libertarians were also quick to point out the continuities. See for example Lee Shelton IV and James Hall, "Patriot Act: Another RICO?," *Enter Stage Right*, 4 February 2002, http://www.enterstageright.com/archive/articles/0202/0202patriot.htm, visited 12 April 2005.

46 This point was made by Richard Doyle at his keynote presentation for the Security Bytes Conference in Lancaster, England, July 2004.

47 While each of these wars represented distinct policy initiatives or defunding protocols, they represented not only a dismantling of welfare entitlements but a sorting of population based upon capacities for risk management. On the dismantling of the social compact see Frances Fox Piven and Richard A. Cloward, *The Breaking of the American Social Compact* (New York: Free Press, 1997). For critical views on the various domestic risk wars see James A. Inciardi, *The War on Drugs III: The Continuing Saga of the Mysteries and Miseries of Intoxication, Addiction, Crime, and Public Policy* (Boston: Allyn and Bacon, 2002); Claire Bond Potter, *War on Crime: Bandits, G-men, and the Politics of Mass Culture* (New Brunswick, N.J.: Rutgers University Press, 1998); Randy Albelda and Nancy Folbre, *The War on the Poor: A Defense Manual* (New York: New Press, 1996); Brigitte Berger and Peter L. Berger, *The War over the Family: Capturing the Middle Ground* (Garden City, N.Y.: Anchor/Doubleday, 1983); Richard Bolton, ed., *Culture Wars: Documents from the Recent Controversies in the Arts* (New York: New Press: 1992).

48 See Mike Males, *The Scapegoat Generation* (Monroe, Maine: Common Courage, 1996), his *Framing Youth: Ten Myths about the Next Generation* (Monroe: Common Courage, 1999), and more recently, Henry Giroux, *The Abandoned Generation: Democracy beyond the Culture of Fear* (New York: Palgrave, 2003), and Lawrence Grossberg, *Caught in the Crossfire: Kids, Politics and America's Future* (Boulder: Paradigm, 2005).

49 Specifically, this form of moral panic is tied to the political backlash which produced Thatcher and then Reagan in Stuart Hall et al., *Policing the Crisis: Mugging, the State, and Law and Order* (New York: Holmes and Meier, 1978).

50 The figure of $17 trillion is taken from Elizabeth Rives, ed., *Powering the Global Economy: Securities Industry Briefing Book* (2001), http://www.sia.com/publications/html/briefing_book.html.

51 Included in this spectrum are Alan Greenspan; Robert Schiller, who wrote the book *Irrational Exuberance* (Princeton: Princeton University Press, 2000); Robert Brenner, *The Boom and the Bubble* (New York: Verso, 2002); and Doug Henwood, *After the New Economy* (New York: New Press, 2003).

52 Robert Guttmann, *Cybercash: The Coming Era of Electronic Money*, 40.

53 This is Robert Brenner's finding in his most recent examination of the bubble and its aftermath, "New Boom or New Bubble? The Trajectory of the U.S. Economy," *New Left Review* 25 (January–February 2004): 57–100.

54 Robert Pollin, *Contours of Descent: U.S. Economic Fractures and the Landscape of Global Austerity* (New York: Verso, 2003), 28.

55 George W. Bush, *2003 Economic Report of the President, Together with the Annual Report of the Council of Economic Advisors* (Washington: U.S. Government Printing Office, 2003).

56 Ibid., 4.

57 For an account of the loss of dream-driving discretionary income to increased housing and educational costs and attendant fixed debt see Elizabeth Warren and Amelia Tyagi, *The Two-Income Trap: Why Middle-Class Mothers and Fathers Are Going Broke* (New York: Basic, 2003). Dream blight affects the very imagination of upward mobility for those at the lower end of the wage scale. For illustrations see David Shipler, *The Working Poor: Invisible in America* (New York: Alfred A. Knopf, 2004), Barbara Ehrenreich, *Nickel and Dimed: On Not Getting By in America* (New York: Henry Holt, 2002), and Beth Shulman, *The Betrayal of Work: How Low Wage Jobs Fail 35 Million Americans* (New York: New Press, 2003).

58 For a look at the industry see David S. Evans and Richard Schmalensee, *Paying with Plastic: The Digital Revolution in Buying and Selling*, 2d ed. (Cambridge: MIT Press, 2005).

59 All figures taken from "Credit Card Debt in America," MSN Money (CNBC), http://moneycentral.msn.com/content/SavingandDebt/p70581.asp?special=0401debt, visited 7 January 2004.

60 Jacob S. Hacker, "Call It the Family Risk Factor," *New York Times*, 11 January 2004, §4, 15.

61 Michael J. Mandel, *The High Risk Society: Peril and Promise in the New Economy* (New York: Random House, 1996). Mandel is but one of the acolytes of risk. For a fuller discussion see my *Financialization of Daily Life* (Philadelphia: Temple University Press, 2002).

62 Michael Perelman, *The Pathology of the U.S. Economy Revisited: The Intractable Contradictions of Economic Policy* (New York: Palgrave, 2002), 143.

63 Risk tolerance, from this perspective, is a freely selected subjective state. As the retirement manager for college teachers put it, "Once you select your savings product(s), the level of investment risk you're willing to accept will be entirely up to you." The pension administrators proceed to offer a series of "calculators" by which you can translate these inchoate sentiments into hard numbers. http://www.tiaa-cref.org/pubs/html/financial_organizer/section_2b.html, visited 26 February 2004.

64 Recent trends in political geography that problematize the inside-outside dichotomy of the national state can be found in Neil Brenner, Bob Jessop, Martin Jones, and Gordon Macleod, eds., *State/Space* (Malden, Mass.: Blackwell, 2003).

65 Albert Hirschman, *The Passions and the Interests: Political Arguments for Capitalism before Its Triumph* (Princeton: Princeton University Press, 1977), 32.

66 Hans J. Morgenthau and Kenneth W. Thompson, *Politics among Nations: The Struggle for Power and Peace*, 6th ed. (New York: McGraw-Hill, 1985 [1948]), 10.

67 Michael G. Roskin, *National Interest: From Abstraction to Strategy*, Report prepared for the U.S. Army War College, 20 May 1994 (Carlisle Barracks, Penn.: Strategic Studies Institute, U.S. Army War College), http://purl.access. gpo.gov/GPO/LPS24653, visited 14 January 2004.

68 Charles A. Kupchan, *The End of the American Era: U.S. Foreign Policy and the Geopolitics of the Twenty-first Century* (New York: Vintage, 2003), 36. Based on a claim that history is "distinctively progressive and evolutionary" (304), Kupchan argues that we are in transition to a new digital age. The transition is a unipolar one that causes internal strife for the United States, but harmony will be restored through the emergence of a new global rivalry that produces the next grand strategy.

69 Benno Teschke, *The Myth of 1648: Class, Geopolitics, and the Making of Modern International Relations* (London: Verso, 2003), 274. Teschke's argument is that international relations emerge from property relations and that domestic and international are mutually determinate.

70 D. Robert Worley, "Waging Ancient War: Limits on Preemptive Force," Strategic Studies Institute, U.S. Army War College (February 2003), http://carlisle-www.army.mil/ssi/pubs/2003/ancient/ancient.pdf, visited December 2003.

71 Robert J. Art, *A Grand Strategy for America* (Ithaca: Cornell University Press, 2003), 5.

72 Ibid., 10.

73 Ibid., 7.

74 George W. Bush, speech and national security statement, 17 September 2002.

75 Harry Harootunian, *The Empire's New Clothes: Paradigm Lost, and Regained* (Chicago: Prickly Paradigm, 2004), 103–4.

76 The adjustment of the prime rate has been regarded as of a piece with the Federal Reserve Board chairman's announcement of it, a discursive formation known as the "Greenspan effect." See David B. Sicilia, *The Greenspan Effect: Words That Move the World's Markets* (New York: McGraw-Hill, 2000).

77 Executive Office of the President, National Security Council, *The National Security Strategy of the United States of America* (2002), 13.

78 Although rising defense spending contributes to deficits that preempt domestic spending, something that Alan Greenspan noted in his recommendation to cut Social Security and Medicare funding. Edmund L. Andrews, "To Trim Deficit, Greenspan Urges Social Security and Medicare Cuts," *New York Times*, 26 February 2004, §A, 1.

79 There are now any number of point-by-point refutations of the arguments made by the Bush administration to invade Iraq. Some web sites have begun to compile them. See for example "The Case against the Invasion of Iraq," http://www.lasg.org/TheCaseAgainstAnInvasionOfIraq.htm; http://www. antiwar.com; and from the conservative Cato Institute, "One Last Time: The Case against a War with Iraq."

80 Noam Chomsky, "Wars of Terror," *Masters of War: Militarism and Blowback in the Era of American Empire*, ed. Carl Boggs (New York: Routledge, 2003), 137.

81 Robert S. Litwak, *Rogue States and U.S. Foreign Policy: Containment after the Cold War* (Baltimore: Johns Hopkins University Press, 2000), 12.

82 Joseph Stephanides, Foreword, *Smart Sanctions: Targeting Economic Statecraft*, ed. David Cortright and George A. Lopez (Lanham, Md.: Rowman and Littlefield, 2002), viii.

83 David Cortright, George A. Lopez, and Elizabeth S. Rogers, "Targeted Sanctions That Do Work," *Smart Sanctions: Targeting Economic Statecraft*, ed. David Cortright and George A. Lopez (Lanham, Md.: Rowman and Littlefield, 2002), 34.

84 Information from http://fincen.gov, visited December 2003.

85 David Cortright, Alistair Millar, and George A. Lopez, "Smart Sanctions in Iraq: Policy Options," *Smart Sanctions: Targeting Economic Statecraft*, ed. David Cortright and George A. Lopez (Lanham, Md.: Rowman and Littlefield, 2002), 201–5.

86 The charges are summarized in Matt Bivens, "Highway Robbery," http://www.thenation.com/outrage/index.mhtml?pid=1028, visited 26 February 2004.

87 Cortright, Millar, and Lopez, "Smart Sanctions in Iraq," 208.

88 For discussion of the history and policy of GSEs from the perspective of their potential privatization see Thomas H. Stanton, *A State of Risk: Will Government-Sponsored Enterprises Be the Next Financial Crisis?* (New York: Harper Collins, 1991), and Stanton's more recent *Government-Sponsored Enterprises: Mercantilist Companies in the Modern World* (Washington: AEI Press, 2002). Figures from page 6.

89 The heavy debt load—now over two trillion dollars—has been the subject of public consternation by none other than Alan Greenspan: "It's basically creating an abnormality, which the system cannot close around, and the potential of that is a systemic risk in—sometime in the future if they continue to increase at the rate at which they are." See Edmund L. Andrews, "Mortgage Giants' Debt Is Big Risk, Greenspan Says," *New York Times*, 24 February 2004, §C, 1.

90 The contours of the accounting scandal in 2004 and 2005 that eroded stock value by 25 percent are tracked by the *Financial Times* in "Fannie and

Freddie under Pressure," http://news.ft.com/cms/50580b0a-1241-11d9-863e-00000e2511c8.html, visited 15 April 2005.

91 These questions will be addressed more fully in chapter 4. Measured narrowly in terms of domestic growth, the long-run impact of empire on development in the imperialist center has, according to some assessments, been small. For various positions see Ronald Chilcote, ed., *The Political Economy of Imperialism: Critical Appraisals* (Norwell, Mass.: Kluwer Academic, 1999).

92 Taken from Robert C. DiPrizio, *Armed Humanitarians: U.S. Interventions from Northern Iraq to Kosovo* (Baltimore: Johns Hopkins University Press, 2002), 3.

93 Allan Gerson and Nat Colletta, *Privatizing Peace: From Conflict to Security* (Ardsley, N.Y.: Transnational, 2002), 1.

94 Noam Chomsky, *The New Military Humanism* (Monroe, Maine: Common Courage, 1999).

95 Ibid., 49.

96 Ibid., 54.

97 Ibid., 63.

98 See Deborah Avant, *The Market for Force: Exploring the Privatization of Military Services* (New York: Council on Foreign Relations, 1999).

99 For a pre-apologist account of arbitrage from one of its masters see Ivan Boesky, *Merger Mania: Arbitrage: One of Wall Street's Best-Kept Money-Making Secrets* (New York: Henry Holt, 1985). More trenchant popular accounts of the errancy of such mastery include Michael Lewis's books *Liar's Poker* (New York: Penguin, 1989) and *Money Culture* (New York: Penguin, 1992) and Connie Bruck's *The Predator's Ball: The Inside Story of Drexel Burnham and the Rise of the Junk Bond Raiders* (New York: Simon and Schuster, 1988).

100 Quoted in Midge Decter, *Rumsfeld: A Personal Portrait* (New York: Harper Collins, 2003), 116.

101 Thomas Frank has argued that the conservative hegemony rests upon a transformation of formerly liberal working people and their alliance with wealthy conservatives. See his *What's the Matter with Kansas* (New York: Metropolitan, 2004).

102 For analysis of income maldistribution see Lawrence Mishel, Jared Bernstein, and Heather Boushey, *The State of Working America: 2002–2003* (Ithaca: Cornell University Press, 2003).

103 The reference here is to Benedict Anderson's now famous formulation in *Imagined Communities*, 2d ed. (London: Verso, 1991).

104 For a look at Reagan's two terms through the lens of this slogan see Gil Troy, *Morning in America: How Ronald Reagan Invented the 1980s* (Princeton: Princeton University Press, 2005).

105 Paul A. Bové, "Can American Studies Be Area Studies?," *Learning Places: The Afterlives of Area Studies*, ed. Masao Miyoshi and H. D. Harootunian (Durham: Duke University Press, 2002), 208.

106 Ibid., 209.

107 U.S. Department of Homeland Security, http://www.dhs.gov/dhs public/theme_home1.jsp, visited 20 January 2004.

108 Figures taken from DHS web site, http://www.dhs.gov/dhspublic/dis play?content=895, visited 20 January 2004.

109 The 2005 appropriation for the agency was $40 billion, with another $30 billion in discretionary spending. See *Homeland Security Budget in Brief, Fiscal Year 2005*, www.dhs.gov/interweb/assetlibrary/FY_2005_BIB_4.pdf, visited 17 January 2005.

110 Michael E. O'Hanlon et al., *Protecting the American Homeland: A Preliminary Analysis* (Washington: Brookings Institution Press, 2002), 10. The EZ Pass system also has a consumer end, to "sort people" by means of a national identity card into those who engage in "routine activities" and those who "show specific troubling patterns of behavior." Michael Cherkasky with Alex Prud'homme, *Forewarned: Why the Government Is Failing to Protect Us— And What We Must Do to Protect Ourselves* (New York: Ballantine, 2003), xvi. Cherkasky, the CEO of Kroll, a transnational risk management firm, offers his own "Proteus Plan," including "government mandated corporate security measures" (xviii), a use of government that would substantially enhance his portfolio. Cherkasky assumes that the borders of the United States are permeable, and that a "layered" (109), technology-driven system can delay the effects of perpetrators.

111 O'Hanlon, *Protecting the American Homeland*, 80–81.

112 Recent examples are David Lyon, *Surveillance after September 11th* (Malden, Mass.: Blackwell, 2003), and his edited volume *Surveillance as Social Sorting: Privacy, Risk, and Digital Discrimination* (London: Routledge, 2003), as well as Christian Parenti's *The Soft Cage: Surveillance in America from Slavery to the War on Terror* (New York: Basic, 2003).

113 "Special Report: Suicide Terrorism: Martyrdom and Murder," *Economist*, 10 January 2004, 22.

114 Within the techno-scientific community, one reputed to be more collaborative than its neighbors at intelligence, the Committee on Science and Technology for Countering Terrorism of the National Research Council has prepared a comprehensive volume, *Making The Nation Safer: The Role of Science and Technology in Countering Terrorism* (Washington: National Academy Press, 2002), which also advocates a "multilayered systems approach" (5), in effect a kind of transcendental interdisciplinarity among the engineers and scientists, with terrorism the great integrator and counterterrorism a "system of systems" (290) that can be factored into "inputs and outputs [that] then enable the building of models that predict the efficacy of risk-management policy options" (290). These models are to be imported from financial services (288).

115 Ibid., 305.

116 The term was given currency by the chairman of the Federal Reserve, Alan Greenspan, during the stock market boom of the late 1990s and has been developed analytically by the Yale economist Robert Schiller in his book *Irrational Exuberance* (Princeton: Princeton University Press, 2000).

117 Ibid., 306.

118 Ibid.

119 Michael Chertoff, who replaced Tom Ridge as secretary of homeland security during Bush's second term, used an early speech to signal the department's risk management approach. Referring to the need to balance security and freedom and not be paralyzed by threats, he argued: "That's why we need to adopt a risk-based approach in both our operations and our philosophy. Risk management is fundamental to managing the threat, while retaining our quality of life and living in freedom. Risk management must guide our decision-making as we examine how we can best organize to prevent, respond and recover from an attack. For that reason, the Department of Homeland Security is working with State, local, and private sector partners on a National Preparedness Plan to target resources where the risk is greatest. We all live with a certain amount of risk. That means that we tolerate that something bad can happen; we adjust our lives based on probability; and we take reasonable precautions." "Remarks for Secretary Michael Chertoff, U.S. Department of Homeland Security, George Washington University Homeland Security Policy Institute" (Washington, 16 March 2005), http://www.dhs.gov/dhspublic/display?content=4391, visited 15 April 2005.

120 Specifically, the sociology of risk associated with the work of Ulrich Beck and Anthony Giddens developed seemingly without awareness of the social effects of finance occurring at the same time. This is discussed in Randy Martin, *Financialization of Daily Life* (Philadelphia: Temple University Press, 2002), chapter 3, "Risking the World." See Ulrich Beck, *World Risk Society* (Cambridge: Polity, 1999); Ulrich Beck, *Risk Society: Towards a New Modernity* (London: Sage, 1992); Ulrich Beck, Anthony Giddens, and Scott Lash, *Reflexive Modernization: Politics, Tradition and Aesthetics in the Modern Social Order* (Cambridge: Polity, 1994); and Mary Douglas and Aaron Wildavsky, *Risk and Culture: An Essay on the Selection of Technical and Environmental Dangers* (Berkeley: University of California Press, 1983).

CHAPTER 2 : DERIVATIVE WARS

1 This is the narrative of Francis Fukuyama's *The End of History and the Last Man* (New York: Harper Collins, 1993), in which global conflict along socioeconomic lines undergoes a cultural displacement. See also Samuel Huntington's *The Clash of Civilizations and the Remaking of World Order* (New York: Simon and Schuster, 1997) and, on those who are for or against globalization, Benjamin Barber's *Jihad vs. McWorld: How Globalism and Tribalism Are Reshaping the World* (New York: Ballantine, 1996) and Thomas Friedman's *The Lexus and the Olive Tree: Understanding Globalization* (New York: Alfred A. Knopf, 2000).

2 Martin van Creveld, *The Transformation of War* (New York: Free Press, 1991), 1.

3 H. Bruce Franklin, *War Stars: The Superweapon in the American Imagination* (New York: Oxford University Press, 1988).

4 The claims for the new economy are articulated and challenged in turn by Doug Henwood in his *After the New Economy* (New York: New Press, 2003).

5 On the trysts and traffic between military and civilian sectors, told with an innocent eye toward mutual benefits, see Daphne Kamely, Kenneth A. Bannister, and Robert M. Samsor, eds., *Army Science: The New Frontiers, Military and Civilian Applications* (Saratoga, Wyo.: Borg Biomedical, 1993); A. D. Van Nostrand, *Fundable Knowledge: The Marketing of Defense Technology* (Mahwah, N.J.: Lawrence Erlbaum, 1997); and Wim Smit, John Grin, and Lev Voronkov, eds., *Military Technological Innovation and Stability in a Changing World: Politically Assessing and Influencing Weapon Innovation and Military Research and Development* (Amsterdam: Vu University Press, 1992).

6 Paul Edwards, *The Closed World: Computers and the Politics of Discourse in Cold War America* (Cambridge: MIT Press, 1996), 207, 364.

7 The notion that war is productive of social matter is developed across a range of historical and cultural examples in Gilles Deleuze and Felix Guattari, *A Thousand Plateaus: Capitalism and Schizophrenia* (Minneapolis: University of Minnesota Press, 1987), especially the "Treatise on Nomadology," 351–423.

8 John Carey, Catherine Yang, Otis Port, and Christopher Palmeri, "Weapons: From Smart to Brilliant," *Business Week*, 27 September 2001.

9 Harlan Ullman and James Wade Jr., *Shock and Awe: Achieving Rapid Dominance* (Philadelphia: Pavilion, 1996), 4.

10 Ibid., 5. Despite the reference to leveraging, Ullman and Wade credit the phrase "shock and awe" to Clausewitz and to Sun Tzu 2,500 years before him (35).

11 For an account of the LTCM debacle see Roger Lowenstein, *When Genius Failed: The Rise and Fall of Long-Term Capital Management* (New York: Random House, 2001), and for the Enron tale see Bethany McClean and Peter Elkind, *The Smartest Guys in the Room: The Amazing Rise and Scandalous Fall of Enron* (New York: Portfolio, 2003), and Mimi Swartz and Sherron Watkins, *Power Failure: The Inside Story of the Collapse of Enron* (New York: Doubleday, 2003).

12 Martin van Creveld, *Command in War* (Cambridge: Harvard University Press, 1985), 96.

13 Chris Hables Gray, *Postmodern War* (New York, Guilford, 1996), 95.

14 Ibid., 107.

15 Ibid., 140.

16 Ibid., 270–74.

17 Manuel de Landa, *War in the Age of Intelligent Machines* (New York: Zone, 1991), 43.

18 Ibid., 97.

19 Van Creveld, *Command in War*, 237–41.

20 De Landa, *War in the Age of Intelligent Machines*, 109.

21 DARPA had cold war origins: it was formed in 1958 as the Advanced Research Projects Agency. See the DARPA web site, http://www.darpa.mil/body/arpa_darpa.html, visited 10 September 2004.

22 Alvin Toffler and Heidi Toffler, *War and Anti-war: Survival at the Dawn of the 21st Century* (Boston: Little, Brown, 1993).

23 Donald Chisholm, "The Risk of Optimism in the Conduct of War," *Parameters* 33, no. 4 (winter 2003–4): 114–31.

24 Steven Metz and James Klevit, "Strategy and the Revolution in Military Affairs" (1995), http://purl.access.gpo.gov/GPO/LPS14295.

25 Ibid., vii.

26 See Midge Decter, *Rumsfeld* (New York: Harper Collins, 2003), 130.

27 See Stephen Peter Rosen, *Winning the Next War* (Ithaca: Cornell University Press, 1991), 205. This book is itself a key text in the self-prophetic turn to American military intervention.

28 Career information on Marshall is taken from an interview with him by James der Derian in der Derian, *Virtuous War: Mapping the Military-Industrial-Media-Entertainment Network* (Boulder: Westview, 2001), 29.

29 "Director of Net Assessment: Department of Defense Directive 5111.11" (22 August 2001), 2, http://www.dtic.mil/whs/directives/corres/pdf/d511111_082201/d511111p.pdf, signed by Paul Wolfowitz, deputy secretary of defense (visited 27 April 2004).

30 Douglas McGray, "The Marshall Plan," *Wired*, 1 February 2003.

31 See for example the web page for 9 December 2003 of the Office of the Secretary of Defense, which lists offices and provides links, http://www.defenselink.mil/osd/.

32 Andrew W. Marshall, Foreword, *The Diffusion of Military Technology and Ideas*, by Emily O. Goldman and Leslie C. Eliason (Stanford: Stanford University Press, 2003), xiv.

33 This account of the Soviet sources of the RMA is taken from Admiral William A. Owens, "Creating a U.S. Military Revolution," chapter 10 in *The Sources of Military Change: Culture, Politics, Technology*, ed. Theo Farrell and Terry Terriff (Boulder: Lynne Rienner, 2002), 208.

34 According to Defense Secretary Cohen, RMA occurs when "a nation's

military seizes the opportunity to transform . . . to achieve decisive military results in new ways." Quoted in Colin Gray, *Strategy for Chaos: Revolutions in Military Affairs and the Evidence of History* (London: Frank Cass, 2002), 1.

35 McGray, "The Marshall Plan."

36 George W. Bush, "Defense Planning Guidance" (April 2003), 3, quoted in Evidence Based Research, Inc., "Network Centric Operations Conceptual Framework Version 1.0," 1, Office of Force Transformation of the Department of Defense, http://www.oft.osd.mil/library/library_files/document_353_NCO%20CF%20Version%201.0%20(FINAL).doc, visited 29 April 2004.

37 Chalmers Johnson, *The Sorrows of Empire: Militarism, Secrecy and the End of the Republic* (New York: Metropolitan, 2004), 188, 4. Total military employment would peak at over fourteen million in 1945, with over eight million active in the Army and over three million in the Navy. After the demobilization that followed the Vietnam War, personnel levels were maintained at roughly the same levels during the rest of the 1970s and 1980s. "Department of Defense Work Force Levels, 1938–present," http://web1.whs.osd.mil/mmid/m01/sms16r.htm, visited 8 June 2004.

38 Between 1987 and 1999 the active duty corps in the Army went from 780,815 to 479,426, in the Navy from 586,842 to 373,046, and in the Air Force from 607,035 to 360,590. Unlike Korea and Vietnam, the two Iraq wars were not accompanied by major troop buildups and demobilizations. Data from "DoD Active Duty Military Strength Levels, Fiscal Years 1950–2002," http://web1.whs.osd.mil/mmid/military/ms9.pdf. During the same period civilian employment was cut by more than a third, as any number of support services from the commissary to base construction were privatized. "DoD Direct Hire Civilian Strength Levels, Fiscal Years 1950–2001," http://web1.whs.osd.mil/mmid/civilian/trends.pdf. Reserves declined during the same period by over 200,000. "Reserve Strength Trends by Reserve Category," http://web1.whs.osd.mil/mmid/M15/R01FILE.HTM. All visited 8 June 2004.

39 Anthony Cordesman, *The Iraq War: Strategy, Tactics, and Military Lessons* (Washington: CSIS, 2003), 167.

40 See Chris Hables Gray, *Postmodern War* (New York: Guilford, 1998).

41 The literature on post-Fordism, spanning over twenty-five years, is by now formidable. For an overview see Ash Amin, ed., *Post-Fordism: A Reader* (Waltham, Mass.: Blackwell, 1994).

42 For a collection of essays on this shift see Mary Kaldor, Ulrich Albrecht, and Genevieve Schmeder, eds., *Restructuring the Global Military Sector*, vol. 2, *The End of Military Fordism* (London: Pinter, 1998).

43 "Network Centric Operations," *Restructuring the Global Military Sector*, vol. 2, *The End of Military Fordism*, ed. Mary Kaldor, Ulrich Albrecht, and Genevieve Schmeder (London: Pinter, 1998), 25.

44 Ibid., 10.

45 The example given is an analysis conducted by RAND of training sorties in which pilots used sensory and computer input to shoot down more enemy planes. Ibid., 9.

46 Ibid., 12.

47 "Statement of Art Cebroski, Director, Office of Force Transformation, Before the Subcommittee on Strategic Forces, Armed Services Committee, United States Senate, March 25, 2004," 2, http://www.oft.osd.mil/library/li brary_files/trends_350_Transformation%20Trends-30%20March%20%20 2004%20Issue.pdf, visited 30 April 2004.

48 Ibid., 3.

49 Ibid., 6.

50 On SDI's genealogies and discontents see Bradley Graham, *Hit to Kill: The New Battle over Shielding America from Missile Attack* (New York: Public Affairs, 2001); Craig Eisendrath, Melvin A. Goodman, and Gerald E. Marsh, *The Phantom Defense: America's Pursuit of the Star Wars Illusion* (Westport: Praeger, 2001); Rebecca S. Bjork, *The Strategic Defense Initiative: Symbolic Containment of the Nuclear Threat* (Albany: SUNY Press, 1992); James J. Wirtz and Jeffrey A. Larsen, eds., *Rockets' Red Glare: Missile Defenses and the Future of World Politics* (Boulder: Westview, 2001); Frances Fitzgerald, *Way Out There in the Blue: Reagan, Star Wars and the End of the Cold War* (New York: Simon and Schuster, 2000); Gordon R. Mitchell, *Strategic Deception: Rhetoric, Science, and Politics in Missile Defense Advocacy* (East Lansing: Michigan State University Press, 2000).

51 "Statement of Art Cebroski," 7.

52 Ibid., 8.

53 Ibid., 9.

54 Chris Hables Gray, "Perpetual Revolution in Military Affairs," *Bombs and Bandwidth: The Emerging Relationship Between Information Technology and Security,* ed. Robert Latham (New York: New Press, 2003), 201.

55 See for example John Gartska, "Implementation of Network Centric Warfare," *Transformation Trends,* 28 January 2004, http://www.oft.osd.mil/ library/library_files/trends_338_Transformation_Trends_28_January_ 2004_Issue.pdf; and Gerry J. Gilmore, "Outgoing Comptroller Cites Transformational Accomplishments," American Forces Press Service, 19 April 2004, http://www.oft.osd.mil/library/library_files/article_359_Outgoing%20 Comptroller%20Cites%20Transformational%20Accomplishments.doc. Both visited 30 April 2004.

56 Juan A. Alsace, "In Search of Monsters to Destroy," *Parameters: U.S. War College Quarterly* 33, no. 3 (autumn 2003): 122–29.

57 This account is taken from Chalmers Johnson, *The Sorrows of Empire: Militarism, Secrecy, and the End of the Republic* (New York: Metropolitan, 2004), 279.

58 Alsace is here referring to a book by Max Boot, *The Savage Wars of Peace: Small Wars and the Rise of American Power* (New York: Basic, 2002).

59 The Small Wars Manual (published in 1940 and declassified in 1958) is available on the web site of the Marine Corps Small Wars Center of Excellence, whose mission is "to provide an unclassified interactive information resource and management tool for the understanding of the history, nature, and relevance of Small Wars in the 21st Century security environment, and for the conduct of Small Wars programs and events," http://www.smallwars.quan tico.usmc.mil/. The earlier British text is by Charles Edward Callwell, *Small Wars: Their Principles and Practice* (London: Printed for H. M. Stationery Office by Harrison and Sons, 1899).

60 Director of Strategic Plans and Policy, "Joint Vision 2020" (Washington: U.S. Government Printing Office, 2000), 32.

61 Quadrennial Defense Review Report, 30 September 2001, http://www.defenselink.mil/pubs/qdr2001.pdf, 57.

62 Ibid., 20.

63 Colonel Richard Witherspoon, writing in the foreword to a report of the Army Tactical Command and Control Center by Elizabeth A. Stanley, "Evolutionary Technology in the Current Revolution in Military Affairs," 28 March 1998 (Carlisle, Penn.: Strategic Studies Institute), noted, "changes largely have been marginal, revolving around the leveraging of technologies into existing systems" (iii).

64 John A. Gentry, "Doomed to Fail: America's Blind Faith in Military Technology," *Parameters* 33, no. 4 (winter 2002–3): 88–103.

65 Robert M. Cassidy, "Prophets or Praetorians? The Utopian Paradox and the Powell Corollary," *Parameters: U.S. War College Quarterly* 33, no. 3 (autumn 2003): 130–43.

66 Ibid., 138.

67 Ibid., 140. See also Conrad C. Crane, *Avoiding Vietnam: The U.S. Army's Response to Defeat in Southeast Asia* (Carlisle, Penn.: Strategic Studies Institute, 2002).

68 Charles C. Moskos and James Burk, "The Postmodern Military," *The Military in New Times: Adapting Armed Forces to a Turbulent World*, ed. James Burk (Boulder: Westview, 1994), 149.

69 Paul Virilio, *Desert Screen* (London: Continuum, 2002), 136.

70 Jean Baudrillard, *The Gulf War Did Not Take Place* (Bloomington: Indiana University Press, 1995), 61.

71 Ibid., 82.

72 Der Derian, *Virtuous War*, xv.

73 Ibid., 219.

74 Harald Kleinschmidt, "Using the Gun: Manual Drill and the Proliferation of Portable Firearms," *Journal of Military History* 63, no. 3 (1999): 601–29, 616. The genealogy of training presented here follows Kleinschmidt's account. On the use of design in command to organize and discipline masses of bodies see "The Means of Correct Training" in Michel Foucault, *Discipline and Punish: The Birth of the Prison* (New York: Vintage, 1979), 170–94.

75 Ibid., 617.

76 Ibid., 629. Victor Davis Hanson identifies a similar self-limiting ethos on the classical Greek battlefield. See his *The Western Way of War: Infantry Battle in Classical Greece* (New York: Alfred A. Knopf, 1989).

77 This theme has been taken up by Barbara Ehrenreich in her *Blood Rites: Origins and History of the Passions of War* (New York: Henry Holt, 1997), where she makes links between predation and contemporary "war worship" in a way that has its own neoprimitivist implications.

78 "Tradoc Begins Major New Initiative: Warrior Ethos," http://www-tradoc.army.mil/pao/Web_specials/WarriorEthos/, visited 19 May 2004. Tradoc, the Training and Doctrine Command, conceives and coordinates the production of soldiers.

79 "Soldier's Creed," http://www.infantry.army.mil/taskforcesoldier/con tent/soldiers_creed.htm, visited 19 May 2004.

80 Julia Simpkins, "Soldiering like a Warrior," *Leader* (Fort Jackson, S.C.), 31 March 2004, http://www-tradoc.army.mil/pao/Web_specials/Warrior Ethos/036504.htm, visited 19 May 2004.

81 Edward Shils and Morris Janowitz, "Cohesion and Disintegration in the Wehrmacht in World War II," *Public Opinion Quarterly* 12 (summer 1948).

82 Leonard Wong et al., "Why They Fight: Combat Motivation in the Iraq War" (July 2003), 10, http://www.carlisle.army.mil/ssi/pubs/2003/whyfight/ whyfight.htm, visited May 2004.

83 David Buckingham, *The Warrior Ethos* (Newport, R.I.: Naval War College, 1999), 22.

84 Stephen P. Ferris and David Keithly, "Outsourcing the Sinews of War: Contractor Logistics," *Military Review*, September–October, 2001. The authors do acknowledge that private firms minimize inventory, promote noncompetitive bidding, and pose security risks to themselves. When these problems do come to pass it is easy to see them as calculable risks.

85 Ibid., 12.

86 See www.todaysmilitary.com.

87 The attention to and assimilationist cast of discussions of gender and racial difference are evident in Dorothy and Carl J. Schneider, *Sound Off: American Military Women Speak Out* (New York: E. P. Dutton, 1988); Mary Fainsod Katzenstein and Judith Reppy, *Beyond Zero Tolerance: Discrimination in Military Culture* (Lanham, Md.: Rowman and Littlefield, 1999); Christopher

Dandeker and Donna Winslow, "On 'The Need to Be Different': Recent Trends in Military Culture," *Backbone of the Army: Non-Commissioned Officers in the Future Army*, ed. Douglas L. Bland (Montreal: McGill-Queens University Press, 2000), 47–67; and the report prepared for the secretary of defense, William Perry, by Susan D. Hosek et al., *Military and Gender Differences in Officer Career Progression* (Santa Monica: RAND, 2001), as well as the collection edited by Mickey R. Dansby, James B. Stewart, and Schuyler C. Webb, *Managing Diversity in the Military: Research Perspectives from the Defense Equal Opportunity Management Institute* (New Brunswick, N.J.: Transaction, 2001).

88 Stephanie Gutmann, *The Kinder, Gentler Military: Can America's Gender Neutral Fighting Force Still Win Wars?* (New York: Scribner, 2000), 114.

89 Ibid., 56.

90 Tradoc Standardized Physical Training Guide PCU 5 (November 2003), 3, http://www.benning.army.mil/usapfs/Doctrine/NewRegs/TRADOC%20Standardized%20PT%20Guide.

91 Ibid., 8.

92 A year after the Iraqi invasion recruiters were finding the military a tough sell, and some Pentagon officials were concerned about not meeting targets. For many recruits, however, the challenge remained "getting through boot camp." See Monica Davey, "Recruiters Try New Tactics to Sell Wartime Army," *New York Times*, 1 June 2004, §A, 1, 14.

93 The attention to the ability to move as a series of arrested body shapes recalls late-nineteenth-century tableaux-vivant practices that anticipated modern dance. See Linda Tomko, *Dancing Class: Gender, Ethnicity and Social Divides in American Dance, 1890–1920* (Bloomington: Indiana University Press, 1999). William H. McNeill has made the larger historical connection between military training and dance in *Keeping Together in Time: Dance and Drill in Human History* (Cambridge: Harvard University Press, 1995).

94 Tradoc Standardized Physical Training Guide, 143.

95 For a discussion of mechanized bodies as a trope of high-industrial warfare see Klaus Theweleit, *Male Fantasies*, vol. 1, *Women Floods, Bodies History*, vol. 2, *Male Bodies: Psychoanalyzing the White Terror* (Minneapolis: University of Minnesota Press, 1989).

96 Tradoc Standardized Physical Training Guide PCU 5, 150.

97 Ibid., 144.

98 See Anne Chapman et al., *Prepare the Army for War: A Historical Overview of Army Training and Doctrine Command, 1973–1998* (Fort Monroe, Va.: U.S. Army Training and Doctrine Command, 1998), 55.

99 Ibid., 101–3.

100 USASOC Special Operations Forces Information, http://www.soc.mil/hqs/hqs_home.htm, visited 28 May 2004.

101 Force structure for combat groups remained constant through the 1990s; see "Special Operations Force Structure," http://defenselink.mil/pubs/almanac. In 2004 the Democratic presidential nominee, John Kerry, promised that he would be "reshaping the military by beefing up the Special Forces." Jodi Wilgoren, "Kerry Says He Will Adapt Military for New Dangers," *New York Times*, 4 June 2004, §A, 23.

102 Figures from Dilip Hiro, *Secrets and Lies: Operation Iraqi Freedom and After* (New York: Nation, 2004), 23.

103 USASOC Primer, http://www.soc.mil/hqs/hqs_home.htm, visited 28 May 2004.

104 USASOC Imperatives, http://www.soc.mil/hqs/hqs_home.htm, visited 28 May 2004.

105 I'm grateful to one of the anonymous readers for suggesting these examples. See Burt Garfield Loescher, *Rogers Rangers, the First Green Beret: The Corps and the Revivals, April 6, 1758–December 24, 1783* (San Mateo, Calif.: Genesis, 1969); and Robert D. Bass, *Swamp Fox: The Life and Campaigns of General Francis Marion* (New York: Henry Holt, 1939).

106 USASOC: A Brief History of Special Operations Forces, http://www.soc.mil/hqs/hqs_home.htm, visited 28 May 2004.

107 Special Forces have been defined from the perspective of "high risk missions." See Ross Kelly, *Special Operations and National Purpose* (Lexington, Mass.: Lexington Books, 1989), xvii. They have also been narrativized as a "precarious value" in a state of renewal since their nadir in the early 1980s. See Susan Marquis, *Unconventional Warfare: Rebuilding Special Operations Forces* (Washington: Brookings Institution, 1997), 7.

108 See for example John Arquilla, *Dubious Battles: Aggression, Defeat, and the International System* (Washington: Crane Russak, 1992); Stephen J. Cimbala and Keith A. Dunn, eds., *Conflict Termination and Military Strategy: Coercion, Persuasion, and War* (Boulder: Westview, 1987); Gideon Rose, "The Exit Strategy Delusion," *Foreign Affairs*, January–February 1998; and Jeffrey Record, "Exit Strategy Delusions," *Parameters: U.S. War College Quarterly*, winter 2001–2, 21–27.

109 Stuart Albert, "Dynamics and Paradoxes of the Ending Process," *On the Endings of Wars*, ed. Stuart Albert and Edward C. Luck (Port Washington, N.Y.: Kennikat, 1980), 9.

110 According to the *OED*, the earliest citation of "exit strategy" dates to 1973. Caspar Weinberger, architect of the decisive force doctrine intended as a corrective after Vietnam, effectively admits that "exit strategy" is a euphemism for losing. Referring to Clinton's adventures in Bosnia he proclaimed, "It is time to stop talking about 'exit strategies' and to concentrate on winning. That is, and should be, the only objective of war." Caspar W. Weinberger, "Losing Track of the Main Objective of War," *New York Times*, 12 April 1999, §A, 25.

1   The role of sheriff is advocated by some as both descriptively and prescriptively appropriate for the role of the United States. See Colin S. Gray, *The Sheriff: America's Defense of the New World Order* (Lexington: University Press of Kentucky, 2004).

2   See Milan Rai, *Regime Unchanged: Why the War on Iraq Changed Nothing* (London: Pluto, 2003). For a benchmark on Iraq's situation before the war see Kamil A. Mahdi, ed., *Iraq's Economic Predicament* (Reading: Ithaca, 2002).

3   National Commission on Terrorist Attacks upon the United States, "Overview of the Enemy: Staff Statement No. 15," 5, http://www.9-11commission.gov/staff_statements/staff_statement_15.pdf, visited 28 June 2004.

4   For an account of this affair see Dennis Hans, "Once They Were Sweethearts: Dick Cheney, the New York Times and the Myth of the Iraq Connection to 9/11" (26–27 June 2004), http://www.counterpunch.org, visited 28 June 2004.

5   The column by "Lexington" in the *Economist* mused, "Judgments on the economy may well be overshadowed by pessimism about the occupation; views on these two largely unrelated subjects seem to move in close correlation." "Poor George: The Case for Pessimism about the President's Prospects," *Economist*, 24 June 2004, http://economist.com/displaystory.cfm?story_id=2792487.

6   The State Department's initial report for 2004 claimed that the number of attacks had declined, but the department later issued a corrective. For this and a more general accounting of the Iraq war's various "costs" see Phyllis Bennis et al., "Paying the Price: The Mounting Costs of the Iraq War" (Washington: DC Institute for Policy Studies, 24 June 2004), http://www.ips-dc.org/iraq/costsofwar/, visited 30 June 2004.

7   For an especially compelling account see Derek Gregory, *The Colonial Present: Afghanistan, Palestine, Iraq* (Malden, Mass.: Blackwell, 2004).

8   Rumsfeld quoted in Rowan Scarborough, *Rumsfeld's War: The Untold Story of America's Antiterrorist Commander* (Washington: Regnery, 2004), 166.

9   Defense Intelligence Agency, "A Primer on the Future Threat: The Decades Ahead, 1999–2020," quoted in Scarborough, *Rumsfeld's War*, 147.

10   See Mahmood Mamdani, *Good Muslim, Bad Muslim: America, the Cold War, and the Roots of Terror* (New York: Pantheon, 2004).

11   See Rashid Khalidi, *Resurrecting Empire: Western Footprints and America's Perilous Path in the Middle East* (Boston: Beacon, 2004).

12   For an accounting of the provision of conventional and unconventional arms to Iraq by the United States see Larry Everest, *Oil, Power and Empire: Iraq and the U.S. Global Agenda* (Monroe, Maine: Common Courage, 2004), especially chapter 4, "Arming Iraq." Details on chemical and biological weapons can be found on page 102.

13 Colonel Walter P. Lang of the DIA quoted in Research Unit for Political Economy, *Behind the Invasion of Iraq* (New York: Monthly Review, 2003), 32.

14 National Commission on Terrorist Attacks upon the United States, *9/11 Commission Report*, 1.

15 Norman Friedman, *Terrorism, Afghanistan and America's New Way of War* (Annapolis: Naval Institute Press, 2003), 55.

16 This distinction between a formal organizational entity and a principle of association is made by Jason Burke to emphasize that terrorism cannot be countered by eliminating individual leaders, but must be addressed through its sociological roots. See his *Al-Qaeda: Casting a Shadow of Terror* (London: IB Tauris, 2003), definitions on pp. 7–8.

17 Friedman, *Terrorism, Afghanistan and America's New Way of War*, 63–66.

18 Burke, *Al-Qaeda*, 16. An analyst for the Marine Corps, J. Noel Williams, likens bin Laden to a "ruthless venture capitalist," who incorporates "many of today's best business practices into his organizational plan." See "Matrix Warfare: The New Face of Competition and Conflict in the 21st Century" (Quantico, Va.: Center for Emerging Threats and Opportunities, 2002), 1, http://purl.access.gpo.gov/GPO/LPS47300, visited 2 July 2004.

19 According to the report of the National Commission on Terrorist Attacks upon the United States, bin Laden never received the larger $300 million inheritance once said to be his share of the family fortune. *9/11 Commission Report*, 3–4.

20 Ibid., 16, 18.

21 "With the Cold War over, Afghanistan was effectively neglected by much of the international community and, since 1992, the UN Consolidated Appeals for Afghanistan remained consistently underfunded, sometimes severely so." Sultan Barakat, "Setting the Scene for Afghanistan's Reconstruction: The Challenges and Critical Dilemmas," *Reconstructing War Torn Societies: Afghanistan* (Houndmills: Palgrave Macmillan, 2004), 8.

22 Friedman, *Terrorism, Afghanistan and America's New Way of War*, 80.

23 Ibid., 21, 81.

24 Ibid., 184–85.

25 Ibid., 193.

26 Anthony Cordesman, *The Lessons of Afghanistan: War Fighting, Intelligence, and Force Transformation* (Washington: CSIS, 2002), 8, 82.

27 See for example Doug Kellner, *The Persian Gulf TV War* (Boulder: Westview, 1992), and for a longer view, Andrew Hoskins, *Televising War: From Vietnam to Iraq* (London: Continuum, 2004).

28 Cordesman, *The Lessons of Afghanistan*, 8.

29 Ibid., 26–27.

30 Martin Shaw, *The New Western Way of War: Risk Transfer and Its Crisis in Iraq* (Cambridge: Polity, 2005).

31 Friedman, *Terrorism, Afghanistan and America's New Way of War*, 200.

32 Cordesman, *The Lessons of Afghanistan*, 42, 36.

33 Ibid., 202.

34 Ibid., 203.

35 Ibid., 205.

36 Anthony Cordesman, *The War after the War: Strategic Lessons of Iraq and Afghanistan* (Washington: CSIS, 2004), 65.

37 Shengman Zhang, "Afghanistan Transitional Support Strategy" (Washington: World Bank, 14 February 2003), http://lnweb18.worldbank.org/sar/sa.nsf/Attachments/TSS2Text/$File/Text.pdf, visited 10 July 2004.

38 Capitol Hill Hearing Testimony, Senate Foreign Relations, Usaid Contracting Policies, Mr. Frederick D. Barton, Co-director of Post Conflict Reconstruction Programs, Center For Strategic And International Studies, 25 February 2004, http://web.lexis-nexis.com/universe/document?_m=f6a5fe083fc1137 11f6614f3a37ccdeb&_docnum=1&wchp=dGLbVzb-zSkVA&_md5=444e40e 86141dc37248b9b0456564bed, visited 4 July 2004. Barton admitted to a deteriorating situation for aid workers: "Many who work in Afghanistan feel that conditions have grown more dangerous, with work in the South slowing down into a shrinking area."

39 Jonathan Goodhand, "Aiding Violence or Building Peace? The Role of International Aid in Afghanistan," *Reconstructing War-Torn Societies: Afghanistan*, ed. Sultan Barakat (Houndmills: Palgrave Macmillan, 2004), 37–59.

40 Jeff Madrick, "Afghans Come Up with an Aid Plan of Their Own Design," *New York Times*, 13 May 2004.

41 "Federal Study Faults Program to Rebuild Afghanistan," PakTribune, 5 June 2004, http://paktribune.com/news/index.php?id=66965, visited 6 July 2004. The study was released by the General Accounting Office on 2 June 2004.

42 David Rohde, "Poppies Flood Afghanistan: Opium Tide May Yet Turn," *New York Times*, 1 July 2004, §A, 13.

43 Afghan Constitution available online at www.constitution-afg.com, visited 6 July 2004.

44 Paul Clammer, "A Place for Tourism in Afghanistan's Recovery," Development Gateway, 8 June 2004, http://topics.developmentgateway.org/afghani stan/sdm/previewDocument.doactiveDocumentId=1000580, visited 6 July 2004. Development Gateway is itself a spinoff of the World Bank and a brainchild of its president, James Wolfensohn, to "build local capacity to empower communities" by using information and communications technologies.

45 Hakim Bey, "For and Against Interpretation," 26 August 1996, www.hermetic.com/bey/millennium/interpret.html, visited 14 July 2004.

46 Eric Shinseki, quoted in Scarborough, *Rumsfeld's War*, 139.

47 Wolfowitz testified to this effect before the House Subcommittee on Appropriations on 27 March 2003 and is quoted in Larry Everest, *Oil, Power and Empire: Iraq and the U.S. Global Agenda* (Monroe, Maine: Common Courage, 2004), 279.

48 For example, in March 2003 Lt. General William S. Wallace made a request to delay any further advance on Baghdad until more troops could be assigned and was threatened with relief of his duties by General Tommy R. Franks; further requests were denied by Donald Rumsfeld. These conflicts were disclosed nearly three years after the invasion. See Michael R. Gordon and Bernard E. Trainor, "Dash to Baghdad Left Top U.S. Generals Divided," *New York Times*, 13 March 2006, §A, 1, 8.

49 The Senate Intelligence Committee's "Report on the U.S. Intelligence Community's Prewar Intelligence Assessment on Iraq, July 7, 2004" found, in the words of its chairman, Senator Pat Roberts (R-Kan.), that "most of the key judgments . . . were either overstated or were not supported by the raw intelligence reporting." Excerpts published in the *New York Times*, "The Senators' Views and Excerpts from the Report on Iraq Assessments," 10 July 2004, §A, 8. Failure to pay heed to what subordinates say is happening is at odds with the command and control protocols claimed by the "revolution in military affairs" but does suggest how intelligence lines of command would find themselves the cognate of military lines of information.

50 Anthony Cordesman, *The Iraq War: Strategy, Tactics and Military Lessons* (Washington: csis, 2003), 58–59.

51 The Army's Center for Army Lessons Learned (call) declassified its study of the war in June 2004. The publicly available Internet version used here was not paginated. Stratman quote from chapter 2, "Prepare, Mobilize Deploy," of "On Point: The United States Army in Operation Iraqi Freedom," http://onpoint.leavenworth.army.mil/ch-2.htm, visited June 2004.

52 Cordesman, *The Iraq War*, 2.

53 "On Point," chapter 4, "The March Up-Country."

54 All quotes taken from "On Point," chapter 2.

55 Tim Weiner, "A New Model Soldier Rolls Closer to the Battlefield," *New York Times*, 16 February 2005, §A, 1, §C, 4.

56 "On Point," Introduction.

57 Ibid., chapter 3, "The Running Start."

58 Ibid., chapter 4, "The March Up-Country."

59 Colonel Pete Bayer, 3rd Army Division, 11 May 2003, quoted in "On Point," chapter 5, "Isolation of the Regime."

60 "On Point," chapter 7, "Implications."

61 As Anthony Cordesman observed, "this integration enabled conventional forces to leverage SOF [Special Operations Forces] capabilities to deal effectively with asymmetric threats." Cordesman, *The Iraq War*, 3.

62 Ibid., 120, 97, 143. The total number of sorties was nearly fifty thousand and the number of precision guided missiles dropped almost twenty thousand (143).

63 Ibid., 365.

64 Crowder quoted in Ibid., 262–63.

65 Ibid., 265–66.

66 Bennis et al., "Paying the Price," iv.

67 Paul Sperry, "U.S. Army Prepares for 9,000 Casualties, Sets Up 'Replacement Center' to Resupply Iraq Combatants," 11 March 2003, http://www.worldnetdaily.com/news/article.asp?ARTICLE_ID=31461, visited 9 July 2004.

68 Andrew Cockburn, "How Many Iraqis Have Died since the US Invasion of 2003?," Counterpunch, 9 January 2006, http://counterpunch.org/andrew01092006.html, visited January 2006.

69 This and subsequent quotes from Army personnel from "On Point," chapter 6, "Regime Collapse."

70 "On Point," Introduction.

71 Larry Everest, *Oil, Power and Empire*, 43.

72 "On Point," chapter 6, "Regime Collapse."

73 Ibid.

74 "On Point," chapter 4.

75 Ibid.

76 Again, this is the Army's own appraisal of its logistical limitations in a section of chapter 4 of "On Point" entitled "Logistics: Setting the Conditions to Win."

77 "On Point," chapter 7, "Implications."

78 Cordesman, *The Iraq War*, 17.

79 Ibid., 174, 369.

80 Everest, *Oil, Power and Empire*, 41.

81 Hence the World Bank formulated what it called an interim strategy that drew on the "Bank's experience with post-conflict countries and countries in transition from a centrally planned economy to a market-economy." "Interim Strategy Note of the World Bank Group for Iraq," 14 January 2004, 1, http://lnweb18.worldbank.org/mna/mena.nsf/Attachments/Iraq+Interim+Strategy/$File/Iraq+Interim+Strategy.pdf, visited 7 July 2004.

82 Christopher Foote, William Block, Keith Crane, and Simon Gray, "Economic Policy and Prospects in Iraq," Federal Reserve Bank of Boston Public Policy Discussion Papers, no. 04-1, 4 May 2004, 2–3, http://www.bos.frb.org/economic/ppdp/2004/ppdp0401.pdf. The authors all worked for the CPA in Baghdad.

83   Ibid., 29.

84   Ibid., 7, 14. Bennis et al. cite the higher figure and add that "the high levels of unemployment fueled the insurgency." "Paying the Price," 28.

85   Results of a poll conducted by the Iraqi Center for Research and Strategic Studies, 20–27 April. At this time 76 percent held an unfavorable view of the CPA as compared to 41 percent who disfavored the UN; 43 percent said they would feel more safe if the coalition left. Quoted in Anthony Cordesman, "The Bush Plan for Iraq: A Risk Assessment" (25 May 2004), 2, http://www.csis.org/feature/iraq-bushplan.pdf.

86   Bennis, "Paying the Price," ii.

87   Cordesman, "The Bush Plan for Iraq," 7.

88   Anthony Cordesman, "The Post-conflict Lessons of Iraq and Afghanistan," Testimony to the Senate Foreign Relations Committee, 19 May 2004, 16, http://www.csis.org/hill/ts040519cordesman.pdf, visited 8 July 2004.

89   Representative Henry Waxman (D-Calif.) succinctly detailed the Halliburton corruptions in a letter to Tom Davis, chairman of the House Committee on Government Reform, on 14 June 2004. Waxman, a committee member, was protesting Davis's prevention of testimony about Halliburton's "waste, fraud, and abuse" from being presented before the committee. Letter on http://www.house.gov/reform/min/, visited 24 June 2004.

90   As reported by the watchdog group Iraqi Revenue Watch in "Iraqi Fire Sale: CPA Giving Away Oil Revenue Billions before Transition," briefing no. 7, June 2004, http://iraqrevenuewatch.org/reports/061504.pdf, visited 8 July 2004. See also Khalid Mustafa Medani, "State Rebuilding in Reverse: The Neoliberal 'Reconstruction' of Iraq," Middle East Report Online 232 (fall 2004), http://www.merip.org/mer/mer232.

91   James Glanz and Erik Eckholm, "Reality Intrudes on Promises in Rebuilding of Iraq," New York Times, 30 June 2004, §A, 1, 11.

92   Steve Negus, "The Insurgency Intensifies," Middle East Report Online 232 (fall 2004), http://www.merip.org/mer/mer232/negus.html, visited 15 February 2005: "Allawi, whose Iraqi National Accord contains numerous former regime officials, and who had long championed the rebuilding of the army and intelligence services, set the erection of an Iraqi security apparatus as his government's top priority. A week before he took power, he announced a dramatic restructuring of the forces at his disposal. The Iraqi Civil Defense Corps was renamed the National Guard, and placed under the authority of the Ministry of Defense. Answering to an Iraqi chain of command, it was believed, would remove some of the taint of collaboration with the foreigners and give the guardsmen more reason to fight. The Guard's ranks, meanwhile, were stiffened with veterans of anti-Saddam militias. The Defense Ministry would also command an elite intervention force and other regular army units in the fight against insurgents."

93 Bathsheba Crocker, ed., "Progress or Peril? Measuring Iraq's Reconstruction," Iraq Update, CSIS, August–October 2004, http://csis.org/isp/pcr/0409_progressperil.pdf, visited 15 February 2005. The CSIS estimated that by the end of 2004 nearly three-quarters of reconstruction money was being spent on security and administering the funds (from fraud monitoring to insurance), with only 27 percent going toward "direct services." Bathsheba Crocker, ed., "Estimated Breakdown of Funding Flows for Iraq's Reconstruction: How Are the Monies Being Spent?" (December 2004), http://csis.org/isp/pcr/iraq_funds.pdf, visited 15 February 2005.

94 Rob Nixon, "Our Tools of War, Turned Blindly against Ourselves," *Chronicle of Higher Education*, 18 February 2005, §B, 7–10.

95 John F. Burns and James Glanz, "Iraqi Shiites Win, but Margin Is Less Than Projection," *New York Times*, 14 February 2005, §A, 1, 11.

96 One study, conducted under Pentagon contract by Andrew Krepinevich, "concluded that the Army cannot sustain the pace of troop deployments to Iraq long enough to break the back of the insurgency." Associated Press, "Report: Army Could Be near Breaking Point: Rapid Troop Rotations Threaten Institution, Pentagon-Sponsored Study Says," 24 January 2006, http://www.msnbc.msn.com/id/11009829/, visited January 2006.

97 Stephen Burd, "Bush Proposes Increase for Pell Grants: But the President's Spending Plan Cuts Loan Program and Services for Needy Students," *Chronicle of Higher Education*, 18 February 2005, §A, 12, 24.

CHAPTER 4 : AN EMPIRE OF INDIFFERENCE

1 Slavoj Žižek, *Iraq: The Borrowed Kettle* (London: Verso, 2004), 2.

2 From Žižek's perspective, these grounds need to be taken together, and correspond as the ideological, the political, and the economic to the tripartite Lacanian scheme of the imaginary, the symbolic, and the real. While Žižek provides a typically intriguing formulation, the elegant alignment of manifest and latent cause does make the task of explanation out to be what we already could surmise from our theoretical frameworks about the world. The war becomes a symptom for an already available unknown known. Žižek advises that we focus on "what kind of society is emerging *here* and *now*" and cautions that the "ultimate result of the war will be a change in *our* political order" (19). He sees an end to the emancipatory potential of the United States as it pursues its national self-interest in the name of empire and uses the export of capitalist revolution to keep Europe divided.

3 Edward Said, *Culture and Imperialism* (New York: Vintage, 1994), 6.

4 Ibid., 10.

5 Fredric Jameson, *The Political Unconscious: Narrative as a Socially Symbolic Act* (Ithaca: Cornell University Press, 1981), 33.

6 In an incisive and sweeping review of the literature to date, Anthony

Brewer persists against his own doubts in evaluating the "predictions" of Marx and others regarding historical outcomes according to different notions of imperialist explanations. See his *Marxist Theories of Imperialism: A Critical Survey* (London: Routledge and Kegan Paul, 1980), 24.

7 "Accumulate, accumulate! That is Moses and the prophets!" An article of faith ascends to the status of law in this insinuation of precapitalist authority for bourgeois dogma. Karl Marx, *Capital*, vol. 1 (New York: International, 1967): 595.

8 Ellen Meiksins Wood, *Empire of Capital* (London: Verso, 2003), 144.

9 Ibid., 151, 153.

10 Ibid., 163.

11 Michael Mann, *Incoherent Empire* (London: Verso, 2003), 13.

12 Ibid., 264.

13 For example, in considering imperialism a permanent stage of capitalism (rather than its ultimate condition), Samir Amin identifies five spheres of monopoly—technological, financial, natural resources, media, and mass destruction—as defining the present incarnation of a collective imperialism of the center against the periphery, whose common interests the United States defends. Samir Amin, "The New Triad Imperialism," *Obsolescent Capitalism: Contemporary Politics and Global Disorder* (London: Zed, 2003), 57–73.

14 Giovanni Arrighi and Beverly J. Silver, *Chaos and Governance in the Modern World System* (Minneapolis: University of Minnesota Press, 1999), 38. For a discussion of this argument in the context of the American war against Iraq see Alex Callinicos, *The New Mandarins of American Power: The Bush Administration's Plans for the World* (Cambridge: Polity, 2003), 106–18.

15 David Harvey, *The New Imperialism* (Oxford: Oxford University Press, 2003), 35.

16 The slogan "no blood for oil" has a root in geophysical arguments about the conditions of limitation on the world's oil supply. "Hubbert's peak" is the point at which new demand is expected to outstrip new discoveries, a point we are now said to have reached. The consequent obligation to secure scarce resources by means of invasion conflates access and control, a historical problem which has destabilized national economies by installing or supporting repressive regimes. For Hubbert's argument see Kenneth S. Deffeyes, *Beyond Oil: The View from Hubbert's Peak* (New York: Hill and Wang, 2005), with a link between scarce oil and population control on page 117. The antinomy of access and control is argued by Toby Shelley, *Oil: Politics, Poverty and the Planet* (London: Zed, 2005). A primer in oil economics, a fully financialized industry, can be found in Sally Clubley's *Trading in Oil Futures and Options* (Boca Raton: CRC, 1998).

17 Ibid., 75.

18 Ibid., 101.

19 Ibid., 179.

20 J. A. Hobson, *Imperialism: A Study* (Ann Arbor: University of Michigan Press, 1965), 71.

21 See Rudolph Hilferding, *Finance Capital: A Study of the Latest Phase of Capitalist Development* (London: Routledge and Kegan Paul, 1981); V. I. Lenin, *Imperialism, the Highest Stage of Capitalism: A Popular Outline* (New York: International, 1969); Nikolai Bukharin, *Imperialism and World Economy* (New York: International, 1929); Rosa Luxemburg, *The Accumulation of Capital* (New York: Monthly Review, 1964).

22 Ibid., 97.

23 Giovanni Arrighi, *The Geometry of Imperialism: The Limits of Hobson's Paradigm* (London: New Left, 1978), 143.

24 These two operations of representation, which we can shorthand as "proxy and portrait," are used by Gayatri Spivak to indissociably link the functional and the figural, political economy and identity. See her "Can the Subaltern Speak?," *Marxism and the Interpretation of Culture,* ed. Cary Nelson and Lawrence Grossberg (Urbana: University of Illinois Press, 1988), 271–313, especially 276.

25 Marx, *Capital,* 1:763.

26 I have explored how this suspicion was abetted by a curiously shared reductive reading of Marx. See Randy Martin, *On Your Marx: Relinking Socialism and the Left* (Minneapolis: University of Minnesota Press, 2001).

27 Michel Foucault, *Discipline and Punish: The Birth of the Prison* (New York: Vintage, 1977), 168.

28 Michel Foucault, *Society Must Be Defended* (New York: Picador, 2003), 14.

29 Ibid., 14.

30 See Nicos Poulantzas, *State, Power, Socialism* (London: Verso, 1978).

31 Foucault, *Society Must Be Defended,* 29.

32 Marx, *Capital,* 153.

33 Foucault, *Society Must Be Defended,* 90.

34 Ibid., 61.

35 Ibid., 216.

36 Ibid., 254.

37 Ibid., 254, 257.

38 Ibid., 79.

39 Arnold Davidson, himself citing Gilles Deleuze's study *Michel Foucault, Philosopher,* makes this point in the Introduction to *Society Must Be Defended,* xvi.

40 Frances Fox Piven, *The War at Home: The Domestic Costs of Bush's Militarism* (New York: New Press, 2004), 11.

41 Foucault, *Society Must Be Defended,* 50.

42 Illustrative here is the work of Erik Olin Wright, who has sought to differentiate Marxist relational notions of class from conventional gradational ideas but remains caught in the hypostasis of interest, location, structure, and action. See Erik Olin Wright, *Classes* (London: Verso, 1985).

43 This has become an assessment within conventional political science approaches. Steven E. Schier summarizes "the high risks for the Bush administration: it seeks to entrench a conservative regime among a public beset by even partisan divisions and without a stable Washington governing coalition." See the Introduction to Steven E. Schier, ed., *High Risk and Big Ambition: The Presidency of George W. Bush* (Pittsburgh: University of Pittsburgh Press, 2004), 9.

44 For the most rigorous presentation of this perspective see Jean Cohen and Andrew Arato, *Civil Society and Political Theory* (Cambridge: MIT Press, 1992).

45 Achille Mbembe, *On the Postcolony* (Berkeley: University of California Press, 2001), 133.

46 Achille Mbembe, "Necropolitics," *Public Culture* 15, no. 1 (winter 2003): 12.

47 Ibid., 15, 40.

48 Ibid., 20.

49 This is a line of reading Marx that extends from Louis Althusser's and Étienne Balibar's *Reading Capital* (London: Verso, 1970) to Gayatri Spivak's *In Other Worlds* (London: Routlege, 1988).

50 Ibid., 20.

51 See Karl Marx, *Capital* 1:630, 632.

52 Giorgio Agamben, *Homo Sacer: Sovereign Power and Bare Life* (Stanford: Stanford University Press, 1998), 170. Agamben draws upon the Greek distinction between zoe and bios and argues that the "politicization of bare life as such—constitutes the decisive event of modernity" (4).

53 The politics of fear as an affective modality has been developed in the work of Brian Massumi. See his *Parables for the Virtual: Movement, Affect, Sensation* (Durham: Duke University Press, 2002) and his edited collection *The Politics of Everyday Fear* (Minneapolis: University of Minnesota Press, 1993).

54 Michael Hardt and Antonio Negri, *Empire* (Cambridge: Harvard University Press, 2000), xii.

55 Ibid., 28.

56 Ibid., 25.

57 Ibid., 28. Gilles Deleuze and Félix Guattari, *A Thousand Plateaus: Capitalism and Schizophrenia* (Minneapolis: University of Minnesota Press, 1987).

58 Hardt and Negri, *Empire*, 32.

59 Ibid., 61.

60 While the idea of just war had a long philosophical tradition (in Aquinas and Grotius), interest was renewed with Vietnam and subsequent interventions in the 1980s and 1990s. See Jean Bethke Elshtain, ed., *Just War Theory* (New York: New York University Press, 1992); Richard J. Regan, *Just War: Principles and Cases* (Washington: Catholic University of America Press, 1996); Michael Walzer, *Just and Unjust Wars: A Moral Argument with Historical Illustrations*, 2d ed. (New York: Basic, 1992); James Turner Johnson, *Can Modern War Be Just?* (New Haven: Yale University Press, 1984); and Robert L. Phillips and Duane L. Cady, *Humanitarian Intervention: Just War vs. Pacifism* (Lanham, Md.: Rowman and Littlefield, 1996).

61 The more empirically based set of critiques can be found in Gopal Balakrishnan, ed., *Debating Empire* (London: Verso, 2003). A collection of more philosophically oriented considerations is Paul A. Passavant and Jodi Dean, *Empire's New Clothes: Reading Hardt and Negri* (New York: Routledge, 2004).

62 Michael Hardt and Antonio Negri, *Multitude: War and Technology in the Age of Empire* (New York: Penguin, 2004), 5. Politically there is a great deal of resemblance between the arguments of Hardt and Negri and those of the "postmarxist" theorists Chantal Mouffe and Ernesto Laclau (among others): see Mouffe and Laclau, *Hegemony and Socialist Strategy* (London: Verso, 1985). Both the work of Hardt and Negri and that of Mouffe and Laclau seek a periodizing break between class-based and newer movements, and a distance between their own politics and the histories of socialism. One curiosity of *Multitude* is the absence on this significant tendency of the American left in the past twenty years.

63 Hardt and Negri, *Multitude*, xv.

64 Manuel Castells, *The Rise of the Network Society* (Malden, Mass.: Blackwell, 1996), 470. Indeed their work is reminiscent of a number of earlier sociological treatments of informational society. See also Daniel Bell, *The Coming of Post-industrial Society: A Venture in Social Forecasting* (New York: Basic, 1973).

65 Ibid., 67.

66 Francesca Polletta has conducted a study of these internal processes aptly called *Freedom Is an Endless Meeting: Democracy in American Social Movements* (Chicago: University of Chicago Press, 2002).

67 Ibid., 249.

68 As is commonly the case, Hardt's and Negri's Marx is itself figural, drawn largely from the Grundrisse. When they turn to discussions of political economy more directly, they miss the kind of nuance that comes from a fuller engagement with the three volumes of *Capital*. Their discussion of exploitation in terms of "the quantity of surplus labor time" is illustrative. They conflate a far more complex discussion of absolute and relative surplus value in which Marx complicates the politics of time in a manner that they would appreciate. See ibid., 150.

69 Mark Gerson, surveying what he considers a generationally based intellectual movement, claims that "neoconservatism is now coming to an end." He has assembled a large number of relevant sources in Mark Gerson, ed., *The Essential Neoconservative Reader* (Reading, Mass.: Addison-Wesley, 1996), xvi.

70 Irving Kristol, *Neoconservatism: The Autobiography of an Idea* (New York: Free Press, 1995), 134.

71 Ibid., 130.

72 Max Boot, "What the Heck Is a Neocon?," *Wall Street Journal,* 30 December 2002.

73 Max Boot, *The Savage Wars of Peace* (New York: Basic, 2002), xx.

74 Andrew Bacevich, *American Empire: The Realities and Consequences of U.S. Diplomacy* (Cambridge: Harvard University Press, 2002), 244.

75 Niall Ferguson, *Colossus: The Price of American Empire* (New York: Penguin, 2004), 170.

76 Ibid., 262.

77 Ibid., 204.

78 Ibid., 294.

79 Ibid., 295.

80 The question of how war attaches to capital is quite different from the premise that new wars "are likely to become an activity apart, ruled for better or worse by their own logic" (28). This is the view of Zygmunt Bauman, who is concerned that when predators don't touch prey, wars lose their function of maintaining solidarity. Bauman was writing with Bosnia in mind, not Afghanistan or Iraq, but still the temptation to accept uncritically the technological claims of the "revolution in military affairs" can lead to an inaccurately antiseptic view of war. See Zygmunt Bauman, "Wars of the Globalization Era," *European Journal of Social Theory* 4, no. 1 (2001): 11–28.

81 For revisionist accounts of suburban politics see Rosalyn Baxandall and Elizabeth Ewen, *Picture Windows: How the Suburbs Happened* (New York: Basic, 2000); Dolores Hayden, *Building Suburbia: Green Fields and Urban Growth, 1820–2000* (New York: Pantheon, 2003); Bruce Haynes, *Red Lines, Black Spaces: The Politics of Race and Space in a Black Middle Class Suburb* (New Haven: Yale University Press, 2001); Sally Helgesen, *Everyday Revolutionaries: Working Women and the Transformation of American Life* (New York: Doubleday, 1998); and J. Eric Oliver, *Democracy in Suburbia* (Princeton: Princeton University Press, 2001).

82 For example, in *Hamdi v. Rumsfeld* the Supreme Court ruled on 28 June 2004 against claimed special rights to hold terrorist suspects without trial. On 1 March 2005 Henry F. Floyd, a federal judge in South Carolina who had been appointed by President Bush, ordered the suspect Jose Padilla charged or released (for court order see http://www.scd.uscourts.gob/Padilla/Images/00000048.pdf).

83 For reflections on recent mobilizations, including the articulation between anti-globalization and anti-imperial movements, see Notes From Nowhere, ed., *We Are Everywhere: The Irresistible Rise of Global Anti-Capitalism* (London: Verso, 2003); Tom Mertes, ed., *A Movement of Movements: Is Another World Really Possible?* (London: Verso, 2004); Jackie Smith and Hank Johnston, *Globalization and Resistance: Transnational Dimensions of Social Movements* (Lanham, Md.: Rowman and Littlefield, 2002); Robin Cohen and Shirin M. Rai, *Global Social Movements* (London: Athlone, 2000); Steven Flusty, *De-Coca-Colonization: Making the Globe from the Inside Out* (New York: Routledge, 2004); Jonathan Schell, *Unconquerable World: Power, Nonviolence and the Will of the People* (New York: Metropolitan, 2003); Joe Bandy and Jackie Smith, eds., *Coalitions across Borders: Transnational Protest and the Neoliberal Order* (Lanham, Md.: Rowman and Littlefield, 2004); Janet Conway, *Identity, Place, Knowledge: Social Movements Contesting Globalization* (Halifax, N.S.: Fernwood, 2004); Robert Jensen, *Citizens of the Empire: The Struggle to Reclaim Our Humanity* (San Francisco: City Lights, 2004); Paul Kingsworth *One No, Many Yeses: A Journey to the Heart of the Global Resistance Movement* (London: Free Press, 2003). The e-journal *Counterpunch*, edited by Alexander Cockburn and Jeffrey St. Clair, closely tracks protests against the imperium, including those convened in New York City against the Republican National Convention. Their web site, http://www.counterpunch.org, archives dozens of dispatches.

84 Gallup asked this question to a population sample thirty times between January 2003 and August 2004, never reproducing the same results. It's instructive to recall that in January 2003, before war seemed certain, 53 percent of respondents thought it worth going into Iraq, while 42 percent reported the sentiment "not worth going." This and similar poll findings are presented at http://www.pollingreport.com/iraq.htm, visited 30 August 2004.

85 See Tariq Ali, *Bush in Babylon: The Recolonisation of Iraq* (London: Verso, 2003), and Alexander Cockburn and Jeffrey St. Clair, *Imperial Crusades: Iraq, Afghanistan and Yugoslavia* (London: Verso, 2004).

86 The notion that imperialism promotes capitalist industrial development, which in turn undermines capitalism, is most closely associated with the work of Bill Warren, *Imperialism: Pioneer of Capitalism* (London: New Left, 1980). The question of what is progressive in the elaboration of mutual interdependence is not itself resolved by these measures of economic growth.

87 Accordingly, with each hand-off of the imperial baton, from the Netherlands to Britain to the United States, the prevalence of finance is asserted and the middle class undergoes an internal crisis. Giovanni Arrighi, *The Long Twentieth Century* (London: Verso, 1994).

88 These themes are explored in Randy Martin, *Financialization of Daily Life* (Philadelphia: Temple University Press, 2002). For an original consideration of just what the labor of the state entails see Stefano Harney, *State Work:*

Public Administration and Mass Intellectuality (Durham: Duke University Press, 2002), and Micki McGee, *Self-Help, Inc.* (New York: Oxford University Press, 2005).

89 See Jasbir K. Puar and Amit S. Rai, "Monster, Terrorist, Fag: The War on Terrorism and the Production of Docile Patriots," *Social Text*, fall 2002, 72, 117–48 [special issue: *911: A Public Emergency?*].

90 The generalizable category of being "at risk" as a condition for a politics of fear—before the terror war as we know it was promulgated—is explored in Frank Furedi, *Culture of Fear: Risk Taking and the Morality of Low Expectation* (London: Cassell, 1997).

91 For an insightful discussion of the complicity with privatizing cleavages of identity and political economy see Lisa Duggan, *The Twilight of Equality: Neoliberalism, Cultural Politics, and the Attack on Democracy* (Boston: Beacon, 2003).

Index ❖

biological weapons, 102

biopower, 132–40, 142–44, 154–55, 165–67

Blackburn, Robin, 36, 175 n. 42

Blount, Buford, 117

blowback, 30–31

Blue Force Tracking, 114

Boggs, Carl, 169 n. 2

Boot, Max, 82, 151–52

Bové, Paul A., 58

Bremer, L. Paul, 62, 99–100

Bretton Woods agreements, 25–26, 28–29, 47

Brewer, Anthony, 127, 197 n. 6

brilliance, paradigm of, 67–73

Brown, Michael E., 171 n. 12

Brown, Wendy, 20

Buckingham, David, 89

Bukharin, Nikolai, 2–3, 129

Burk, James, 85

Burke, Jason, 103, 192 n. 16

Bush, George W., 5, 40, 171 n. 8; domestic agenda of, 49; Iraq war and reconstruction planned by, 12–13, 171 n. 14; military policies of, 21, 110–11; national security policy of, 9–10, 47–55, 58, 83; Social Security privatization plans of, 39; transformation paradigm and policies of, 76–78

business cycle, 25

Camp Rhino (Afghanistan), 105

capabilities-based force paradigm, 81–82

Capital (Marx), 134, 140, 171 n. 12, 201 n. 68

capitalism: accumulation by dispossession paradigm and, 129; binary aspects of, 147–51; imperialism and, 126–32, 198 n. 5, 198 n. 13, 203 n. 86; indifference to human associations in, 140–46; neoconservative view of, 151; politics and, 156, 202 n. 81; progressive aspects of, 162–67; social implications of, 14–15, 128–29; taxation and, 129; war as tool of, 154–67, 202 n. 80. *See also* financialization

Carter, Jimmy, 27

Cassidy, Robert M., 84

Castells, Manuel, 145

casualties, 84–86, 106–10

Cebrowski, Art, 78–79

Center for Army Lessons Learned, 112

Center for Strategic and Budgetary Assessments, 67

Center for Strategic and International Studies, 105

chemical weapons, 102

Cheney, Richard, 13, 75, 99, 152, 171 n. 8

Cherkasky, Michael, 181 n. 110

Chertoff, Michael, 182 n. 119

China, 30

Chomsky, Noam, 56

Christian, Jason, 114

citizenship, 36–37

civil society, 139–46

Civil War, 90

class struggle: Foucault on, 136–38, 200 n. 42; Marx on, 140

Clausewitz, Carl von, 51, 132–33, 135

Clinton, Bill, 40, 51, 190 n. 110

Coalition Provisional Authority, 51, 105, 119–23, 196 n. 85

coercive networks, 78–82

Cohen, William, 76, 184 n. 34

cold war: Marxism in context of, 140; military strategy during, 55–56; securitization paradigm and, 51; socioeconomic impact of demise of, 64; systems approach to policymaking during, 72–73; war on terror influenced by, 102

Halliburton: corruption in Iraqi reconstruction and, 121, 196 n. 89; government ties to, 13; price gouging allegations against, 53

Hamdi v. Rumsfeld, 202 n. 82

Hanson, Victor Davis, 188 n. 76

Hardt, Michael, 14, 142–46, 148, 201 n. 62, 201 n. 68

Harootunian, Harry, 48

Harvey, David, 128–30, 162

hegemony: fission of military and financial power and, 128; leveraging of, 58–63; national interest and, 43–47; revolution in military affairs (RMA) and, 65; risk strategies and, 8–9; war as means of achieving, 154–67

Henwood, Doug, 21, 172 n. 8

Hilferding, Rudolf, 1–2, 129, 170 n. 4

Hirschman, Albert, 42

Hobbes, Thomas, 134–35, 145

Hobson, J. A., 129–30

homeland security: economic aspects of, 17–18; globalization and meaning of, 42–47; military intervention as strategy for, 55–63, 180 n. 91; risk management and, 59–63, 182 n. 119; securitization of state and, 48–55

home ownership: citizenship linked to, 175 n. 43; derivatives development and, 34–37; mortgage-backed securities and, 54; as speculation, 40–41

"Hubbert's peak," 198 n. 16

Hudson, Michael, 32

humanity, imperialist indifference to, 5–8

Hurricane Katrina, 60

Hussein, Saddam, 10–12, 50, 67, 85, 100–102, 111, 118–19

"imagined community," 58

imperialism: accumulation by dispossession paradigm and, 129, 143–46; binary aspects of, 146–51; capitalism and, 126–32, 198 n. 5, 198 n. 13, 203 n. 86; delocalization of, 161–62; of finance, 169 n. 1; globalization of, 142–46; indifference and, 156–67; Marxist critique of, 2–3, 127–28, 170 n. 6; mass resistance to, 157–64; neoconservative embrace of, 151–53; resurgence of, 124; Said on, 125; "surplus," 127; territory and, 128; unsustainability of, 127–28; utopian promise of, 4–8; war as tool of, 132–38, 154–67

Imperialism and the World Economy (Bukharin), 2–3

income stagnation, 40–41, 177 n. 57

indifference: empire of, 13–14; imperialism and, 157–67; securitization and, 8–16

Individual Retirement Accounts (IRAS), 34

inflation: defined-contribution plans and, 36; economic growth and, 4; government policies toward, 10–12, 28–30, 40–41

informal empire, 130

informatics, 66, 73

"information pathology," 72

information processing, 9–12

information technology: civilian-military collaboration on, 78–79; in Iraq war, 113–19; military policy and, 72–73; revolution in military affairs (RMA) and, 64–66

institutional risks, 83

intellectual labor, 143

intercontinental ballistic missiles, 78–82

interest rates, 39–40

international currency system: derivative development and, 31–37; dominance of dollar in, 26; U.S. debt financing and, 154

International Monetary Fund (IMF), 26, 29, 151; Iraqi reconstruction and, 120

International Monetary Market, 32

international relations, 43–47, 176 n. 69. *See also* foreign policy

International Telephone and Telegraph (ITT), 32

internet, 145

interoperability: coercive networking and, 82; Special Operations Forces and, 94–96

intervention, imperialist motives for, 4–8

investment: citizenship and, 57–58; influence on government policy of, 36–37; morality of, 22; national security as, 17. *See also* stock market investment

investor class, 34–37

Iran, 98, 102

Iran-Iraq war, 11–12

Iraqi Center for Research and Strategic Studies, 196 n. 85

Iraq Liberation Act (1998), 51

Iraq war: Allawi government after, 121–23, 196 n. 92; al-Qaeda and, 103; control of oil as motive in, 128, 198 n. 16; corruption in reconstruction and, 121, 196 n. 89, 197 n. 93; as dispersed warfare, 98–102, 110–19, 123, 159–67; economic centralization in, 119–23; economic sanctions and, 52–55; "effects-based bombing" in, 115–16; financial reasons for, 13; imperialist motives for, 5, 124–25; indifference in management of, 159–67; insur-

gency movement in, 157–58; local elections after, 100, 122–23; looting during, 116–19; military employment trends during, 185 n. 38; military planning strategies and, 84–86, 110; military recruitment shortages and, 189 n. 92; military training doctrine and, 89–93, 189 n. 92–93; paramilitary forces in, 113–14; preemptive strategy in, 49–55, 179 n. 79; public opinion on, 158–59, 203 n. 84; reconstruction failures and, 100–102; revolution in military affairs (RMA) and, 110–19; risk transfer paradigm in, 106; as self-managed colonialism, 97–98; self-management ethos of occupation and, 100–102; social and economic costs of, 100, 191 n. 6; Special Operations in, 114–19; U.S. troop shortages in, 110–11, 122–23, 194 n. 48, 197 n. 96

"irrational exuberance," 62, 182 n. 116

Islamic Movement of Uzbekistan, 103

Islamist Mujaheddin, 103–4

isolationism, interventionism vs., 149–51

Jameson, Fredric, 125–26, 169 n. 1

Jefferson, Thomas, 82

jointness: in Afghanistan occupation, 107–10; Special Operations Forces and, 94–96

Joint Vision 2020, 81–82

"just-in-time operations": in Iraq war, 111–12; military troop reductions and, 77

just war theory, 143–44, 201 n. 60

Kansas City Board of Trade, 34

Karzai, Hamid, 109–10

Keithly, David, 188 n. 84

Keynesian economics, 22, 24, 36

McNamara, Robert, 72
mechanized body imagery, 91–92, 189
   n. 94
Medicare, 178 n. 78
mercantilism, 54
Metz, Steven, 74
micro-credit, 32
microsatellite technology, 79–82
middle class: financial capitalization
   of, 32–37, 203 n. 87; idealization of,
   8–9; speculative investment by,
   27–30
Military Assistance Command, 72
military command: expansion of
   U.S. military by, 76–77, 185 n. 37;
   financial models applied to, 72–73;
   revolution in military affairs
   (RMA) and paradigm of, 69–73
military forces: in combat operations, 90; costs of, 112–13; derivatives' impact on, 164–67; history
   of, 86–87, 187 n. 74; irrelevance
   after cold war of, 64–65; as labor,
   69, 73, 76–77, 86–87, 184 n. 37; in
   noncombat operations, 90; shortages in Iraq war of, 110–11, 194 n.
   48; specialization of, 89–93; training of, 87–89
"military humanism," 56
military intervention: binary aspects
   of, 149–51; financial capital and, 9–
   12; history of warfare and, 86–87;
   imperialist motives for, 4–8, 127;
   liberation paradigm of, 97, 101–2;
   as national branding, 165–67;
   national interest and, 43; neoconservative embrace of, 152–53; oil
   supply and, 128, 198 n. 16; as preeminent strategy, 55–63; as risk
   management, 38–41; securitization
   through, 47–55; selective engagement strategy and, 45–47; "small

wars" legacy and, 82–83, 187 n. 59;
   sociology of, 85–86, 89–93; strategic failures of, 96; systems approach to, 74, 184 n. 27
military spending, 21–25
Mitchell, Bill, 65
Moltke, Helmut von, 70
monetarism: deregulation and, 27–
   28; disequilibrium and, 29–30;
   federal economic intervention
   and, 3–4; securitization of nation-
   state and, 47–55
monopoly: Amin's five spheres of,
   198 n. 13; Foucault's analysis of
   power and, 137–38
moral economy, money economy vs.,
   23
moral hazard, 56
moral theory, 18–25
Morgenthau, Hans, 43
mortgage-backed securities, 54
mortgages, 40–41
Moskos, Charles C., 85
Mouffe, Chantal, 201 n. 62
multiculturalism, in military training, 90–91
multilateralism, 143–44, 201 n. 60
multinational corporations, 121
multitude, capitalism and role of, 155
Multitude (Hardt), 14, 144–45, 201 n.
   62
mutual funds, 26

Napoleon I, 69–70
National Commission on Terrorist
   Attacks upon the United States,
   99–100, 192 n. 19
national interest: binary aspects of,
   148–51; disavowal of cooperation
   and, 72; monetary interest vs., 42–47
National Research Council, 62, 181 n.
   114

national security, as economic investment, 17

nation-state: binary aspects of, 147–51; as enemy, 57–58; Foucault's analysis of power and, 135–38; globalization and, 127, 169 n. 2; political geography and, 42, 177 n. 64; public rituals of, 140; securitization of, 47–55

Navy Seals, 94–95

necropolitics, 141

Negri, Antonio, 14, 142–46, 148, 201 n. 62, 201 n. 68

Negroponte, John, 121

neoconservatism: economic theory and, 21–25; generational limits of, 202 n. 69; imperialism and, 151–53; racial injustice and, 137–38

neo-isolationism, 44–47

neoliberalism: economic theory and, 20–25; imperialism and, 151–53

net assessment, 74–78

network theory: coercive networks, 78–82; internet social connectivity and, 145–46; Iraq insurgency and, 118–19; military planning and, 76–78

New York Times, 99

Nicaragua, 55

Nixon, Rob, 122

Nocera, Joseph, 27

No Child Left Behind act, 38–39

Northern Alliance (Afghanistan), 104–6

North Korea, 98

Office of Force Transformation, 76, 78

Office of Net Assessment, 74–76

Office of Strategic Services (oss), 95

Office of Systems Analysis (osa), 72–73

055 Brigade, 104

Ogarkov, Nikolai, 75

oil prices, 26–27, 29–30

oil supply, 128, 198 n. 16

Omar, Mullah, 100

"On Point" lessons, 112–13

operational risk, 83

Operation Anaconda, 105–10

Operation Iraqi Freedom, 116

Operation Phantom Fury, 121–22

opium, 104, 109–10

Order of Things, The (Foucault), 132–33

organizational sociology, 29–30

Organization of Petroleum Exporting Countries (OPEC), 26

Overseas Private Investment Corporation (OPIC), 56

Pakistan, 104

Panama, 55

Panel Study of Income Dynamics, 41

Patriot Act, 144; Financial Crimes Enforcement Network, 52–55; risk wars and, 38–41

Pax Americana, 152; globalization and, 25–30

Paxson, Ed, 71

peacekeeping, 81–82

Pell Grants, 123

pension funds, 34–37

People's Democratic Party (Afghanistan), 103

Perelman, Michael, 41

Perkins, David, 117

Perkins loans, 123

Pieterse, Jan Nederveen, 169 n. 2

Piven, Frances Fox, 137

political realism, 43–47

political unconscious, 125–26

politics: debt management and, 156; demographics of participation in,

financing and, 35–37; political power and, 137–38; risk management and, 37–41; tourism and, 109–10

September 11 Commission, 99–100, 192 n. 19

severe acute respiratory syndrome (SARS), 81–82

Shapiro, Michael, 23, 172 n. 11

Shaw, Martin, 106

"sheriff" operations, 97, 191 n. 1

Shinseki, Eric, 110

shock and awe paradigm, 68, 73, 113

Silver, Beverly, 128

singularity, imperialism and, 143–44

Small Wars Manual (U.S. Marine Corps), 187 n. 59

small-war strategy: in Iraq war, 111–19; military intervention and, 82–86, 187 n. 59; revolution in military affairs (RMA) and, 96; Special Operations Forces and, 94–96

smart weapons, 67–68; in first Gulf War, 105

Smelser, Neil, 62

Smith, Adam, 23

social contract: financial capitalism's breach of, 24–25, 130; risk management and dismantling of, 38–41, 176 n. 47

socialism, globalization and, 156

socialization: capitalism and, 155, 163–67; defined, 7–8; imperialism and, 161–67; internationalism and, 150–51; war as regulation of, 141–46

Social Security, 35–36; funding cuts for, 178 n. 78; privatization proposals for, 39–40, 123

social welfare: capitalism's depletion of, 128–32; defined-contribution plans as end to, 36–37; Foucault's

analysis of power and, 135–38; labor as social production and, 146, 201 n. 68

Society Must Be Defended (Foucault), 33

Southern Alliance (Afghanistan), 105

South Korea, 82

sovereignty: in financial capitalism, 26; Foucault's analysis of power and, 134–38; globalization of, 142–46; internal violence and, 169 n. 2; Patriot Act and concepts of, 144; preemptive terror strategy and, 46–47; self-management ethos and, 100–102; war as tool for, 139–46

Soviet Union: Afghanistan war and, 102–4; demise of, 64–65; market transition after fall of, 49; net assessment strategy and, 75–76

space technology, 78–79

Special Operations Forces, 10–12; definition and value of, 190 n. 107; in Iraq war, 114–19; risk model of, 93–96, 190 n. 101; transformation paradigm and, 76–78

Special Warfare School, 95

Specifically Designated Nationals (SDNS), 52–53

Spinoza, Baruch, 143

Spivak, Gayatri, 199 n. 24

Stalinism, 140

"Standardized Physical Training Guide," 91–93

State Department, U.S., 100, 191 n. 6

state rationality, 43–47

Stephanides, Joseph, 52

stock index futures contracts, 34

stock market investment: burst bubble in, 39, 66; limits on, 35; pension financing and, 35–37. See also investment

Strategic Defense Initiative (SDI), 78–80

Stratman, Henry, 111

suicide bombers, 61–62

superweapons technology, 65

"surplus imperialism," 127

surveillance technology, 107–121

Syria, 98

systems analysis: homeland security and, 62–63; imperialism and, 130–31; in Iraq war, 112–19; military policy shaped by, 72–75

Tabb, William K., 169 n. 1

Taliban, 101, 103–10

tax policy: class division through, 57–58; imperialism and, 129; national security and, 151; wealth redistribution through, 40–41

territorialism, 128–30

terrorism, 102–3, 192 n. 16

Teschke, Benno, 44, 178 n. 69

Thierry, Augustin, 136

third world nations: bailout programs for, 29–30; financial capitalism and, 26–30; interstate conflicts in, 55–56; national interests and relations with, 45–47; securitization paradigm and, 51–52

Thomas, Clarence, 137

"thunder runs," 116

Toffler, Alvin, 73

Toffler, Heidi, 73

tourism, in Afghanistan, 109–10

training doctrine (TRADOC), 87–93

transformation paradigm: generalizable applicability and, 79–82; revolution in military affairs (RMA) and, 75–78

Treasury Department, U.S.: Financial Crimes Enforcement Network, 52–53; international bailouts by, 29–30

Ullman, Harlan, 68, 73

uncertainty, in military planning, 70–73, 77

unilateral coercion: game theory and, 72; imperialism and, 128

United Iraqi Alliance, 122

United Nations, 52–55

United States: constitutional basis for sovereignty in, 142–46; as debtor nation, 28; elections of 2004 in, 100; financial dominance of, 25–30; fiscal policy in, 49, 178 n. 78; imperialist roots of, 4–8, 170 n. 7; military expansion in, 76–77, 185 n. 37–38

U.S. Constitution, 142–46

U.S. War College, 43–44

utilitarian logic, security tradeoffs and, 19, 172 n. 3

value: financial planning and, 9–12; imperialist view of, 6–8, 153–54; Marxist theory of, 134; meaning and, 172 n. 11; morality of risk and, 22–25

van Creveld, Martin, 69–71

Venezuela, 29

Vietnam syndrome, 46, 84, 157–58; body counts as symptom of, 106; revolution in military affairs (RMA) and, 159

Vietnam War: combat and logistics in, 90; mathematical modeling and policies during, 72; military demobilization after, 185 n. 37–38; military technology revolution during, 75; political legacy of, 84, 157–58

violence: commercialization of, 72–73; financial capitalism and, 128; globalization and, 169 n. 2; postcolonial sovereignty and, 139–46

Virilio, Paul, 85
"visionary capitalism," 26
vision as truth paradigm, 70
Volcker, Paul, 27–28

Wade, James, Jr., 68, 73
Wallace, William S., 117, 194 n. 48
Wall Street Journal, 151
war: binary aspects of, 149–51; capitalism and, 154–67, 202 n. 80; financial capital and, 9–12; Foucault on, 132–38; history of, 86–87; imperialist motives for, 4–8, 127, 154–67; liberation paradigm of, 97, 101–2; national interest and, 43; neoconservative embrace of, 152–53; oil supply and, 128, 198 n. 16; as preeminent strategy, 55–63; as risk management, 38–41; securitization through, 47–55; selective engagement strategy and, 45–47; "small wars" theory, 82–83, 154, 187 n. 59; sociology of, 85–86, 89–93; strategic failures of, 96; systems approach to, 74, 184 n. 27. *See also* derivative war
War on Poverty (1964–68), 38
war on terror: capabilities-based force paradigm and, 81–82; derivative methods in, 165–67; as derivative war, 100; foreign policy and, 17–18; globalization and, 1–2; historical models of, 9; insurgencies in response to, 12; liberation paradigm of, 97; as liberation theology, 23–25; national and international views of, 8; paradox of, 159–67; politics of fear and, 141–42; privacy

risks and, 61; securitization of state and, 47–55, 101
warrior ethos, 85–93
"war worship," 188 n. 77
Waxman, Henry, 196 n. 89
Wayne, John, 95
wealth creation: imperialism as tool for, 126; Marxist view of, 127, 140–41, 197 n. 6, 198 n. 7; morality and, 23–25; reactive indifference and, 161–67; securitization and, 19–25; tax reforms and, 40–41
weapons of mass destruction: end of cold war and, 64; Iraq war predicated on, 50–55
Weinberger, Caspar, 55, 84, 190 n. 110
welfare reform, 38–39
Wells, Linton, II, 76
Whitehead, Carnelia de Groot, 90
Wiener, Norbert, 71
Williams, J. Noel, 192 n. 18
Wohlstetter, Albert, 71
Wolfensohn, James, 193 n. 44
Wolfowitz, Paul, 13, 75, 82, 97, 110, 152, 195 n. 47
Wood, Ellen Meiksins, 127
Woolsey, R. James, 62
World Bank, 26; Iraqi reconstruction and, 120, 195 n. 81; "Transitional Support" scheme for Afghanistan of, 108–10, 193 n. 44
World Is Flat, The (Friedman), 169 n. 2
Worley, D. Robert, 44–45
Wright, Erik Olin, 200 n. 42

Zawahiri, Ayman al-, 61
Žižek, Slavoj, 124–25, 197 n. 2

: RANDY MARTIN

is director of the graduate program
in arts politics and a professor of art and
public policy at the Tisch School of the Arts,
New York Unversity.

Library of Congress Cataloging-in-Publication Data
Martin, Randy, 1957–
An empire of indifference : American war and the financial
logic of risk management / Randy Martin.
p. cm. — (Social text books)
Includes bibliographical references and index.
ISBN-13: 978-0-8223-3979-3 (cloth : alk. paper)
ISBN-13: 978-0-8223-3996-0 (pbk. : alk. paper)
1. War on Terrorism, 2001—Finance—United States. 2. War
—Economic aspects—United States. 3. Government spending policy
—United States. 4. Risk management—United States. 5. National
security—United States. I. Title.
HV6432.M378 2007
973.931—dc22   2006027825